DISCOVER·NATURE

in the
Garden

DISCOVER·NATURE
in the
Garden

Things to Know and Things to Do

Jim Conrad

Illustrations by Jim Conrad

STACKPOLE
BOOKS

Published by
STACKPOLE BOOKS
5067 Ritter Road
Mechanicsburg, PA 17055

Printed in the United States of America

Cover design by Mark Olszewski with Kathleen D. Peters

First Edition

10 9 8 7 6 5 4 3 2 1

Library of Congress Cataloging-in-Publication Data

Conrad, Jim.
    Discover nature in the garden : things to know and things
to do / Jim Conrad ; illustrations by Jim Conrad. — 1st ed.
      p.   cm.
    Includes bibliographical references.
    ISBN 0-8117-2442-5
    1. Garden ecology. 2. Nature study. 3. Gardening.
QH541.5.G37C66   1996
574.5—dc20
                                          95-46473
                                            CIP

CONTENTS

PREFACE

Usually I write about ecotourism in Latin America. Among my customary topics are ancient Maya ruins deep in the jungle, animals such as howler monkeys and army ants, and plants like wild orchids and banana trees. More than one friend has wondered why I've suddenly switched from this exciting stuff to the less romantic subject of home gardening.

My reply is that the two topics—exotic natural history and backyard gardening—are fundamentally the same. The main difference is that one involves a great deal of traveling; the other flourishes best when we stay at home.

Wondrous plants and animals? How about the recent drama right below my kitchen window, among my snap beans, when a big argiope spider snared a grasshopper in its web? It was a struggle to the end between two innocent beings brought into conflict by their very natures. It was thought provoking, and their deadly dance was starkly beautiful.

Like a walk in the jungle, a visit to the garden awakens us to the basic fundamentals of planetary ecology. For what's more insightful into the way nature is put together than learning how to manage the relationship between carbon and nitrogen in a pile of compost?

Like a walk along a tropical beach, working in a backyard garden or flower bed heals and renews the human spirit. You'll see for yourself what salutary effects come not only from outdoor exercise, but also from rubbing shoulders with vegetables, pretty flowers, bugs, and soil. Just thinking of sunflowers and of healthy, benevolent earthworms tunneling through rich soil rejuvenates the soul and makes us happier.

Henry David Thoreau wrote that nature "invites us to lay our eye level with her smallest leaf, and take an insect view of its plain." The backyard garden and flower bed enable us to do exactly that. The Mexican bean beetle beneath a ragged bean leaf urges us to share its view of the blue sky beyond corn blades rustling in summer breezes. The backyard's mellow, friendly character invites us to tarry awhile and let our minds drift among clouds of yellow and black butterflies attending zinnias at the end of the house.

With this book, then, I continue guiding readers into the most gorgeous, pregnant corners of nature. My goal is to shake up the reader's spirit by exposing eyefuls of color and form, by eliciting unaccustomed thought processes, and by opening doors to the garden's thousand unforeseen enchantments.

The garden of this book is less the garden of production and home economy than the garden of the open mind.

ACKNOWLEDGMENTS

Thanks to Eva Rae Gill of Semiway, Kentucky, for permitting a glance into her garden notebook; to Marie Taylor, my grandmother, for long talks about gardening in the old days; and to my mother, for sharing one or two secrets on how she usually grows the season's first ripe tomato.

INTRODUCTION

This book in the Discover Nature series is for people who want to know what's going on among the rustling rows of corn in the backyard garden or the pansies planted around the birdbath. As with other volumes in this series, this book deals with knowing and *doing*. It's for young people, parents, students, teachers—everyone who knows that even things that are close at hand can be interesting.

Each chapter looks at a different aspect of the garden environment. Hands-on projects are scattered here and there. You don't necessarily need to begin at the beginning in this book. If you just happen to be fascinated by bugs, then chapter 8 is a fine place to start! What you learn there likely will arouse your curiosity about other aspects of backyard nature, and then you'll go on to read about those topics. Before you know it, you'll have read the whole book!

Once you've sat cross-legged in your backyard figuring out the differences between monarch butterflies and the mimicking viceroys—and understand why these two unrelated species are so similar in the first place—your newly acquired insights should send you roaming beyond the backyard realm.

Area woods, fields, roadsides, marshes—wherever plants and animals commune—are appropriate destinations for those of us who have learned the pleasures of naturalizing in our own backyards.

TOOLS FOR BACKYARD NATURALIZING

A walk through a garden always reveals a few interesting bugs, diseases, and curious blossoms and fruits. For our purposes, however, that isn't enough. We need something that can come only from within; we need a *burning curiosity* about what's going on beneath those leaves, inside those blossoms, on the other side of everything that placidly shows us its superficial face.

This means plopping onto our stomachs, nosing around, and taking the time to peep into holes and corners and beneath things. Because that's where the timid cricket awaits night's darkness; where soft-bodied insects cower, hoping to escape marauding dragonflies; and where the smaller scale of things makes roving centipedes into rampaging monsters with diabolical intentions and fangs dripping with venom.

The backyard, then, is a stage on which a million mostly hidden dramas are taking place.

We just need to have the curiosity, wit, and talent to search them out, and then calmly sit and think about what it all means.

Many, maybe most, of the dramas taking place in our gardens and flower beds occur at a level of existence that our naked eyes are poorly equipped to see. We must possess a tool for seeing those things that live on a much, much smaller scale than we. Otherwise, we'll never behold the grasshopper's wondrously complex mouthparts, the superfine root hairs that enable garden plants to acquire water, or the surprisingly bright crystal faces of quartz grains in garden soil. We need a *magnifying glass.*

Maybe the best kind of magnifying glass is the one called a *hand lens,* or *jeweler's loupe.* Hand lenses typically consist of two small lenses mounted one above the other in such a way that the whole apparatus swings into a metal handle for storage. A good hand lens has a magnification power of about 10X. Such lenses purchased in jewelry shops or stores specializing in optical equipment may cost $75 or more; hand lenses good enough for beginning naturalists often can be found in toy shops for $5 or less. If you buy one that's part of a detective kit, you'll get a free false mustache to boot.

If you take this book's advice and pay attention to hummingbirds sipping nectar from your flower bed's tube-shaped blossoms, and to house sparrows that frolic in the dust between your bean rows, *binoculars* can be a lot of fun. A good power is 7.5X. Big, bulky binoculars are easier to use for spotting things than smaller, lighter ones.

Field guides are special kinds of books that enable you to look up all kinds of plants and animals. The looking-up process is so much fun, so enlightening, and so important that chapter 11 is dedicated to it. Basically, looking up entails matching a plant or animal with its illustration in a field guide. A more technical approach is to use identification keys, which also are described in chapter 11.

Most books that deal with insect identification encourage readers to collect, kill, and mount specimens as part of the identification process. Admittedly, it's easier to identify a bug mounted on a pin in a box than one busy stalking an aphid beneath a squash leaf. In this book, however, becoming sensitized to the backyard's living things is considered more important than merely knowing technical facts about them. Killing and pinning living things accomplishes just the opposite of that: It desensitizes us to life. And if anything is needed on earth today, surely it's greater human sympathy to all other forms of life, whether they're other humans, animals, or crabgrass.

Anyone who still wishes to collect insects or any other living feature of the garden environment can learn the appropriate techniques from the field guides listed in the Bibliography.

THE BACKYARD NATURE NOTEBOOK

It's magical the way nature-oriented notebooks work. Few of us can remember everything we see or read. If a TV nature program reveals to us the life cycle of an aphid, most of us will have forgotten all or part of the complex cycle by the next day. But if we diagram the aphid's cycle in a notebook as we watch the program, then that information stays handy for as long as we keep the notebook.

Everyone has his or her own way of organizing a backyard nature notebook. For example, my cousin, Eva Rae, put together one that was completely different from mine. When she heard I was writing this book, she brought me an old, dog-eared, spiral-bound notebook bearing the words *Garden 1981* on the cover. Inside was a hodgepodge of gardening tips, notes about her garden, and articles clipped from magazines. On the first page, she'd taped a poem that spoke of "the seed catalog itch" and "squealing, bawling new life."

I am more interested than Eva in the names and life cycles of plants and animals in my backyard, and my notebook includes more information on the plants and animals I encounter. I use a loose-leaf binder so that I can insert new pages here and there. It never occurred to me to include a poem in my notebook, but maybe, after seeing Eva's notebook, I'll do that . . .

Eva didn't mind having a page on strawberry cultivation next to a page on how ladybird beetles spend their winters. She enjoyed just thumbing through her creation, skipping here and there, and of course, there's nothing wrong with that.

If you like your information organized for fast retrieval, however, and you want all your bug information in one place and all your weed info in another, you might consider using subject headings.

My notebook is divided into ten sections: Projects, Gardening Tips, Garden Plants, Weeds, Insects, Spiders, Other Invertebrates, Birds, Mammals, and Herps (amphibians and reptiles).

In the projects section, I describe the procedures and results of projects such as those suggested in this book. For example, I might have data from an experiment to see if planting marigolds really keeps bugs off nearby crops. In the next section, I list gardening tips I've collected from various sources, such as TV gardening shows, friends, and family. For instance, the other day, a friend told me to put a matchstick right next to a tomato set's stem to prevent cutworm damage.

In the garden plants section, I designate one page to each plant I grow. I then record as much information about the plant as I can find. For example, notes on my kale page remind me of the following: Kale is a member of the mustard family; a study in China found that women who eat lots of kale are less likely to develop lung cancer; kale likes cool weather, and in my area it often survives the whole winter; and it's loaded with vitamin A, vitamin B complex, and vitamin C.

Each of the remaining seven sections of the notebook is dedicated to a particular kind of plant or animal. Within each section, one page is dedicated to each organism. I arrange each page alphabetically according to the organism's name, with the exception of the part on insects. You'll see in chapter 9 that, because of the sheer numbers of insect species inhabiting our gardens, I suggest that you organize the insects a little differently.

Every time I positively identify a plant or animal, I know it took a lot of work and brainpower, and placing the page into my notebook is like putting a trophy on my wall. Except that the plants and animals I "captured" are still alive.

Often, once I've identified a species, I sketch it, drawing little arrows to various parts of the body and labeling them. I make notes that in the future will help me distinguish this from similar creatures. "Beak fits into groove in prosternum," I might write about an assassin bug. This will help me distinguish between it and the rather similar ambush bug.

The main rule for *all* of your notebook is this: *The best part of what you put there will be what you have discovered yourself, through your own observations, in your own backyard.*

PART I

LOOK AT THAT PLANT!

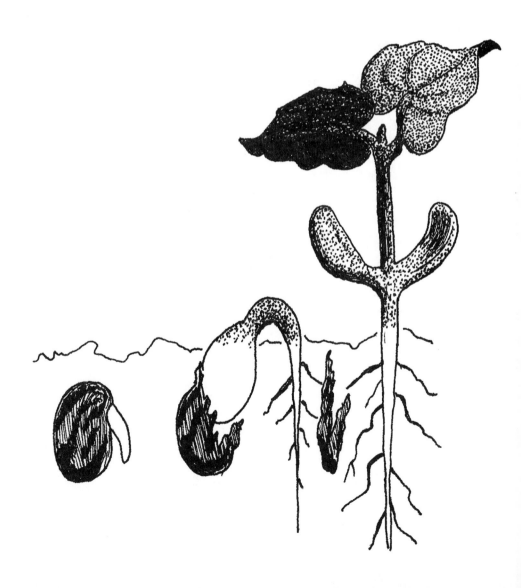

There is a lot more to the plants of our backyard gardens and flower beds than our being able to eat them or make bouquets from them. Every plant has its own unique story, and each interacts with all other plants and animals in special, important ways.

On the following pages, you will see how plants are put together and how they work. As if you were going to a three-ring circus to see lions, tigers, and elephants, you'll get a look at different kinds of plants and find out what's so interesting about them.

By no means do these pages tell all or even most of the secrets of garden and flower bed plants. What's written here is just a sample of what can be known; it's only a start, to whet your appetite and show you how to continue, for the rest of your life, relating what you learn in your own backyard to what you will see in the many different environments, habitats, and entire new worlds you will encounter in your future.

CHAPTER 1

The "Standard" Backyard Plant

The best way to develop a feeling for what is special about any plant in your garden is to form in your mind's eye an idea of a "standard" backyard plant. This plant should be so unspecialized and average that it is painfully bland and unimaginative. Of course, no such plant exists, but let's imagine it anyway.

The idea is that in the future, anytime you take a look at a plant that's new to you—a garden plant, a new weed that has made its way into your garden ecosystem, or even a native plant in the wild—you'll be able to form an opinion of what that new plant is like by noticing how it differs from the "standard" backyard plant. Those differences are the features that define what is special about the new plant.

The "standard" backyard plant is composed of four main different parts: roots, stem, leaves, and reproductive parts (flowers and fruits).

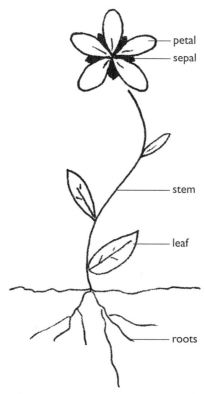

The "standard" backyard plant possesses average traits: one flower with five identical petals and sepals; unbranched stem; alternate, simple leaves; and fibrous roots.

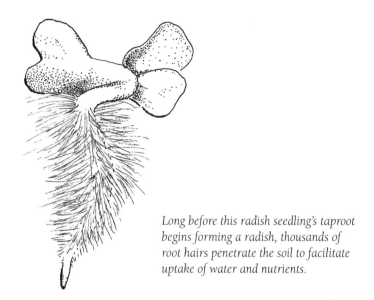

Long before this radish seedling's taproot begins forming a radish, thousands of root hairs penetrate the soil to facilitate uptake of water and nutrients.

ROOTS

When a seed germinates, typically just one little, white root, called a *radicle,* emerges at first. Looking like a grain of rice protruding from the seed coat, this little root is drawn downward by gravity. Before long, the radicle branches, then these new branches branch, and often those branches continue to branch and rebranch into an extensive network of roots and *rootlets* (small roots).

It's hard to imagine how the efforts of one little radicle eventually lead to an effective root system. A classic study by H. J. Dittmer found that one rye plant about waist-high grew approximately 380 miles of roots. Most of that length was produced by rootlets that were branches of branches of branches of main roots. If all of this rye plant's roots had been sliced open and pressed flat on a basketball court, their combined surface areas would have covered approximately half of the court!

Even before the radicle began branching, hundreds of extremely slender *root hairs* had grown from its sides, looking like some kind of fuzzy fungus. Later, all the hundreds of rootlet tips at one time or another were equipped with root hairs, always located immediately behind the root tip. As the root tip advanced through the soil, the root hairs left behind grew old, collapsed, and sloughed off. New root hairs appeared right behind the advancing root tip, so there was always a small root-hair zone near the root tip.

This information is worth thinking about, because in all our flowering backyard plants, water and dissolved nutrients are absorbed into the plant nearly entirely by root hairs.

This means that the large, branching roots we see when any bush, grass, or garden plant is pulled from the ground do not soak up water and nutrients. They mainly anchor the plant in the soil and conduct water and dissolved nutrients from the root hairs to the main plant body. Root hairs do the soaking up.

Therefore, if you have a large, thirsty tomato plant, but only a cup of water, where should that water be poured? If you know that most of the plant's root tips have penetrated the soil to two or three feet away from the tomato stem, that this is where the root hairs are, and that only root hairs soak up water it wouldn't make much sense to pour the water right around the stem, would it?

Our "standard" backyard plant's roots are threadlike and divide a couple of times; such slender, branching roots are called *fibrous roots*. Many herbs and most grasses that live for just one year (called *annuals*) have fibrous roots.

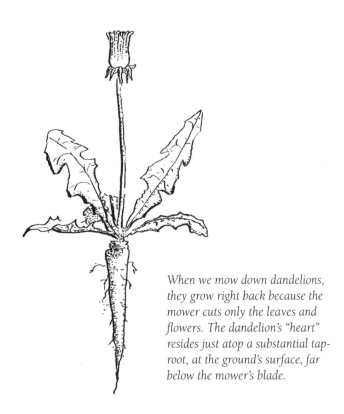

When we mow down dandelions, they grow right back because the mower cuts only the leaves and flowers. The dandelion's "heart" resides just atop a substantial taproot, at the ground's surface, far below the mower's blade.

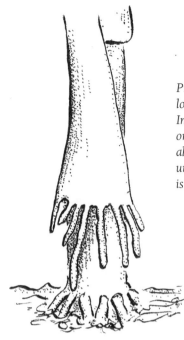

Prop roots emerge from the lower nodes of a corn plant. In any plant or animal, an organ that occurs in an abnormal position or at an unusual time of development is said to be adventitious.

Other plants, however, have much more exotic kinds of roots, especially those that live for two years (called *biennials*) or for more than two years (called *perennials*).

For example, some plants have *taproots*—single, much-thickened central roots that grow straight down. Dandelions and alfalfa, as well as many oaks, hickories, and coniferous trees, possess tap roots, at least when young.

Some taproots are particularly fleshy and serve as food-storage areas for the plants that have them. When you eat carrots, you're eating fleshy taproots in which food is stored for the frilly leaved carrot plants. The stored food is carbohydrate, which you'll learn a lot more about in chapter 4.

In our gardens, carbohydrate-rich taproots are found beneath not only carrot plants, but also turnips, beets, radishes, and parsnips. Not all taproots become fleshy storage roots, however, and there are many kinds of storage roots other than taproots.

Maybe the most interesting kind of root is the type produced on stems above the ground; these are called *aerial roots*. In tropical forests, aerial roots are common on such plants as orchids and peperomias, which grow on trees. In many of our backyards, two common plants with aerial roots are corn and English ivy. The ivy's aerial roots anchor climbing stems as they creep up walls and trees. Corn's aerial roots arise on the stem right above the ground and grow downward, where they grow into the soil, branch profusely, absorb water and nutrients, and help prop up the stems. These particular kinds of aerial roots are also known as *prop roots.*

STEMS

Stems can do a lot more than simply grow straight up and hold leaves and reproductive parts, though that's all they seem to do for our "standard" backyard plant.

Of course, in real plants, the stem is not just a black line the way it is in our drawing. In real plants, every place a leaf arises from a stem, a certain thickening and hardening usually occurs. This connection area is referred to as a *node.* In many *herbaceous,* or nonwoody, plants, you know that a node is present only because a leaf arises from it. In other plants, however, especially woody ones, nodes are much more conspicuous, as in bamboos, where each thickened "joint" is a node. One reason it's important to understand about nodes is this: When you try to identify plants, it's very important to know whether one, two, or more leaves arise from each node.

Though the stem of our "standard" backyard plant simply rises into the air, the stems of other plants may branch, twine up poles, or lean onto the ground. Sometimes plant stems produce shoots at their bases that develop into long, slender *runners* that grow atop the ground or just beneath it; runners often bear leaves and roots along their entire lengths. The more technical name for a runner is *stolon;* crabgrass has stolons, as do strawberry plants.

In some plants, underground stolons develop swollen food-reserve areas called *tubers.* White potatoes are tubers developed on stolons. This means that potatoes are actually growths of the stem, not of roots.

When gardeners dig up their thick, starchy iris or canna "roots" in the fall so that the plants won't be killed by the cold, those aren't really roots at all, but rather underground stems called *rhizomes.* Rhizomes differ from runners or stolons in that whereas runners or stolons are just side shoots of a main plant that grows upright, rhizomes are actually the plant's main stem, growing horizontally below the ground.

This means that the irises or cannas we see in the summertime, from a botanical point of view, are actually just temporary, summer-appearing side shoots off the perennial plant's stem, which stays underground. In a sense, the main, long-lived iris and canna plants are never seen unless they are dug up.

If you take a horizontal rhizome, shorten it, and make it grow vertically below the ground, you have a *corm.* In our flower beds, plants that produce corms include the gladiolus, crocus, and tuberous begonia.

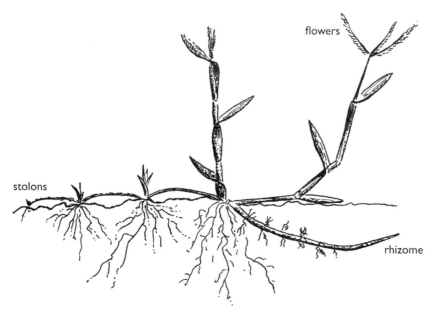

One reason crabgrass is so hard to control is that it uses three reproductive methods: sexual reproduction with flowers and seeds, asexual reproduction with underground rhizomes, and asexual reproduction with stolons, which arch atop the ground.

Bulbs, botanically speaking, are very short corms encased in thickened, fleshy scales, which are actually modified leaves. Unlike the carrot, where the tap root is the main site of food storage, in a bulb the scales hold the carbohydrate.

Two main kinds of bulbs can be found in our backyards. When bulb scales form a series of concentric rings that can be seen when the bulb is cut across, as in onions and hyacinths, the bulbs are called *layered;* when the scales do not encircle the stem, but rather are thick and fleshy and group together rather loosely, as in most lilies, the bulbs are said to be *scaly.*

LEAVES

Leaves come in a multitude of shapes and configurations. Referring to the accompanying drawing, we can figure out that our "standard" backyard plant has leaves that are lanceolate to ovate, with acute tips and obtuse bases. Also, they are alternate (one leaf per node) along the stem.

Sometimes it's not so easy to figure out what a plant's leaf is; sometimes what we think of as the leaves are actually mere leaf subdivisions or maybe even shoots consisting of stem material and several leaves.

Our "standard" backyard plant has simple, undivided leaves, called, logi-

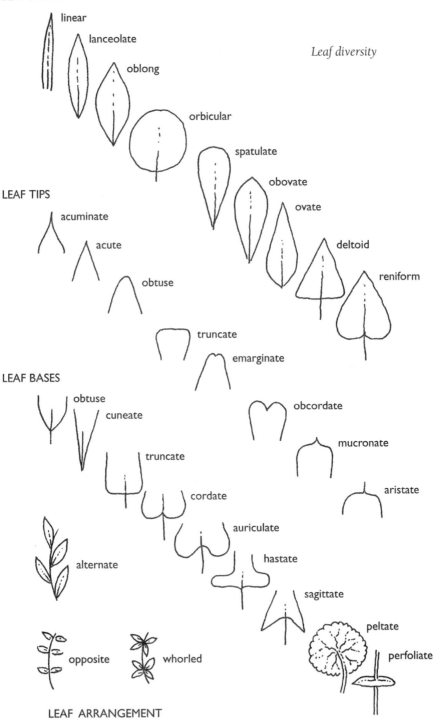

LEAF SHAPES

linear
lanceolate
oblong
orbicular
spatulate
obovate
ovate
deltoid
reniform

Leaf diversity

LEAF TIPS

acuminate
acute
obtuse
truncate
emarginate
obcordate
mucronate
aristate

LEAF BASES

obtuse
cuneate
truncate
cordate
auriculate
hastate
sagittate
peltate
perfoliate

alternate
opposite
whorled

LEAF ARRANGEMENT

cally enough, *simple leaves.* Leaves that are divided into two or more blades are known as *compound leaves.* Subdivisions of compound leaves are referred to as *leaflets.* When leaflets are arranged within the leaf like fingers arising from the palm of a hand, as in the case of the lupine and the horsechestnut, they are *digitately,* or *palmately, compound;* when they arise along the compound leaf's midrib, as with ash trees, they are *pinnately compound.* Most backyard plants bear simple leaves, but those of beans, tomatoes, marigolds, and a few other common ones are compound.

On some plants, leaves bear special features. The upper leaflet of the garden pea's pinnately compound leaves are modified into *tendrils* that curl around whatever is at hand and help hold the pea plant upright. The clematis vine has leaves on stems, or petioles, that twine around like tendrils.

LEARNING ABOUT THE
LEAVES ON A PLANT

What you will need

a variety of plants

---

1. Choose a plant in your garden and try to locate one of its leaves. Keep in mind that most backyard plants other than conifer trees bear leaves that are flat in cross section, not round. Therefore, look for a blade or cluster of blades that is flattish, as if scissored from a sheet of paper. Anything that is round in cross section is probably one or more stems or leaves, or clusters of flowers or fruits.

2. Once you think you've found a leaf, confirm your decision by reflecting on how leaves are attached to the main plant body. In the angle between a leaf's *petiole,* or stalk, and the main plant stem, there often arises a small, buttonlike *bud;* these buds hold future stems, leaves, or perhaps flowers. This information is relevant because *buds never occur on a leaf, on a petiole, or between the leaf and its petiole.* Therefore, anything with a bud on it must *not* be a leaf.

3. Now figure out if what you have is a simple or compound leaf. If you've found a bud and a petiole, this step is easy. If just one flat blade is appended to the petiole, then you have a simple leaf; if there are two or more blades, then you have a compound leaf, and each of those blades is considered a leaflet.

4. Double check that your leaf is a leaf by considering its symmetry. If you

Where are the leaves on this young tomato plant? Sometimes this simple question is hard for beginning naturalists to answer. This young plant bears three developed, compound leaves. Can you find them?

cut most simple or compound leaves down the middle—through midrib and petiole—you'll end up with one side of the leaf more or less being the mirror image of the other. Does this apply to your leaf? Some leaves have one side that bulges downward a little more than the other side. This last step won't prove anything, but if one side of your leaf is a fair mirror image of the other side, then that's one more piece of evidence that you really do have a leaf.

Sometimes it's next to impossible for the beginning naturalist to be sure what's leaf, leaflet, or something else. If you have problems with one species, try another, until you've found something on which the leaves are easy to discern—probably a species with simple leaves and conspicuous buds.

CHAPTER 2

The "Standard" Backyard Blossom

For the same reason that we imagined a "standard" backyard plant, it's also helpful to visualize a "standard" backyard blossom—the most average, unspecialized, nondescript, absolutely boring blossom we can think of.

As was the case with our "standard" backyard plant, in nature, nothing exists exactly like this one. Nonetheless, this blossom will cue us to what's special about real blossoms we meet in our backyards, when we see how those real blossoms differ from our imaginary one.

First of all, let's review a few flower terms. Don't think of these words as simply vocabulary to be memorized; a word like *filament* behaves like a magic chant that can draw our minds into the perfumy, other-worldly zone beneath bouquets of stamens sprouting like weird-shaped, translucent trees deep inside tiny flowers.

flower: term used interchangeably with *blossom*

pedicel: the stem of an individual blossom

calyx: the usually green, cuplike part of the flower below the corolla

sepal: a lobe or division of the calyx

corolla: usually the bright, pretty part of a blossom located immediately above the calyx

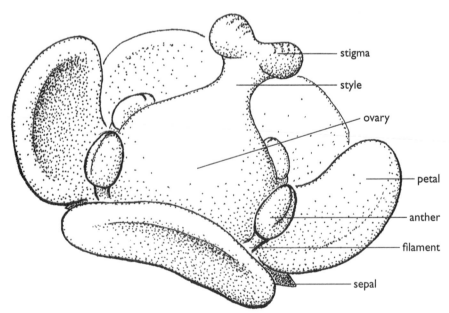

The "standard" backyard blossom possesses average traits: five identical sepals, petals, and stamens, and a plump ovary with a short style, beneath a shallowly lobed stigma.

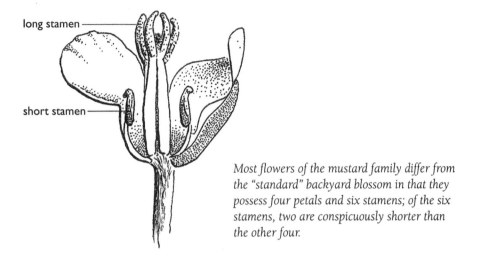

long stamen

short stamen

Most flowers of the mustard family differ from the "standard" backyard blossom in that they possess four petals and six stamens; of the six stamens, two are conspicuously shorter than the other four.

petal: a lobe or division of the corolla

stamen: the male part of a flower, composed of the anther and filament

anther: the upper part of a stamen; produces pollen

filament: the stalk of a stamen, supporting the anther

pistil: the female part of the flower, composed of the stigma, style, and ovary

stigma: the pistil's summit, where pollen grains germinate

style: the part of the pistil connecting the stigma with the ovary

ovary: the swollen, basal portion of a pistil; ovaries eventually develop into fruits

ovules: the egglike items inside an ovary that, once fertilized, develop into seeds

The corolla of our "standard" backyard blossom is composed of five separate petals. Its hardly visible calyx is divided into five sepals, and there are five stamens (in the drawing, one lies behind the pistil). Therefore, our "standard" backyard blossom subscribes to the old saying that "nature loves the number five."

Moreover, our "standard" blossom's pistil possesses a roundish ovary, a short style, and a bilobed stigma. Let all this information crystallize in your brain. You will have fun seeing how your backyard blossoms differ from this simple design.

Let's give this kind of flower comparing a try by relating a drawing of a tomato blossom to our "standard" backyard blossom.

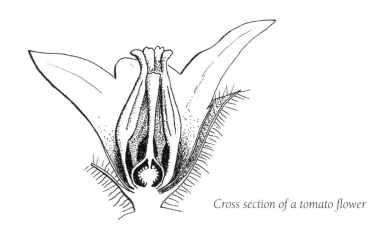

Cross section of a tomato flower

COMPARING A DRAWN TOMATO BLOSSOM WITH THE "STANDARD" BACKYARD BLOSSOM

What you will need
nothing but this book

1. Maybe the most interesting difference between the drawing and our "standard" backyard blossom is that the tomato's five stamens are enlarged, and the anthers are grown together into a kind of tube or cylinder surrounding and concealing the small ovary. Once the ovary begins growing into a tomato, it will burst through this encirclement; only the pedicel and calyx will continue growing with the tomato.

2. Notice that the tomato flower's petals are not separate, as in our "standard" blossom, but rather are united at their bases, forming a funnel-shaped corolla with lobes. Many kinds of flowers have corolla lobes instead of distinct petals.

There are many other differences as well, but for a beginning, this will do.

Actually, relative to many other kinds of blossoms found in our backyards, the tomato flower is fairly similar to our "standard" backyard blossom; having big stamens is no big deal.

If you can find a bean flower, for instance, you can see for yourself a prime example of how very common flowers can differ drastically from the "standard" blossom. In bean blossoms, the five petals are separate from one another as in our "standard" blossom, but each of the bean flower's five petals are shaped differently from one another.

Blossoms in which all petals, sepals, and stamens are shaped alike, as with our "standard" blossom, are referred to as *regular* flowers. Blossoms in which at least one petal, stamen, or sepal is different from the others are said to be *irregular*. In our gardens and flower beds, besides members of the bean family, most plants in the mint family also have irregular blossoms. One difference between irregular bean blossoms and irregular mint blossoms is that bean flower petals are usually separate from one another, but mint flower petals are united.

Well, see how this blossom-comparing business works? Now every time you see a new flower, you can compare your new discovery with our "standard" backyard blossom.

For example, if you encounter a hibiscus flower, a little voice in your head will spout off, "Wow! Look at how that flower has many more than the 'standard' five stamens, and all the stamens' filaments are smushed together into a cylinder surrounding the style. Weird!"

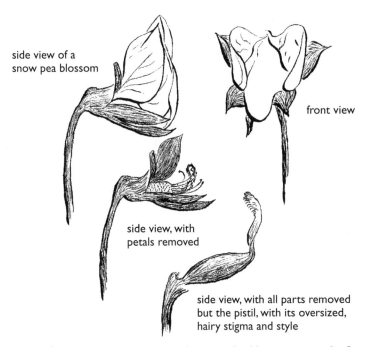

side view of a
snow pea blossom

front view

side view, with
petals removed

side view, with all parts removed
but the pistil, with its oversized,
hairy stigma and style

A member of the bean family, the snow pea has irregular blossoms. Once the flower is pollinated, the petals shrivel and fall away, and the ovary enlarges into a legume.

One of the weirdest things a backyard flower can do is to come in either a male or a female form; such blossoms are said to be *unisexual*. The male blossoms just produce pollen, and female flowers only possess a pistil. Sometimes female flowers do have male stamens, but they are very reduced and nonfunctional, and the same holds true for pistils in male flowers. In our gardens, the most common species with separate male and female flowers are corn and members of the gourd family, such as squash, cucumbers, watermelons, cantaloupes, pumpkins, and gourds. Observe how squash (this includes zucchini) usually have both male flowers, which open and soon fall off, leaving just a naked pedicel, and female blossoms, which develop into fruits.

By the way, another strange feature of flowers in the gourd family is that instead of their ovaries arising above the corolla, as in our "standard" blossom and most other flowers as well, they arise below it. A blossom with its ovary above the corolla is said to be *superior,* while one with an ovary below the corolla is *inferior.*

Yet another curious feature of gourd family members is that their flowers often seem to have three stamens instead of five. In reality, the blossom does have five stamens; however, four of the stamens are united into two pairs.

There are two main flowering strategies for species bearing unisexual flow-

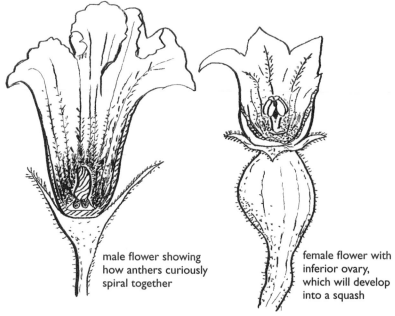

male flower showing
how anthers curiously
spiral together

female flower with
inferior ovary,
which will develop
into a squash

Squash flower cross sections

LOOK AT THAT PLANT!

ers. If a species consists of plants that possess only male flowers or only female flowers, so that a male plant is needed to pollinate the female plant, the plant is said to be *dioecious*. If a species has plants that bear both male and female flowers, then the plant is said to be *monoecious*. Corn and most members of the gourd family are monoecious; spinach and asparagus are dioecious. Sometimes the boundary between monoecious and dioecious plants isn't clear. Red maple trees are usually dioecious, but sometimes you can find a branch or two bearing flowers of the "wrong" sex.

When sepals, petals, stamens, and pistils all occur in one blossom, the flower is said to be *complete*. A flower with one or more of these parts missing is *incomplete*. In our backyards, the most common plants with incomplete blossoms are the grasses, which have no corollas. Trees with flowers lacking corollas include oaks, hickories, elms, and willows. The blossoms of castor bean plants, sometimes marketed in the United States as "mole killers," also bear no corollas.

Now that you've had more practice comparing flowers, let's make a project of examining a real flower in your own backyard.

COMPARING A REAL FLOWER
WITH THE "STANDARD" BACKYARD BLOSSOM
What you will need
an easy-to-see backyard flower

---

1. Using the "standard" backyard blossom drawing as a reference, try to locate each of the following flower parts.

pedicel	anthers (maybe with pollen)
calyx	filaments
sepals	pistil or pistils
corolla	ovary or ovaries
petals or corolla lobes	style or styles
stamens	stigma or stigmas

2. Now go back and note how each of the above parts is the same as or different from those of the "standard" backyard blossom.

3. Reflect for a moment on how your concept of the backyard flower you just examined has changed. Earlier, it probably was just a mass of miscellaneous shapes and colors, but now it has assumed a real personality—an

individuality that will be hard to forget. Moreover, allowing the terms to draw your mind deep into the miniature, surreal world of the flower's filaments and ovaries should have simply been jolly good fun!

There's a whole level of blossom-comparing fun beyond the process you've just accomplished. People who pay close attention to a great number of flowers eventually discover that every family of flowering plants has its own "standard" family blossom.

For instance, there is a "standard" gourd family blossom, with the features mentioned above. There are about seven hundred species in the gourd family, however, and all the blossoms of these seven hundred species, though possessing the same basic gourd family flower structure, are nonetheless just a little different from one another. What a pleasure it is to see how many variations on the gourd family theme Mother Nature has thought up! And the gourd family is just one of dozens of plant families we can find in our backyards.

COMPOSITE FLOWERS

If you try to relate sunflower blossoms to the "standard" blossom, you'll have a hard time. That's because nature has done something bizarre with the flowers of the composite family, to which sunflowers belong. These plants have flower heads composed of a kind of stage or platform, called a *receptacle,* upon which are packed together many tiny flowers. In other words, when you look at a sunflower, the big, bright thing atop the stem that looks like a blossom with many petals is actually a *composite blossom* composed of *hundreds* of tiny flowers.

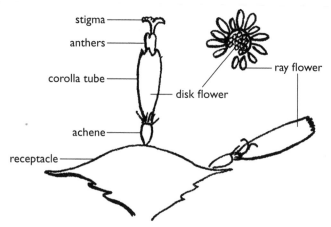

Simplified diagram of a composite flower

LOOK AT THAT PLANT!

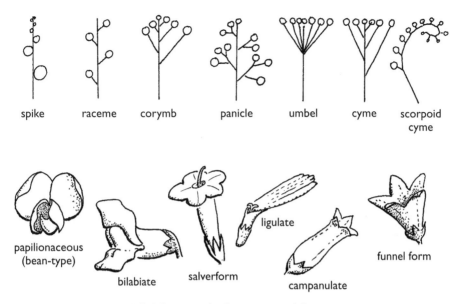

| spike | raceme | corymb | panicle | umbel | cyme | scorpoid cyme |

papilionaceous
(bean-type)

bilabiate salverform

ligulate

campanulate

funnel form

Simplified diagram of inflorescence and flower types

Moreover, in the sunflower's composite blossom there are two distinct categories of tiny flowers. Each flat, yellow, strap radiating from the sunflower's center is a *ray flower*. The dark face of the sunflower is composed of hundreds, if not thousands, of tiny, cylindrical blossoms called *disk flowers*. Each disk flower possesses five minute lobes, and each flower sits atop a fruit called an *achene*, which is the thing popularly known as the sunflower seed.

Not all composite flowers possess both ray and disk flowers. Dandelions, lettuce, and marigolds have composite blossoms composed strictly of ray flowers; eupatorium, ageratum, and bachelor's buttons possess only disk flowers. But daisies, chrysanthemums, coreopsis, cosmos, asters, goldenrod, Jerusalem artichokes, and most other composite family species have both ray and disk flowers.

The composite family is huge. In my little county in western Kentucky, I've listed sixty-three species of wildflowers and weeds belonging to this family, and each year I find more.

MONOCOT FLOWERS

Flowering plants are divided into two great groups: the *monocots* and *dicots*. Monocots, such as corn and other grasses, usually have parallel-veined leaves, but the veins of dicot leaves usually spread and branch, termed *net veined*. Monocot flowers are distinct from dicot flowers in several fundamental ways.

Our "standard" backyard blossom is strictly a dicot flower, whereas some of the most important, showy plants in the backyard are monocots.

One way that all monocot flowers differ from all dicot flowers is that instead of loving the number five, they love the number three, and multiples thereof. Look at any lily, amaryllis, or iris flower, and notice that most conspicuous parts number three or six. Also, especially among these families, often the sepals and petals are so similar—both large, colorful, and fleshy—that they are indistinguishable from one another.

Sometimes petals and sepals that are indistinguishable from one another are called *tepals.* Crocus blossoms, for instance, seem to have six colorful petals and no sepals. In truth, however, the three petals and the three sepals are so similar that they are practically the same, so we can say that crocuses possess six tepals. Just as several petals form a corolla, several tepals compose a *perianth.*

Corn blossoms do a great job of showing us just how exotic monocot blossoms can be. First of all, the corn plant is monoecious, so its flowers are unisexual. Male flowers are clustered toward the top of the plant, in the *tassel;* female flowers make up the ear. Individual male corn blossoms possess perianths composed of chafflike, folded-together scales. Similar to the manner in which composites have more than one blossom squeezed together on a receptacle, corn is one of many, many members of the grass family in which two or more flowers occur in one flowerlike *spikelet.* Usually two male corn flowers, or *florets,* are found in each male spikelet, and the corn ear is a packed-together bunch of female florets. Peel back the shucks on a ripening ear of corn, and here is what you see: Each kernel of corn is an ovary. Arising from each kernel is a silk, which runs to the ear's top and hangs out of the shucks;

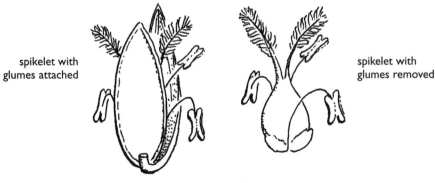

spikelet with
glumes attached

spikelet with
glumes removed

A simple grass flower

LOOK AT THAT PLANT!

a spikelet with one floret above two glumes

a spikelet with several florets above two glumes

The two basic grass-flower arrangements

each of these silks is a style. The tips of the hanging-out silks serve as stigma areas, and the ear's shucks are modified perianth segments.

The interesting thing here is that even though an ear of corn hardly looks at all like our "standard" backyard blossom, it is in fact structurally similar. Corn does have stigmas, styles, and ovaries—but what stigmas, styles, and ovaries they are!

Once you begin paying attention to grass flowers, you'll like them. A randomly chosen grass blossom looks similar to all other grass flowers, but once you begin noticing its tiny features (a good hand lens is needed), any grass flower soon takes on its own unique personality, just like the gaudiest lily. The sheer numbers of different kinds of grasses are staggering. Just in my county, I've identified fifty-five grass species, and each year I find more!

I love using field guides, such as *How to Know the Grasses* (see the Bibliography), to identify grass species. It's fun to see how flower parts that are usually so big and gaudy in dicot flowers become so reduced and understated in grasses. If flower blossoms are like music, then showy lilies are loud, rambunctious heavy metal, but grass flowers are elegant little violin solos. John James Ingalls wrote that "Forests decay, harvests perish, flowers vanish, but grass is immortal." Somehow I feel that more than just referring to how grass is so hard to get rid of in a garden, Ingalls was remarking on the timeless nature of grass's refined simplicity.

The monocots' preference for three is hard to see in grass flowers. If you can find a grass flower with anthers or stigma protruding from close-packed, scalelike parts, notice that, probably, the flower has three stamens and the stigma is three-lobed.

PLANT REPRODUCTION

Don't get so bogged down in counting stigma lobes and figuring out whether something is a petal or a tepal that you forget to ask this fundamental ques-

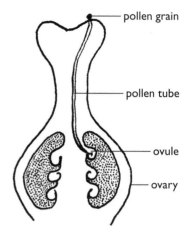

pollen grain

pollen tube

ovule

ovary

In this cross section of a pistil with a germinated pollen grain on its stigma, the pollen grain's pollen tube has grown down through the style into the ovary. Here, its tip, carrying male sex germs, has penetrated an ovule, fertilizing it. Fertilized ovules develop into seeds; ovaries develop into fruits.

tion: Why flowers? Why do flowers exist? Why are they pretty and why do they smell good? Why do so many plants have them?

The short answer is that of all the things nature wants its plants and animals to do, procreating, or reproduction, lies close to the top of the list. And among the vast majority of plants in our gardens and flower beds, flowers are the sexual organs that enable procreation to take place. Here is what flowers do:

Male sex germs are carried in the anthers' *pollen,* which in many flowers appears as a yellow, dusty material. When pollen lands on a stigma, *pollination* occurs. Pollen grains on the stigma germinate rather like seeds, sending a rootlike tube, called the *pollen tube,* down through the style into the ovary, where ovules reside, holding inside them the female sex germs.

The pollen tube's tip carries the male sex germ or germs with it. When the tip penetrates an ovule, the male sex germs migrate from the pollen tube into the ovule, sexual union takes place, and fertilization occurs. As ovules develop into seeds, the ovary swells and becomes a fruit.

This seed- and fruit-producing process is the reason for all flowers to exist; it is a creative process that occurs again and again throughout nature, and it is one of the most fundamental and beautiful processes in all of life.

Everything about a flower—its color, form, size, location on the plant—is related to plant reproduction. Look at how flower design can be dictated by the kind of pollination strategy it uses:

Wind-pollinated blossoms, such as those of corn, produce abundant, lightweight, dusty pollen that the wind can carry. Stigmas on wind-pollinated flowers are usually feathery, so that they expose much more surface area than single, slender stigmas and therefore can catch more pollen. Pollen from wind-pollinated flowers often causes hay fever.

Insect-pollinated blossoms produce pollen that is heavy and gummy, so that it sticks to insect bodies. Stigmas of these flowers are often positioned so that as an insect enters a flower, the stigma touches the part of the insect body on which pollen from another flower is being carried. If a flower depends on butterflies for pollination, it will possess a slender tube to accommodate the butterfly's thin proboscis, but if it's pollinated by bees, the blossom's throat will be spacious enough to accommodate entry of a big bee—there will be no slender tube. Large, open flowers with musky odors, like certain squash blossoms, often depend on beetles that follow the stinky odor into the flower and then walk around aimlessly, accidentally transferring pollen. Heavy, sticky pollen from insect-pollinated blossoms doesn't cause hay fever because it has no way to get into our nostrils.

Once a flower is pollinated and its ovules are fertilized, watching the transformation of one or more pistils into a fruit is a fascinating process.

WATCHING A FLOWER PISTIL DEVELOP INTO A FRUIT

What you will need

a flowering plant

small ribbons or other markers

---

1. Find a newly opened flower; bean or pea plants make good candidates. Tie a small ribbon or other marker below or near the blossom so that later you can easily find it.

2. Observe this blossom from day to day and notice how the pistil changes. As the pistil enlarges into a fruit, what happens to the stamens and corolla? Do the stigma and style enlarge as the ovary grows?

FLOWERLESS PLANTS

Though the vast majority of plants in our backyards possess flowers, by no means do all plants in nature possess them. Flowering plants are just one kind of plant, referred to by botanists as *angiosperms*. In terms of the history of life on earth, flowering plants are newcomers. About 150 million years ago, though plants had been around a long time, no plant bore a flower.

The first more or less plantlike life forms appeared on earth about 2 billion years ago; these were very primitive algaelike organisms called *uralgae*. The uralgae probably reproduced somewhat like today's algae. For many millions of years, earth's main plant communities looked more like green paste than forests.

Plants did not develop true stems for another 1.5 billion years. The first stemmed plants were the ancestors of plants known today as club mosses and horsetails. These plants reproduce by spores, not by flowers, fruits, and seeds. Leaves evolved next. Earth's first plant leaves appeared on the ancestors of today's ferns about 390 million years ago; they also reproduced with spores.

About 345 million years ago, the first seed-producing plants appeared, even though flowers still were not on the scene. These first real seeds occurred on the *gymnosperms,* represented today by conifers, such as pine, spruce and fir trees. If you have these trees in your backyard, you may know that they produce hard *cones.* These cones are not considered real fruits. Conifers have sexual organs vaguely resembling real flowers found on such trees as willows and poplars, but botanists don't regard them as true flowers. Gymnosperm seeds are classified as real seeds, however, so it is accurate to say that seeds came before fruits.

The first real flowering plants, known as *angiosperms,* appeared about 135 million years ago. Flowering plants were so successful at adapting to earth's conditions that over much of the face of the planet they shoved the more primitive kinds of plants aside.

Eventually the angiosperms split into the big subgroups known today as the monocots and dicots. Today it's estimated that there are more than fifty thousand species of monocots and more than two hundred thousand species of dicots. This compares with only about ten thousand species of ferns, fourteen thousand species of moss, and maybe five hundred species of conifers. Clearly, flowering plants now rule the world, not only our backyard gardens and flower beds.

CHAPTER 3

Fruits and Seeds

TYPES OF FRUIT

The next time you slice across a tomato, notice that its interior is separated into several wedge-shaped compartments and that seeds, rather than being randomly and evenly distributed throughout the tomato, tend to be clustered inside these compartments.

In botanical terms, these compartments are referred to as *carpels*. In everyday life, we never speak of carpels, but you need to know about them to get a handle on understanding the differences between the kinds of fruit. In a way, the tomato with its wedge-shaped compartments holding clusters of seeds can represent the "standard" backyard fruit.

If you cut across a snap bean or pea pod, you'll see that the pod possesses no tomatolike interior walls, because beans are fruits with just one carpel. In contrast, a cross section of an iris fruit pod reveals three carpels, and a cut across an okra pod discloses five.

Flower ovaries have carpels too. When botanists in the jungle need to identify a newly encountered plant by its blossom, often the first test he or she conducts is to bring out a very sharp knife, cut across the ovary, and

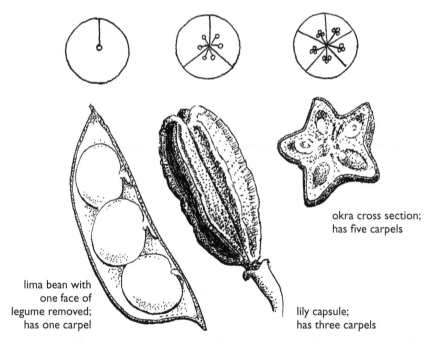

okra cross section; has five carpels

lima bean with one face of legume removed; has one carpel

lily capsule; has three carpels

In nature, carpel number is very constant within plant groups. In horticultural crops, however, as in domesticated animals, there are often surprising variations. For example, the ancestral tomato has two carpels, but modern hybrid tomato fruits may have five or more.

LOOK AT THAT PLANT!

count the carpels. This is because the members of a certain family or genus of plants often all have the same number of carpels.

Now let's take a look at the different kinds of fruits found in our gardens and flower beds.

Legumes are dry fruits (not fleshy like a tomato) derived from a single, one-carpel pistil but with two fruit faces coming together along two *sutures,* or seams. Bean and pea plants produce legumes.

Capsules, like legumes, are dry fruits derived from a single pistil, but they are partitioned into more than one carpel and open in various ways. Irises produce capsules.

Drupes are fleshy, one-seeded fruits that do not open at all. Their seeds are enclosed in woody cases. Peaches are drupes.

Berries are fleshy fruits with few to many seeds. The seeds are not enclosed in woody cases. This means that, botanically speaking, tomatoes are berries, but strawberries and blackberries are not!

Aggregate fruits are derived from several to many one-carpel pistils, all occurring in one flower. Strawberries and blackberries are aggregate fruits, not berries.

We'd have to get too technical to say why sunflowers, marigolds, and other members of the composite family produce seedlike fruits referred to as *achenes* (yes, sunflower seeds are fruits!) and why corn seeds are *grains.*

This is a good time to ask whether a tomato is a fruit or a vegetable. We've just spoken of tomatoes as fruits, but English speakers generally regard them as vegetables.

We have seen that a fruit is the item that develops from a pistil—the flower part with one or more seeds inside it. Therefore, technically, tomatoes are certainly fruits. But then, so are cucumbers, muskmelons, squash, ears of corn, and many other kinds of produce that don't seem particularly "fruity."

Vegetable is a very general term applied to plants. In its broadest sense, even trees are vegetables. Well, a language is the way people use it, and languages can often be self-contradictory, as well as vague, so there's no point in arguing the matter. We'll just say that tomatoes can be both fruits and vegetables, depending on who's talking.

Often we don't associate any flowers or fruits with certain garden plants. For example, where are the flowers and fruits for cabbage and lettuce? We don't usually see these plants' reproductive organs because they are harvested before flowers and fruits form. If we should leave the plants alone as summer progresses, however, they would indeed send up a perfectly typical stem, and flowers and fruits would eventually develop.

If you plant your cabbage so late in the spring that they have not begun forming heads before really hot weather arrives, you may end up with nothing but cabbage flowers and fruits. When a plant is composed of a rosette of overlapping leaves, like a head of lettuce or cabbage, and then heat or perhaps changing lengths of night cause it to very rapidly send up a flowering shoot, the process is referred to as *bolting*.

We have seen that potatoes develop on underground stolons, have nothing to do with flowers, and therefore cannot be considered any kind of fruit. Nonetheless, potato plants usually do produce attractive flowers that are very similar to tomato and pepper flowers, because potatoes, tomatoes, and peppers all belong to the same plant family, the nightshade family. Curiously, potato blossoms very seldom produce fruits. Once in a blue moon, however, a potato flower does manage to set fruit. Be sure to watch for potato fruits on your own plants. If your fruits contain seeds, try to germinate them.

SEEDS

In the previous chapter, we saw that seeds develop from fertilized ovules, which reside inside flower ovaries. One interesting thing to do with seeds is to cut across them to see what's inside.

Inside most kinds of seeds found in our gardens and flower beds, there are two general areas. First, there is a relatively large zone of whitish, unstructured, starchy or oily material; this is food for the future germinating seedling. When the embryo first begins growing, extending its shoot up through the sunless soil, it will not be able to manufacture its own food the way mature green plants do, because that requires sunlight; at this critical time, it will tap the energy stored in this high-calorie "seed food."

To one side of this area, there lies a relatively small *embryo*, composed of exceedingly tiny structures—the first hints of folded leaves, stem, and root.

We humans tend to eat so many seeds (corn and corn products, wheat products, beans, peas) precisely because seeds contain these food-storage areas and embryos. By eating the energy-rich starchy or oily material, we take advantage of the energy nature put there for the future developing seed embryo. When we eat the embryos themselves, we take into our own bodies the proteins and other nutrient elements inside the developing embryos.

By the way, when wheat flour or cornmeal is advertised as *degermed*, it means that the embryos have been removed, leaving behind just the calorie-rich starchy or oily material. Degermed wheat flour may be whiter and make a lighter bread than whole-wheat flour, which contains the ground-up embryos, but degermed flour is significantly less nutritious, because it lacks the embryos' protein.

A seed's embryo and the large food-storage area can be associated in two basic ways. In corn and other cereals, castor beans, and buckwheat seeds, for instance, the embryo is simply embedded in the storage area. In other seeds, probably the majority of them, the large storage area is actually part of the future plant, usually in the form of special leaflike items called *cotyledons.*

When a bean, or nearly any of our common garden plants except corn and other monocots, first emerges from the soil, two green, thick, kidney-shaped, leaflike things first appear, and then the stem with regular-shaped and normal-textured leaves emerges from between the two leaflike things. Those first two leaflike things are the cotyledons.

In such plants, starchy or oily food material meant for the germinating seedling is stored in the cotyledons. When the seed germinates, the cotyledons are pulled out of the seed coat and thrust upward, fueling the seedling as all this happens. Finally, aboveground, they spread apart and may even turn green; then from between them, the plant's stem and leaves begin developing.

EXAMINING A BEAN

What you will need
a large bean, such as a lima

---

1. Soak the bean overnight to make opening it easier.

2. Holding the soaked bean, notice that its skin, or *seed coat,* is smooth and continuous all over except in one place, which may look a little like a tiny, closed mouth with thick lips. This tiny thing, called a *hilum,* is the scar remaining from when the seed was an ovule attached to its ovary with a placenta. If you picked a fresh fruit hanging on a bean plant, opened the fruit's husks, and removed the bean yourself, it probably was still attached to the pod via the placenta, which you broke, leaving the hilum, as you pulled the bean away.

3. Remove the seed coat, which may already have ruptured.

4. Most of a bean seed consists of the two cotyledons, both full of starchy or oily material, pressing against one another, joined together only in the vicinity of the embryo. Thus maybe 99 percent of the bean in your hand is

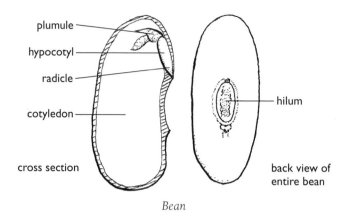

plumule
hypocotyl
radicle
cotyledon

cross section

hilum

back view of
entire bean

Bean

made up of the two cotyledons. Remove one of the cotyledons. If the cotyledons don't separate easily, squeeze on the bean as you roll it between your fingers.

5. When the cotyledons are separated, one of them will carry the embryo embedded in it. In a good-sized lima bean, you will be able to see the embryo with your naked eyes. It will reside near the hilum. Discard the other cotyledon.

6. With your hand lens, maybe you can see the embryo's very tiny, tightly folded-together "baby leaves," more properly called *plumules*. Right below the plumules resides a smooth item looking like a tiny, shiny grain of rice; the broad part of this is referred to as the embryo's *hypocotyl*. The hypocotyl's end opposite the plumule is pointed and is considered to be the radicle; the division between hypocotyl and radicle is not well defined. Later the radicle will enlarge, grow out of the seed, and become the seedling's first root, its *primary root.*

Monocots and Dicots. All germinating seedlings beginning life with two cotyledons—beans, cabbage, squash, marigolds, and most other garden and flower bed plants—are known as *dicots.* Those with one cotyledon are *monocots.* The grass (including corn), lily, amaryllis, iris, orchid, canna, water lily, banana, arum, palm, and cattail families are monocots.

The word *dicot* is actually a shortened form of the word *dicotyledon,* which means that the plant has two cotyledons. Similarly, *monocot* is short for *monocotyledon,* referring to the single cotyledon that pops up when a monocot seedling emerges.

Sprouting Seeds. One thing that is nearly as much fun as planting seeds in a garden is sprouting them inside the house. Not only is this a form of indoor gardening, but it also can provide nutritious food.

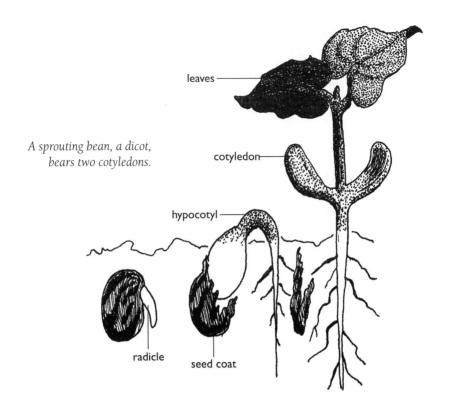

leaves

A sprouting bean, a dicot, bears two cotyledons.

cotyledon

hypocotyl

radicle

seed coat

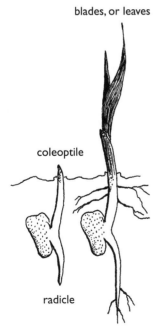

blades, or leaves

coleoptile

A sprouting corn kernel, a monocot, sprouts just a single first blade. Corn and other grasses, evolved only recently in the history of flowering plants, have developed specialized parts. Their first shoot is actually a coleoptile, a sheath protecting the unfolding blades; the coleoptile has evolved from the single simple cotyledon.

radicle

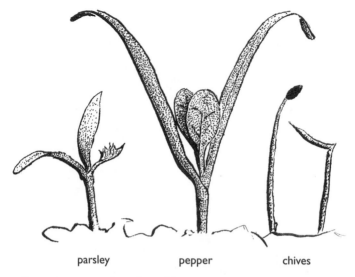

parsley   pepper   chives

Each seedling as it emerges from the soil has its own unique appearance. In your notebook, sketch each seedling as you identify it, and learn to distinguish it from all others.

Sprouting seeds undergo chemical changes that make the sprouts much more nutritious than the unsprouted seeds. Research has shown that sprouting wheat seeds significantly increases amounts of niacin and vitamins B_1 and C. Folic acid and vitamin B_2 concentrations were increased four times.

GROWING SPROUTS IN A JAR

What you will need
a wide-mouth gallon jar
old nylon stockings or piece of cheesecloth
rubber band
beans or seeds for sprouting (alfalfa, mung, lentil, garbanzo, soy, or other)

---

1. Various kinds of beans or seeds for sprouting can be purchased at a health food store. They should be fairly new ones meant for sprouting, or else they may be dead or weak and will not germinate properly. Don't use beans meant to be sown; these may be treated with toxic fungicides and insecticides.

2. Cut a circular nylon or cheesecloth cover for the jar's mouth, about six inches across. Make sure the jar and covering are clean.

3. Pour some beans or seeds into the jar. A surprisingly small amount goes a long way—about one and a half cups of large beans such as soy, one cup of smaller mung beans, or a half cup of tiny alfalfa seeds will do.

4. Stretch the covering across the jar's mouth so that it is taut, and secure it with the rubber band. The rubber band should be tight enough to hold the covering on when the sprouts are being washed.

5. Wash the beans by filling the jar one-quarter full with tap water, swirling, then pouring off the excess water through the nylon or cheesecloth.

6. Fill the jar two-thirds full of water, and soak the seeds. Soak soybeans overnight. Smaller mung and alfalfa seeds can be ready in about six hours, but soaking overnight won't hurt.

7. After soaking, pour out all the water. If using small seeds, which tend to clump together, roll the jar so that the seeds will adhere to the jar's wet inner surface instead of clumping; the idea is to make free air available to all seeds. Soybeans are so big that air circulates around them as they lie on the jar's bottom.

8. Store the jar in its sprouting place. No light is needed; anyplace will do, even inside a cabinet, as long as it's neither too hot (fungi will grow) or too cold (slows down germination). A corner shelf in the laundry room is good.

9. Wash the beans each morning and night by running tap water into the jar, sloshing the contents around, and pouring out the liquid, repeating this procedure three or four times.

10. Alfalfa sprouts are ready for harvesting once they reach one to two inches long. Mung sprouts should be two to three inches, and soybean sprouts about one and three-quarter inches. When the sprouts are big enough, spread them on a tray and place them in the sunlight for half an hour or so; on cloudy days, let them stay out longer. This activates photosensitive enzymes, which make the sprouts more nutritious. Also, the chlorophyll thus produced will add a green coloration, making them look more appetizing.

11. Eat your sprouts! Don't just shyly sprinkle a few onto salads, in soups, or in sandwiches—use them by the handfuls. Nothing is as good as a crunchy heap of alfalfa sprouts on whole-grain bread, maybe smeared with a little salad dressing.

Here's another project for those of you who are reading this in the middle of winter, have no gardening equipment, and just can't wait to begin germinating and growing plants *in the ground!* This project will at least give you a taste of seedling starting.

1. Prepare a sterile seed-starting soil mixture. Regular garden soil is undesirable because it contains disease organisms that can kill sprouting seeds. Mix one part store-bought peat moss with two parts potting soil, or mix equal parts of peat moss and vermiculite. Moisten this mixture, and add a little fertilizer.

2. Now fill the cup to about half an inch from the rim.

3. Atop the soil mixture, place one to three seeds of a garden plant of your choice. If you have seeds packaged for the current year and proper, sterile soil mixture, the seeds will almost invariably sprout. If you want insurance, however, plant two or three seeds, then later snip down the less vigorous.

4. Cover the seeds with soil mixture. As a general rule, the appropriate depth is usually three to four times the seed's diameter. (This depth is generally given on the seed packet.) Firm down the soil with a couple of gentle pats, making sure that the seeds make good contact with the moist mixture.

5. Place the cup inside a sealed plastic bag. At this point, the soil mixture should be moist but not so wet that water is running out the hole. Thus covered, the cup will require no further watering until the seedling is well established.

6. Once the seedling has sprouted and is well established, remove the bag, and begin occasional sprinkling with fertilizer-enriched water. Sprinkle once a day, just enough to keep the soil mixture moist and spongy. The sterile soil is low in nutrients, so it is important to use fertilizer. A balanced liquid fertilizer with an N–P–K (nitrogen, phosphorus, and potassium) analysis of 15–30–15 is fine. (See chapter 12.) Notice the high phosphorus content, which we'll see later is good for cell division and root formation.

CHAPTER 4

A Plant's Inner World

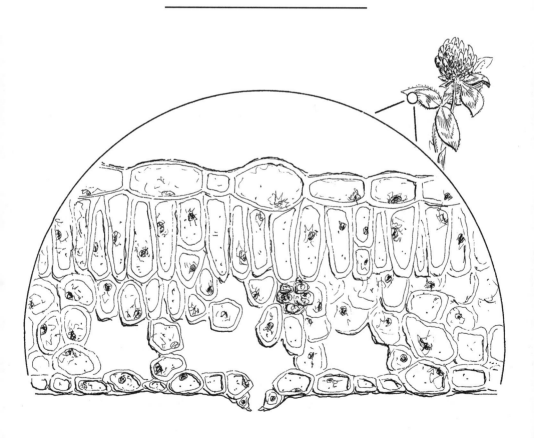

PLANTS AND SUNLIGHT

Probably nothing on earth is more mind-boggling—and certainly nothing is more important for earth's living things—than something that happens every day among all green plants, including those in our backyards.

The thing that happens is this: Energy in the form of sunlight flows across the vast emptiness of space between earth and the sun, and when this energy floods onto earth's surface, some of it is captured by green plants and stored for later use.

Green plants capture sunlight's energy by *photosynthesizing* air and water into a *simple carbohydrate,* which is then stored in various ways. Here is the simplified chemical formula for the photosynthesis process:

$$6CO_2 + 6H_2O \xrightarrow[\text{energy}]{\text{sunlight}} C_6H_{12}O_6 + 6O_2$$

What this formula says is that in photosynthesis, *energy from sunlight is used to combine molecules of the gas called carbon dioxide with molecules of water to produce a white, starchy carbohydrate and oxygen gas.*

This is worth thinking about. The formula says that when we look at a green plant, be it a tomato or a giant sequoia, we're seeing something concocted mostly from a gas and water. Nature has brewed two transparent, yielding materials with sunlight, plus tiny amounts of a few nutrient elements (discussed in chapter 12), to produce plants with a wide variety of leaves, blossoms, and fruits.

Green plants photosynthesize only when they have light to fuel the chemical reactions. When the sun goes down, plants still need energy, so they use up some of what they have stored in the process of *respiration.* The simplified chemical formula for respiration is the photosyntheses formula in reverse:

$$C_6H_{12}O_6 + 6O_2 \longrightarrow 6O_2 + 6H_2O + \text{energy}$$

This formula says that in the respiration process, *the carbohydrate produced by photosynthesis is "burned" with oxygen to form gaseous carbon dioxide, water, and energy.*

The reason that green plants go to all this trouble is that they need energy to grow and to produce flowers and fruits.

The physics and chemistry behind all these goings-on are fun to think about. We get to stretch our minds. Don't worry if you don't understand these principles the first time; just get ready to think *big,* and hold on!

Now, the science of physics has a law that states that nothing is ever really destroyed; it just changes form. In the sun's core, for instance, it looks like matter is being obliterated because at one time it's there but then suddenly it isn't. What's actually happening, however, is that, as the sun's core matter disappears, it is being transformed into heat, light, and many other things, like X rays and gamma rays. These then flow through space, some of them reaching earth. And the sunlight energy is magically used by plants to put invisible things together into matter that can be touched.

Through photosynthesis, earth's green plants capture sunlight energy by bonding together carbon, hydrogen, and oxygen atoms from carbon dioxide and water to form a carbohydrate. Scientifically, a carbohydrate can be defined as molecules composed of carbon, hydrogen, and oxygen. As we perceive it, a carbohydrate is a white, starchy material. The starchy part of the

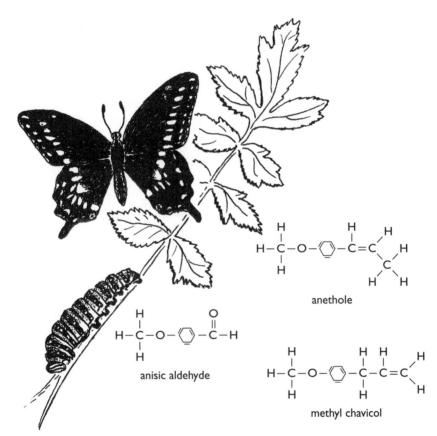

anethole

anisic aldehyde

methyl chavicol

Many of a garden's most fascinating events occur at the unseen chemical level. For example, black swallowtail butterfly larvae are attracted to parsley, carrots, celery, and other plants in the parsley family containing the three essential oils diagrammed here. Orange tree leaves also contain these oils and thus are eaten by the larvae as well.

stored food found in seeds is mostly carbohydrate. The white part of white potatoes is practically pure carbohydrate.

When dietitians speak of *complex carbohydrates* as being good to eat, they are referring to very long carbohydrate molecules—molecules composed of thousands of carbon, hydrogen, and oxygen atoms. It takes time for the body to break these long molecules down, and thus energy is released in a slow, methodical way. Simple carbohydrates, such as sugars, on the other hand, are made of short molecules, maybe with only a couple dozen atoms of carbon, hydrogen, and oxygen. These short molecules break down at the same time and assault the body with a brief, intense flush of energy.

In a way, plants storing energy in photosynthesized carbohydrates and then using that energy later is like a person lifting a rock onto a table, and then later pushing the rock off the table to crack a nut on the floor.

Once the rock is on the table, it has *potential energy*. That abstract energy has been transferred into the rock from the person as he or she used energy to lift the rock. Once the rock is pushed off the table, its potential energy is used in the act of smashing the nut.

Happily for us animals who need oxygen, green plants produce much more oxygen during the daytime photosynthesis process than they use during their nighttime respiration process. Were it not for green plants producing more oxygen than they need, we animals would suffocate as earth's oxygen ran out.

This is why some of us are very concerned about earth's oxygen-producing forests being destroyed and the oceans being polluted by chemicals that damage oxygen-producing algae.

TESTING FOR
SUNLIGHT-PRODUCED CARBOHYDRATE

What you will need

a sunny day

a growing herbaceous leaf in full sunlight

stiff, black paper about the size of an index card (three by five inches)

a large paper clip or adhesive tape

rubbing alcohol (isopropyl)

an electric stove with a functional ventilation hood

ten drops of tincture of iodine (the kind used on cuts or scrapes)

---

1. The day before you do this experiment, locate a broad leaf that remains in sunlight all day long and that you can clip off at the end of this experiment. A fast-growing leaf of a bean plant would be perfect. A fast-growing leaf is a young leaf about two-thirds grown, rapidly expanding in size. Mark the leaf so that you can find it later.

2. Fold the stiff, black paper across the middle, with the fold parallel with the short sides. (The paper should be thick enough that sunlight will not penetrate, but not so thick that it cannot be easily folded.) In one half, cut a simple design, such as a circle, a diamond, or a star.

3. In the early morning before the sun comes up, sandwich your chosen leaf between the halves of the folded card so that the cutout design faces the sky. You want sunlight to be blocked from all parts of the leaf except for what passes through the cutout design. Secure the paper onto the leaf with paper clips or adhesive tape.

4. At day's end, remove the whole leaf. Inside the house, remove the folded paper.

5. In a small pan, pour about half an inch of rubbing alcohol. Drop the leaf into the pan.

6. On an *electric* stove, bring the alcohol to a boil. Use a lower heat than is needed for boiling water, because alcohol boils at a much lower temperature. The *medium* setting should be adequate. An electric stove is required because alcohol is flammable. *Important: Don't heat the alcohol over an open flame or at too high a temperature, or you may cause a fire!* An easygoing boil will do. If the boiling becomes too vigorous, lift the pan off the burner until the boiling calms down. Since odoriferous, eye-burning fumes rise off boiling alcohol, use the stove's ventilation hood.

7. Once the alcohol has become dark with chlorophyll boiled from the leaf and the leaf itself is much paler than before, remove the pan from the heat. Carefully remove the leaf and place it on a saucer.

8. Using a Q-tip or an eyedropper, apply iodine evenly over the leaf's surface. If the experiment is a success, a dark design matching the pattern cut into the paper should appear on the blanched leaf.

9. Keeping in mind that iodine stains carbohydrate a very dark purple color, reflect on the meaning of the dark purple pattern.

The experiment had you affix the paper to the leaf in the early morning because at that time stored carbohydrate in leaves is at a low point, some having been consumed as the leaf respired during the night, and some having been transported to the plant's food-storage areas. Late in the afternoon of a sunny day, those parts of the leaf that have received sunlight will contain a maximum amount of carbohydrate because it will have been photosynthesized by the leaf over the course of the day.

For many chemical experiments, you don't even need the simple equipment called for in the above project. Each person carries his or her own personal chemical laboratory in the form of the eyes, tongue, and nose. For example, consider the next project, in which the apple is analyzed.

ANALYZING APPLES

What you will need

an unripe and a ripe apple

1. Slice open an unripe apple, and take a small bite of it. Your tongue should quickly inform you that there's very little apple taste there. In fact, the apple is so sour that it may sting your tongue. This sourness indicates that unripe apples are full of various kinds of acids.

2. Smell the unripe green apple. You should detect very little, if any, "apple" odor. This indicates that the acids present are not the kind that evaporate and waft into the nose; they are *nonvolatile* acids, such as malic and citric acids.

3. Nibble on the unripe apple's skin. Your lips should pucker a little. This is caused by tannic acid, famous for its pucker-causing quality.

4. Now go through the above steps with a ripe apple. You will find, of course, that the apple not only tastes like an apple, but also is sweet, smells fruity, and will not pucker the lips. Obviously, enormous chemical changes have taken place.

To the practiced nose of a chemist, the ripe-apple odor reveals the presence of a kind of easy-to-evaporate, or *volatile,* chemical compound called an *ester.* Esters are formed by combining acids, like those found in unripe apples, with alcohol.

We know from our experiment that there were acids in the unripe apple, but where did the alcohol come from? The respiration formula showed that when carbohydrates break down (apples are mostly carbohydrate, even unripe ones), oxygen is needed. Well, inside an unripe apple there is very little oxygen, so a different kind of chemical reaction is needed to break down the apple's carbohydrate. This special kind of reaction, which occurs throughout nature when carbohydrate needs to be broken down without the aid of oxygen, also occurs when beer is brewed or homemade bread is set out to rise; we call this process *fermentation*. And alcohol is a product of fermentation.

The apple's sweetness reveals the presence of sugars. So where did the sugars come from? Well, in unripe apples, the stored carbohydrate is so complex that it isn't sweet. As an apple ripens, however, the long carbohydrate molecules break down to much shorter ones, and the shortest carbohydrate molecules are nothing less than the simple sugars known as sucrose (table sugar) and fructose. And table sugar and fructose are very sweet indeed.

In your garden, most immature fruits will taste bitter, but mature ones will be sweet. It's the same breaking-down process of complex carbohydrate to sugar just described for apples. Gardeners who raise parsnips and turnips know that these root crops are sweetest when a good freezing helps smash complex carbohydrates into simple sugars.

PLANTS AND WATER

As we saw in the photosynthesis equation, water is one of the most important chemicals for plants. If a plant becomes too thirsty, it becomes stunted or even dies. Therefore, it seems surprising that through a process called *transpiration,* garden plants lose about 99 percent of all the water they take up through their roots. Transpiration takes place both through the varnishlike *cuticle,* a film covering the plant's entire body, and even much more through *stomata,* which are tiny openings or pores on the plant body surface.

On a sunny day, hold a thin bean leaf or a blade of corn up to the sun and look closely at the leaf's undersurface, using a magnifying glass if you have one. Stomata should be just barely visible, causing the leaf's surface to look a little grainy. Beneath a microscope, stomata look like tiny lips. The lower surface of a blade of corn holds about 64,000 stomata *per square inch,* and the lower surface of a bean plant about 160,000!

MONITOR TRANSPIRATION TAKING PLACE

What you will need
a vigorously growing potted plant
a plastic bag

---

1. Choose a fast-growing potted plant and water it moderately—not so much that water runs through the drainage hole. A large, healthy geranium in a smallish pot filled with crumbly potting soil would be perfect.

2. Place the entire pot, but not the plant, into a plastic bag of appropriate size. Tie the bag's mouth around the base of the plant's stem so that no water in the pot can escape unless it's transpired by the plant.

3. Precisely weigh the whole assemblage, note the date and time, and place it outside. The sunnier and warmer it is, the better the experiment works.

4. Prepare a line graph so that you can plot weighings over a period of several days. The graph's vertical axis should show weight, and the horizontal axis should show time.

5. Weigh the assemblage every day at the same time, and plot the falling weight on the graph. Assuming a cow isn't coming during the night to nibble on your geranium, any weight loss will be nearly entirely attributable to transpiration.

Transpiration isn't the only way plants lose water. The next time you are up early and the grass and other plants are wet with dew, take out your magnifying glass, get onto your hands and knees, and look closely at how the dew rests upon the individual blades of grass and leaves of your backyard herbage. If the herbage is simply wet, then that's dew. But if leaf blades are adorned with large pearls of water at their tips, and leaf margins are beaded with similar crystal-clear droplets, then you're seeing the results of *guttation*. Guttation occurs when plants exude water but the air is so moist that instead of evapo-

Most water is lost from plants as water vapor, but it may also leave in liquid form, in the process called guttation.

rating, the water beads up in large droplets. Guttation is one way plants get rid of excess water.

Excess water is one thing, but we all know that often, during dry weather, plants die for need of water. Remembering that plants transpire, even when they are thirsty, a question arises: Why would plants have evolved so that they lose so much precious water through transpiration? It's true that transpiring helps hot plants cool off, just as sweating helps overheated humans cool off. But even vigorously transpiring leaves cool by only three to six degrees Fahrenheit. Leaves lose most of their excess heat through radiation, the way a hot brick does when left in a cool room.

Neither does the transpiration process pull water from the roots to where it's needed above. Experiments show that plants transport water upward even when no transpiration takes place.

It appears that plants transpire largely because they can't avoid doing so. The photosynthesis formula shows that photosynthesizing plants need carbon dioxide as much as they need water, and the only way they can obtain all the carbon dioxide they need is to open their stomata. Needed carbon dioxide flows in, but needed water flows out, even if the plant is thirsty.

Therefore, the situation represents a compromise between two conflicting needs. It's hard to believe that nature would be forced into such an awkward, dangerous situation with regard to such a fundamental matter as a plant's need for water, but that's the way it's turned out.

Actually, it makes me feel a little good, knowing that even Mother Nature from time to time must make uncomfortable, messy compromises.

LIGHT AND DARKNESS

Back in the 1920s it was discovered that if flowering plants were grown in light chambers in which the relative lengths of day and night were manipulated, the plants' flowering and fruiting schedules were thrown off. Some plants tended to flower when day length was twelve hours or less (short-day plants), while others flowered only when day length was twelve hours or more (long-day plants). The flowering of others didn't seem to be affected at all by day-length variations (day-neutral plants). Botanists refer to the period of time that light is provided to an organism as the photoperiod. If a short-day or long-day plant doesn't receive the right period of light, even if it receives abundant light otherwise, it may not flower at all or its flowers may develop very late.

Today we know that really it's the length of the period of darkness that triggers flowering, not light. By the time this was discovered, however, terms like short-day and long-day were already in common use, so they are still used.

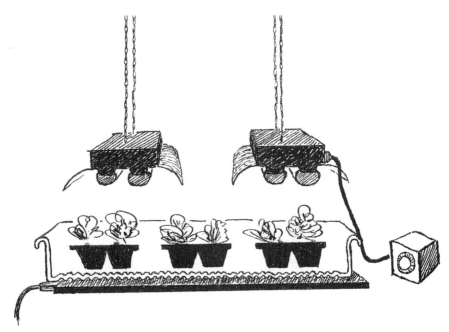

Simple growth chambers for conducting photoperiod experiments, or simply to grow your own seedlings, can be constructed for less than $100. Four four-foot-long fluorescent lights illuminate a growing area four feet long and sixteen inches wide. Such a unit burns about 160 watts of electricity and costs approximately $4 per month. The lights should hang no closer than two or three inches above the top leaves. Bottom heat can be provided with a special heating mat with a built-in thermostat, keeping the soil between seventy and eighty degrees. For regular seedling growing, the timer should be set for at least twelve hours of light a day, but no more than sixteen.

Anyone who knows how to make a Christmas cactus adorn itself resplendently with red blossoms at Christmas knows how to deal with photoperiod requirements. It happens that the Christmas cactus has been programmed by nature to create flower buds when days become shorter. Therefore, a gardener who wants flowers at Christmas must decrease the cactus's hours of sunlight (increase the hours of darkness) during September and October. One of my friends whose Christmas cactus is fully flowering every Christmas says that her secret is to put the cactus behind the piano on September 15 every year, and forget about it until mid-December.

In the Christmas cactus's native environment, when nights become longer, a dry season occurs. Therefore, watering also must be diminished drastically.

Besides flowering, photoperiod governs other events as well. Some trees don't begin preparing for fall unless shorter autumn days cue them to do so.

Thus, if a tree from Canada is planted closer to the equator, such as in Mexico, where fall days are longer, but atop a mountain, where winters still can be severe, the tree may not develop the cold-resistance it needs, even though nights become gradually colder as winter approaches. This tree may die during the Mexican winter, simply because in Mexico, even at high elevations, nights are never as long as those in Canada.

Similarly, potato formation proceeds best during short days (long nights). Thus if a potato is planted so that its main potato-making time occurs during summer's long days, potato production may suffer.

In seed catalogs, notice that onion seeds and sets are often characterized as short-day or long-day. Short-day and long-day varieties have been bred because during the northern summer, night length changes much more drastically than in the South. If a northerner plants a short-day bulb, the onion will begin producing its bulb too early, before its green leaves have grown enough to photosynthesize all the food the bulb needs, and the bulb will turn out runty. Therefore, northerners should plant long-day varieties, and southerners short-day ones.

PLANTS AND COLD WEATHER

Gardeners who start seedlings indoors or buy plants from greenhouses need to know this: Seedlings that have always lived sheltered lives assume that they'll have it soft for the rest of their lives and don't bother to toughen themselves up for such things as cold nights, intense sunlight, and the drying-out effect of wind.

Plants that have always lived indoors but now must live outdoors must be toughened up slowly, in a process called *hardening off*. Let's make a project of this.

HARDEN OFF INDOOR-RAISED PLANTS

What you will need
indoor-raised plants

---

1. A couple of weeks before setting the plants in the garden, stop fertilizing them and reduce their water.

2. A week before transplanting, set the plants outside *in a shady place* for two or three days. If at any time during the entire period the night temperatures are forecast to drop below forty degrees, bring the plants in overnight.

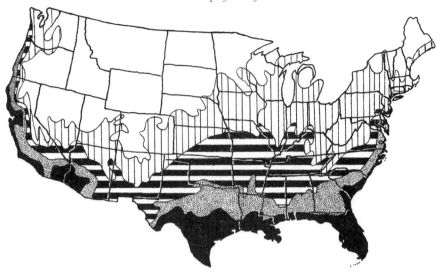

Generalized map of U.S. frost zones

First expected frost in fall

☐ before October 1

▥ October 1–October 20

▬ October 20–November 10

▦ November 10–November 20

■ after November 20

Last expected frost in spring

☐ after May 1

▥ April 25–May 1

▬ March 5–April 25

▦ March 1–March 5

■ before March 1

3. For the next two or three days, keep the plants in a spot receiving two or three hours of daily sunshine.

4. For two or three more days, place them where sun hits daily for four or five hours.

Note: If the seedlings are especially spindly, or if overcast skies greet your plants instead of sun, double the above times.

Hardening off isn't a gardener's only defense against spring's cold weather. One of the most enlightened approaches is to make good use of the *greenhouse effect*. In a greenhouse, sunlight enters and the air warms up, but the warm air can't escape back outside because of the greenhouse's glass panes. On earth, the greenhouse effect comes into play when sunlight strikes the earth, warms things up, and the resulting heat can't escape back into outer space because of an ever-increasing layer of carbon dioxide, which behaves like a greenhouse's glass panes. The reason that sunlight's heat energy can enter through carbon dioxide, but heat energy reradiated from things that have been warmed up can't leave the earth through the same carbon dioxide is this: Sunlight's energy is of a short wavelength that can penetrate carbon dioxide, but reradiated energy is of a longer wavelength that cannot.

Cold frames work like greenhouses, except that they are smaller. A typical cold frame is about six feet long, three feet wide, and about a foot high; has glass on top and wooden sides; and opens onto garden soil below. Its top is tilted so that maximum sunlight enters. Since on a chilly, sunny day temperatures inside a cold frame can soar above one hundred degrees Fahrenheit, the glass top is usually fixed so that it can be cracked open or removed once temperatures rise above eighty degrees.

Plants inside cold frames get a jump on spring. A well-functioning cold frame can be chock full of green onions, mature radishes, lettuce, and spinach while the rest of the garden is still frost-nipped and dead. On especially cold nights, a blanket or thick layer of straw over a cold frame helps protect the tender plants inside.

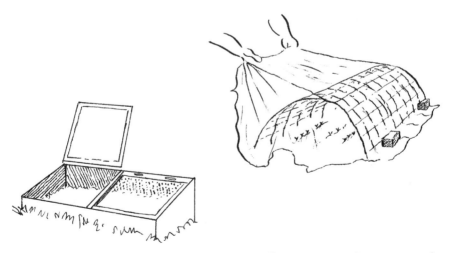

Cold frames and tunnels make use of the greenhouse effect to capture radiant energy and warm the soil below them, stimulating early spring growth. Cold frames constructed of red cedar with hinged Plexiglas lids may cost more than $100, but tunnels made with spare plastic sheeting spread over unused lengths of fence may not cost anything.

Cold frames also can be used to harden off plants. As transplant time approaches, just open the glass top wider and wider over a period of time.

THE FIVE THINGS A PLANT NEEDS

After reading about water problems, photoperiod, hardening off, and the rest, you might feel as though growing plants is like embarking on a "mission impossible." Of course, that's not so, because if it were, gardening wouldn't be America's favorite pastime, and agriculture couldn't be done on such a large, impersonal scale.

One way to think about growing plants is this: Plants need only five basic things. Supply those five things, and the plant will take care of the rest and will flourish. So what are those five things? They are sunlight, air, water, nutrients, and protection from outside threats. Notice that "having a green thumb" isn't on the list.

Let's think a little about each of the above items, in terms of how we must deal with them in our gardens and flower beds.

With a proper soil mixture, careful watering, appropriate sunlight, and protection from outside threats, plants such as this tomato can be grown nicely under just about any circumstances—even in a broken plastic bucket.

LOOK AT THAT PLANT!

Late frosts can be deadly for many garden and flower bed plants. Plastic milk jugs with the bottoms cut out can be set over tomato plants to provide excellent, inexpensive protection.

Sunlight. The vast majority of vegetable-garden plants need all the sun they can get, except lettuce, which may become bitter if it receives too much. Among flower bed plants, however, the following are famous for needing shade or at least semishade: anthurium, begonia, caladium, dieffenbachia, dracaena, fuchsia, maranta, monstera, pandanus, peperomia, philodendron, pilea, podocarpus, schefflera, selaginella, and spathiphyllum. Many ferns need shade, as well.

Most flower bed plants survive in places that are sometimes in the sun, sometimes in the shade, but they may do best in full sun. Be sure to pay attention to any plant's sunlight needs when putting it out.

Air. If soil around a green plant's roots is too compact or wet, air won't circulate properly, carbon dioxide will concentrate and oxygen levels will plummet, roots won't form right, and complex soil chemistry will be unable to take place. The soil air problem is addressed in chapter 12. You'll see that it's usually a simple problem to deal with, though it may require a lot of work, adding organic material to the soil and tilling it.

Air pollution certainly damages some plants, but garden and flower bed species seem to be more tolerant than many native species. I'd think twice, however, about eating produce that has been covered by toxic wastes from local smokestacks.

Water. If a soil is too sandy, water drains right through it, becoming unavailable to plants. But if soil is too clayey, rainwater runs off instead of soaking in. This problem is also addressed in chapter 12, and you'll see that managing soil water is very closely related to managing soil air.

Nutrients. Some soils hold more nutrients than others. Fertilizers can enrich soil, but which fertilizers should be used, and how much? Sometimes too much causes plants to grow luxuriously but produce very few fruits; too much can even burn and kill plants. Chapter 12 also looks at soil's essential nutrients in detail.

Protection against Outside Threats. Garden plants must be protected against animals that would eat them, cold temperatures that would chill them, dry winds that would wilt them, diseases that would weaken or kill them, weeds that compete with them for sunlight and water, and a host of other enemies. This may sound like a grab bag of nearly uncontrollable problems. It's surprising, however, how few of these problems appear in properly managed gardens and flower beds. A hallmark of proper management is keeping soil healthy by incorporating into it a lot of organic matter (discussed in chapter 12), using mulch, and paying attention to the plants' special needs, such as building trellises for beans that twine.

CHAPTER 5

Vegetable Portraits, A to Z

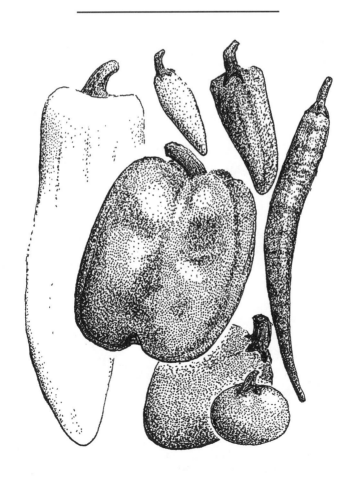

Directions on how to grow specific vegetable plants appear on seed packets, on flowerpot and seed-tray labels, and in gardening books. This kind of information is not repeated below. What follows is information you won't find on the seed packets.

You can gather much, much more of this kind of information by looking up plant names in encyclopedias and dictionaries. In libraries, fascinating facts can be unearthed by thumbing through gardening books. You can look up plant names in the *Guide to Periodical Literature,* which will direct you to magazine articles. If your library has computer terminals tied to a data bank listing magazine and book topics, use it to look up some plant names, and see what happens.

ASPARAGUS

Most North American wildflower lovers know the wild asparagus, a waist-high, ferny-leaved member of the lily family. It often grows as a weed along roadsides, producing tiny (less than a quarter inch long), greenish white, bell-shaped flowers and red, spherical fruits about five-sixteenths inch across. Not many people familiar with wild asparagus's tough, wiry shoots would think of eating them, even though wild asparagus is in the very same genus and species as garden asparagus. Garden asparagus is simply a horticultural form developed by mankind.

The garden asparagus's edible shoots are actually the plant's stem, and the triangular scales along asparagus stems are modified leaves. If there's a potted plant called *asparagus fern* in your house, look at how it's put together, for it's a real asparagus, having nothing at all to do with ferns. Garden asparagus and wild asparagus are *Asparagus officinalis;* asparagus fern is *Asparagus plumosus.*

BEANS

One reason that American Indian cultures such as the Aztec and Maya of Mexico and Central America and the Inca of Peru developed such advanced cultures was that they possessed the wisdom to eat corn and beans together.

The human body manufactures protein by combining different kinds of amino acids. It's like putting together pieces of a puzzle. It happens that corn possesses one array of amino acid puzzle parts, and beans provide the "missing" amino acids. In other words, when corn or beans are eaten alone, all the amino acids the body needs for synthesizing protein aren't there, but when corn and beans are eaten together, they are.

Of course, the ancient Maya, Aztec, and Inca Indians didn't know about

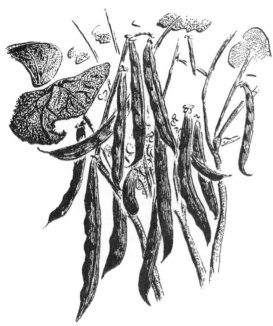

Snap beans often hang in clumps; resist the urge to pull them off by the handfuls, lest you damage the bean plant. Do not harvest the beans when the plants are wet; wet plants are brittle and break easily, and waterborne disease organisms are easily transmitted among wet plants.

amino acids. They just knew that eating beans and corn together was good for their bodies.

Beans have been around for such a long time that there is a puzzlement of names surrounding them. Lima beans are the same as butter beans; if you should see the quantity of butter my mother dollops into her cooking lima beans, you'd understand why.

Don't forget our earlier botany lessons revealing that individual, roundish beans are nothing but seeds and that the fruits containing the beans are referred to as *legumes*. The legume's leathery cover enclosing the beans is often called a *pod*.

Green beans, string beans, and snap beans, which are actually legumes, are all the same thing. Each name is appropriate, because the legumes are green; when they are bent, they snap; and in some varieties a tough, thread-like string forms along the mature fruit's midrib. Removing these strings from the old varieties was a tedious task that used to occupy me on many summer afternoons, but nowadays horticulturists have developed "stringless" string beans. Wax beans are almost the same thing, except that they are yellow instead of green, taste slightly different, and have a waxy texture.

When legume fruits are allowed to develop until the beans inside are fully mature, but not yet truly hard, and then the beans are shelled from their leathery pods, the resulting beans are called *shell beans*. Lima and certain kinds of snap and wax beans also can be used as shell beans.

Kidney, pinto, great northern beans, and cowpeas are all *dry beans,* which are not harvested until the husks are dried out and leathery and the beans are hard and dry. Dry beans were important to our ancestors because they could be kept through the winter. Before being used, dry beans are soaked so that they swell back to their shell-bean size, and then they are used as shell beans.

BEETS

Beets are fine examples of storage roots. Sunlight falls upon beet-plant leaves, carbohydrates are produced through photosynthesis, and those carbohydrates are mostly stored in the beets. Beet plants, being biennials, think that next spring they'll be able to use the stored-up carbohydrate energy in their bloated roots to produce vigorous, second-year beet plants, but we humans frustrate the plants' plans by stealing that stored carbohydrate for ourselves.

BROCCOLI

The branched, smooth parts of the broccoli plant are stems, and the bumpy, granular masses at the stems' tops are hundreds and thousands of unopened flower buds.

When we eat broccoli, we're actually munching on flowers.

The part of the Brussels sprout plant that we eat is the vegetative bud.

BRUSSELS SPROUTS

Brussels sprouts get their name from Brussels, the capital of Belgium. They are close relatives of broccoli, but the edible parts of Brussels sprouts—those little cabbagelike heads—are vegetative buds that grow in the axils of leaves along a tall stem. (Vegetative buds are buds from which vegetative parts like leaves and stems arise, rather than flowers.)

CABBAGE

Whereas Brussels sprouts are lateral vegetative buds, cabbage heads are derived from the plant's terminal vegetative bud.

Expanding cabbage heads sometimes are afflicted with an interesting problem: A head may develop deep cracks extending from the outside to near the heart. This happens when the cabbage's heart grows faster than its outer leaves, usually because the gardener has been watering and fertilizing too much.

There's a gardener's trick for stopping this splitting. The trick is to grasp the cabbage's head and twist the whole thing halfway around. As this is taking place, disconcerting pops and snaps can be heard as roots shatter. That is the point, however—to disrupt the cabbage's plumbing enough to slow down the intake of water and nutrients.

CANTALOUPES

Though people often use the words *cantaloupe* and *muskmelon* interchangeably, experts say that there's a difference. *Muskmelon* is a general term for the many varieties of *Cucumis melo,* whereas *cantaloupe* is reserved for the particular variety of muskmelon going by the Latin name of *Cucumis melo* var. *cantalupensis.* Real cantaloupes are derived from ancient melons grown in the area of Cantaluppi, near Rome, and those Italian cantaloupes had been grown from seed imported from Southwestern Asia. Thus, all cantaloupes are muskmelons, but only some muskmelons are cantaloupes.

CARROTS

The garden carrot's wild ancestor, Queen-Anne's lace, or wild carrot, grows abundantly along North America's weedy roadsides. The scientific name for both wild carrot and garden carrot is *Daucus carota.* In other words, they're nearly the same thing. If you have a wildflower book, look up this weed and try to find it in your area in late summer. Its large, lacy flower clusters are so easy to spot and to recognize that you shouldn't have too much trouble.

If you do locate a wild carrot, pull it up by its root, snap the long taproot in two, and smell it. Smells like a carrot, right? When you see how tiny and woody the wild carrot's tap root is, you'll have a lot of respect for the horticulturists who over the centuries have developed the good-tasting carrots we have today. Carrots, like parsnips and celery, are members of the parsley family.

CAULIFLOWER

Botanically, cauliflower is practically the same thing as broccoli, except that cauliflower's edible stalks and immature flower buds lack green pigment for photosynthesis. The cauliflower's whiteness is not natural; gardeners intentionally keep sunlight from hitting developing cauliflower heads to keep the bitter, green pigment chlorophyll from forming.

The process of blocking the sun from developing cauliflower heads is called *blanching.* A traditional blanching technique is to tie a cauliflower's own long lower leaves over the mature heads, which are usually six to twelve inches across.

CELERY

What garden vegetable, when we eat it, is *not* a root, stem, leaf, flower, or fruit? Celery is the answer. When we eat celery, we're actually consuming grossly oversized leaf petioles. Petioles are the parts of a plant that connect stems to their leaf blades.

COLLARDS

Collards are greens that grow like leaf lettuce but are much larger. Unlike most greens, they thrive in heat without turning tough and bitter. In southeastern states, collards are *the* greens to grow. Anyone wishing to experience a Southern culinary high should fix a meal of cornbread, black-eyed peas, and a heap of butter-smothered collards.

CORN

Eating sweet corn at the precise moment when grain sweetness is at perfect equilibrium with kernel firmness must rank as one of our most pleasurable and civilized undertakings.

One secret to enjoying a perfect homegrown ear of sweet corn is to cook and eat it as soon after picking as possible. Sweet-corn connoisseurs often have their water boiling as they step into the garden to pick their ears. Once the ear is picked, its grains begin to mature and harden. The sweet-tasting sugars combine into starchy-tasting complex carbohydrate, which stores better than sugars.

As described in chapter 2, corn plants possess very strange flowers. Male flowers are found in the tassels, and female blossoms make up the ears. Each corn kernel is a mature ovary, and the silks are styles.

The silks lead outside the husks so that pollen grains floating in the air can land on the silks' stigmatic surfaces, germinate, send their pollen tubes down through the silks, and fertilize the immature ovary that will become the kernel.

If you think about this, a problem for the corn plant becomes apparent. What if, on the day or days the male flowers are producing pollen, the wind blows all the pollen away before it can land on receptive silks? If this happens, the corn's immature ovaries won't get fertilized, kernels won't form, and the plant's ears won't fill out.

This is exactly why gardeners plant at least four rows of corn side by side; this way, usually enough pollen fills the air to assure that every silk receives at least one grain.

Few garden crops have had their chromosomes more shuffled around than corn. Seed catalogs are full of high-sugar hybrids and super-sweet hybrids, such as the Kandy Korn and Cotton Candy varieties. To my mind,

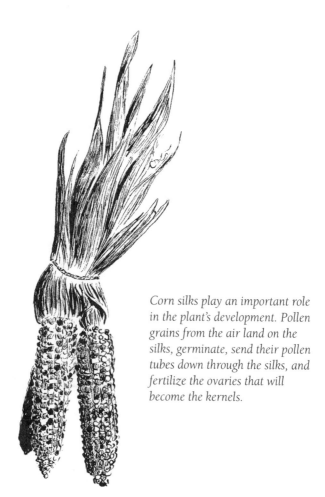

Corn silks play an important role in the plant's development. Pollen grains from the air land on the silks, germinate, send their pollen tubes down through the silks, and fertilize the ovaries that will become the kernels.

such corns cater to a perverse streak in Western taste equating goodness with sugary. Corn should taste like corn, not sugar!

CUCUMBERS

In seed catalogs, notice that some cucumber varieties, such as Hybrid Sweet Success, and Hybrid Olympian, are referred to as *gynoecious*. Gynoecious plants are those bearing only female flowers. The advantage of gynoecious cucumber plants is that since they don't waste energy developing male flowers, they can concentrate all their efforts just producing female flowers and thus yield more fruits. A disadvantage is that because all cucumber flowers must be pollinated with male pollen before fruits develop, a second cucumber variety—one that isn't gynoecious—must be planted nearby to supply the pollen.

MAKING CUCUMBER-END BEAUTY CREAM

What you will need

a fresh cucumber

1. Cut a one-half-inch piece off each end of a medium-size or large cucumber.

2. For a couple of minutes, rub the flat faces of the cucumber ends together in fast little circles, as if trying to start a fire with friction.

3. When finished, look for tiny amounts of a white, creamy substance around the edges of the flat faces.

4. Run a finger around the rims, collecting the cream; expect a total production about the size of a small match head.

5. Rub the cream on dry skin or wrinkles. This cream supposedly is a skin softener and wrinkle remover.

EGGPLANT

Eggplants are big, purplish black, polished, gorgeous pearls. Even eggplant flowers are pretty. Eggplant blossoms are structurally similar to tomato and potato flowers because eggplants, tomatoes, and potatoes are all in the same family, the nightshade family.

GARLIC

Anyone who eats garlic bread or pizza knows that garlic imparts a unique, robust odor. But when coppery smelling "garlic breath" is exhaled later, the scent is anything but pleasant. Obviously, garlic undergoes profound, somewhat mysterious chemical changes once inside our bodies.

Though we don't hear of many doctors prescribing garlic as medicine, people have been talking about garlic's almost magical medicinal value for a long time. During World War I, the English government ordered tons of garlic bulbs for use on the battlefield. Raw garlic juice was squeezed from the bulbs, diluted in water, and applied as an antiseptic to wounds. Supposedly wounds so treated seldom became infected; garlic is credited as having saved the lives of thousands of soldiers. Nowadays, some people claim that "garlic syrup" is especially good for relieving hoarseness, coughs, and asthma and other breathing difficulties. I really don't know if garlic is healthy for the body or not, but I do eat a lot of it, and I feel great and seldom get sick.

You can braid garlic to produce kitchen decorations that are both beautiful and useful. Garlic leaves should be braided when they are beyond the green stage but not yet completely dried out. Unless you're an expert braider, you may need to reinforce the braid with ribbon or nylon thread.

JERUSALEM ARTICHOKES

Don't confuse Jerusalem artichokes with the green, bristly globe artichokes. Jerusalem artichokes are the white tubers of *Helianthus tuberosus;* globe artichokes are the flower heads of *Cynara scolymus.* Both plants are members of the composite family.

The word *Jerusalem* in Jerusalem artichoke has nothing to do with the plant's geographic affinities but is what early English speakers thought they heard when Spanish speakers called the plant *girasol,* which means "sunflower."

Jerusalem artichokes are indeed sunflowers, as you'll see if you grow them. In late summer, the plant produces numerous sunflower blossoms two to three inches across. A clump or row of robust Jerusalem artichokes is a pretty sight, and in the fall, goldfinches love foraging among their fruiting heads.

Jerusalem artichokes are native American plants; they, along with potatoes, tomatoes, corn, chocolate, and many other goodies, were introduced to the Europeans by the Indians.

I prepare a strong-tasting soup with Jerusalem artichoke tubers by boiling them; pureeing them with a food processor; adding milk, a chunk of butter, sautéed onion, garlic, salt, and pepper; and then slow-cooking. The full-flavored taste can be softened by adding flour.

KALE

Kale is highly esteemed in some parts of the world not only for its fine taste and availability in cold weather, but also because of its phenomenal nutritional value. It's loaded with vitamin A, the B complex vitamins, and vitamin C. Lately a lot of attention has been given its very high beta carotene content—twice that of spinach!

KOHLRABI

Kohlrabi deserves mention because it's seldom bothered by pests and diseases, thrives in nearly any soil, isn't fussy about temperature, and therefore is a natural candidate for beginning gardeners.

Kohlrabi's edible "bulb" is actually the plant's swollen stem. It tastes just like the lower part of the stem of a broccoli plant, to which it is very closely related. Once the tough rind is pared off, the green stem material can be eaten raw, sautéed, or steamed. I like steamed kohlrabi smothered with an onion gravy.

LETTUCE

Lettuce comes in two main forms: head and leaf. The typical head lettuce available in supermarkets is a variety called iceberg. Leaf lettuce makes no head; the plant is a small rosette of leaves loosely arising from a tiny stem.

When summer's long, hot days arrive, lettuce tends to bolt, quickly producing tall stems with flowers. These flowers will clue savvy gardeners in to the fact that lettuce is a member of the composite family.

MUSTARD GREENS

Yellow mustard smeared on hot dogs is concocted from ground-up seed of black mustard, *Brassica nigra,* of the mustard family. Mustard greens are the cooked leaves of leaf mustard, *Brassica juncea,* also of the mustard family. Mustard greens don't taste anything like mustard out of jars. They are just good, wholesome greens that cook up like spinach.

ONIONS

Bulb-producing onions spend the first part of the summer growing green leaves. Then, at a precise moment in midsummer that is defined by the length of nights, they stop producing tops and begin storing photosynthesized carbohydrates in their bulbs, causing the bulbs to grow. Thus the green

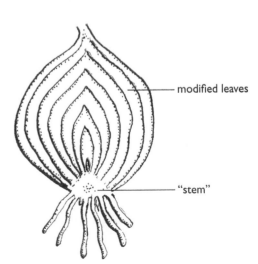

This cross section of an onion bulb shows the bulb's layers, which are modified leaves. As with other plants, the onion bulb's leaves arise from a stem; in the bulb's case, the stem hardly exists.

modified leaves

"stem"

One of the first signs of spring for a gardener: fresh, prepared green onions in a glass of water set on the table for nibbling.

tops of bulb-producing onions shouldn't be harvested as green onions, because doing so cripples the plant's bulb-building capacity.

Spring onions, or green onions, can be chopped into salads or just eaten by themselves. To harvest green onions, pull them up, cut off their roots and leaf tips, peel off the dirty outer skin, and wash them. Green onions thus prepared can be kept in plastic bags in the refrigerator's crisper for a week or more. I love putting green onions on egg sandwiches, adding them to bean soup, sautéeing them in stir-fries, or just eating them by themselves.

PEAS

Peas, including snow peas and snap peas, are members of the bean family. And both peas and beans have a special kind of flower, one with *papilionaceous* corollas. This term is derived from the Latin word *papilio,* which means "butterfly," referring to the flower's vaguely butterflylike shape. In papilionaceous flowers, the large top petal is called the *standard,* or *banner,* the two side petals are referred to as the *wings,* and usually the two lowermost petals are completely or partially united into a single scooplike petal termed the *keel.*

PEPPERS

First of all, forget about the black pepper found in a shaker next to the salt on your kitchen table; that pepper is derived from fruits of a plant originally from Asia, in the black pepper family. The peppers we're talking about are native American red and green peppers, of the same family as tomatoes, potatoes, and tobacco, the nightshade family.

The green and red peppers shown in the accompanying illustration represent just a small fraction of the many kinds of peppers that can be grown and eaten. My latest Stokes seed catalog offers fifty-six kinds—forty-five sweet varieties and eleven hot ones. All of these can be traced to wild ancestors that were being grown by the Aztecs and other native American cultures before the arrival of the Europeans.

Unless you know the varieties by sight, it is difficult to judge a pepper's hotness by its shape or color. The degree of hotness ranges from not hot at all, as in the sweet bell peppers, to hot enough to make a grown man cry, as in habeneros and jalapeños.

The diversity of sizes, shapes, colors, and degrees of fruit hotness is even more surprising when we realize that most of the pepper varieties are very

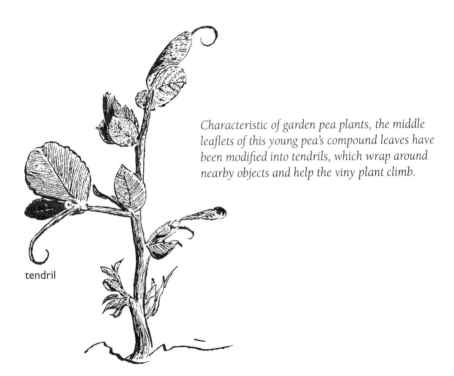

Characteristic of garden pea plants, the middle leaflets of this young pea's compound leaves have been modified into tendrils, which wrap around nearby objects and help the viny plant climb.

tendril

VEGETABLE PORTRAITS, A TO Z

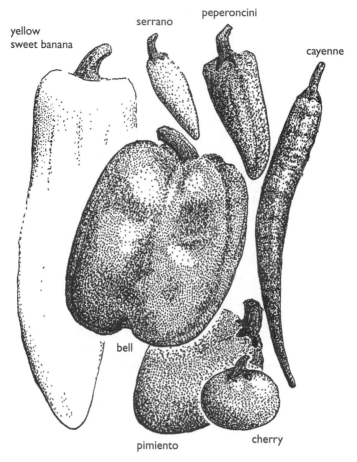

A miscellany of pepper fruits

closely related. I learned this the hard way. Once I planted sweet banana peppers next to some fiery hot jalapeños. When I eventually harvested my sweet banana peppers, I sliced some into a salad, which I served to dinner guests. After they began to eat, my guests suddenly scrambled for water. Obviously, some jalapeño pollen had made its way onto the stigmas of my banana pepper flowers. Cross-pollination like this can only occur between very closely related plants.

Cayennes are slender, lipstick red, hot peppers. To string cayennes, pick several peppers with about an inch of the stem attached. Use a large needle to thread monofilament nylon fishing line through the stems. Hang the strung peppers in a cool, arid place so that they will dry without rotting. They will become so crisp that they can be crumbled like crackers into pots of cooking food. And nothing is prettier than a string of crimson cayennes hanging by a kitchen's white curtains.

Once you've handled hot peppers, be sure to wash your hands fastidiously before rubbing your eyes.

POTATOES

The word *potato* came into English via the Spanish word *patata*, which was derived from the American Indian name for the vegetable, *batata*. The term *spud*, sometime used to refer to potatoes, traces back to the days when Northern Europeans grubbed roots from the ground. *Spud* is from Middle English, spoken from about A.D. 1050 to 1450, and denotes any sharp, narrow spade used for digging up large-rooted weeds. When potatoes were introduced into Europe from the Americas in the 1500s, they probably were dug with spuds. People would go "spudding," and eventually one may have come to "spud spuds."

A potato's surface is dimpled with several eyes, each of which possesses a tiny bud or incipient sprout whose goal in life is to become a whole new potato plant. Therefore, instead of planting potato seeds, chunks of potato bearing two or more eyes are planted. Do not try planting eyes from store-bought potatoes sold for eating, however, because these usually have been treated with chemicals to prevent spouting.

PUMPKINS

Nowadays a few people grow pumpkins for pies, but most gardeners seem to plant them just for the fun of watching the big, friendly-looking fruits develop, and then having them on hand at Halloween.

GROWING A COLOSSAL-SIZE PUMPKIN

What you will need

*pumpkin seeds of a hybrid developed for size,
such as Atlantic Giant or Big Max*

compost, aged manure, or commercial fertilizer

---

1. In the spring, once the ground is thoroughly warm and all danger of frost is past, dig a hole about two feet across and two feet deep in a well-drained spot that receives sunlight the whole day.

2. Next to the hole, mix equal parts of well-digested compost or aged

If you follow these directions, you too can grow a humongous pumpkin.

barnyard manure with the soil just removed from the hole. If you do not have compost or manure, mix about a pound of balanced fertilizer, such as a 10–10–10, with a bushel of soil. If the soil is very clayey, add enough sand or peat moss to make it loose and crumbly.

3. Shovel the soil mixture back into the hole. If you've enriched the soil with compost or manure, mound it into a hill about a foot high. If the soil is enriched with commercial fertilizer, make the mound about eight inches high, then add about three inches of loose, crumbly unfertilized soil atop that.

4. Plant three or four pumpkin seeds in the hill.

5. Once the plants bear three or four leaves, cut (don't pull) all plants except the biggest one.

6. After your remaining plant has produced three or four pumpkins, pick off all blossoms and all vine tips; there's no use having the plant waste energy on future pipsqueak pumpkins and wide-ranging vines.

7. When the pumpkins are about softball size, grit your teeth and cut off all but the best one. Be delicate here; damaging the stem could wreck plumbing needed for a smooth, regular conduction of water and nutrients into the future giant.

8. Big pumpkins flatten as they grow. If you want a perfectly shaped one and you're willing to live dangerously (the danger being that you might damage the stem or leaves), every couple of weeks *delicately* shift the fruit's position.

9. Harvest the pumpkin when it seems to be finished growing. Don't remove the stem from the pumpkin; this causes the fruit to deteriorate. If you have a hard time getting the pumpkin unattached from its vine, use pruning shears or even a saw.

RADISHES

If you don't harvest your radishes, they eventually will produce a stem two or three feet tall, and little white to lilac flowers appear. These flowers reveal that radishes are members of the mustard family, whose flowers are characterized by their four petals and six stamens, two stamens of which are shorter than the others.

SPINACH

Ever since Popeye, we've known about spinach's outstanding nutritional value. It's especially high in minerals, as well as vitamins A and C. In ancient Persia, spinach was grown as a medicinal plant.

SQUASH, SUMMER

The word *squash* is of American Indian origin: In Algonquian, *askoot-asquash* means "eaten green." Today, various squashes are exceedingly important to isolated American Indian communities, especially in Latin America. In southern Mexico's Indian markets, sometimes the large, orange squash flowers are sold as food.

FRYING SQUASH BLOSSOMS TO EAT

What you will need

ten freshly opened squash flowers

cooking oil

one cup self-rising flour

one egg

water, milk, or buttermilk

salt and pepper

skillet and stove

---

1. Pick flowers just unfurling into open blossoms, and wash them. If the stamen filaments feel stiff, remove them.

2. Oil a skillet and heat it up on medium. Some people deep-fry their

Summer squash flowers

flowers in a pool of very hot oil or grease; I prefer using just enough to keep things from sticking. A cooking spray like Pam works fine.

3. Mix the flour, salt, pepper, and egg into a bowl, then beat in enough water, milk, or buttermilk to form a loose batter of the consistency proper for pancakes.

4. Dip the blossoms into the batter, covering them entirely.

5. Fry until the batter is golden brown. If the batter begins burning on the outside but remains wet next to the flowers, turn the heat down. Once one side looks done, flip the blossom and fry the other side.

Try fried flowers with sliced fresh tomatoes and a salad. An easier and much less caloric way to eat squash blossoms is to simply sauté them in a little butter, perhaps along with garlic and diced onion.

SQUASH, WINTER

Winter squashes come in a wide variety of beguiling shapes and colors, are easy to grow, and store well. Some winter squashes are so pretty that we display them as Thanksgiving decorations.

One winter squash that's growing in popularity is the spaghetti squash. Cook this like any winter squash, slice it down the middle, stick a fork into its flesh, twirl, and—behold!—the flesh is transformed into tasty spaghettilike strands, with less than half of spaghetti's calories! Vegetable spaghetti may not please pasta purists, but it remains a fine, low-cal candidate for glorification with tomato sauce seasoned with sautéed onion, celery, garlic, and fresh basil.

STRAWBERRIES

Gardeners don't plant strawberry seeds; they set out plants with leaves, stems, and roots already formed. After the plants have grown awhile, like crabgrass they issue stolons, or runners, that arc over the soil's surface, ending in entirely new *daughter plants,* which root, grow, and send out their own runners. Sometimes you find one generation after another of such daughter plants, all linked together by runners. A good gardener takes care of these daughter plants and multiplies the garden's strawberry population year after year.

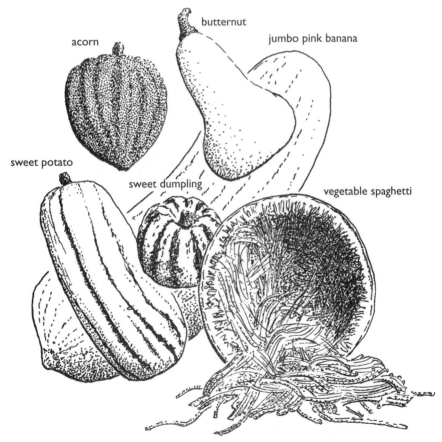

Winter squashes are a variety of colors—green, gold, and buff.

Another peculiar thing is the strawberry fruit itself, an aggregate fruit. If you try to relate a strawberry fruit to any "standard" fruit type you might have in your head, you'll get confused. That's because the red strawberry we think of as a fruit isn't a fruit at all, but the swollen strawberry flower's much-modified receptacle—a blossom part that usually is very inconspicuous and unimportant, essentially serving as a platform for the pistils.

The actual strawberry fruits are those multitudinous dark, gritty dots on the red, fleshy receptacle's surface. If you look closely at these minuscule fruits, which are technically classified as achene fruit types, you'll see slender styles attached to the top of each. Every achene bears inside it a single seed.

SWEET POTATOES

Though both sweet potatoes and white potatoes are food storage sites for the parent plant, they are fundamentally different. White potatoes are tubers, and are part of an underground stem, while sweet potatoes are really storage roots. Moreover, sweet potatoes don't belong to the same family as white potatoes. White potatoes are included in the nightshade family, along with tomatoes, peppers, and eggplants. Sweet potatoes are members of the morning glory family—just notice the similarities between sweet potato and morning glory blossoms. Some varieties of sweet potatoes may be referred to as *yams*.

Sweet potatoes are propagated by *slips*—little green-stemmed sprouts with roots on them sprouted from sweet potatoes. These slips are available at garden centers and from seed catalogs. They can also be grown from store-bought sweet potatoes, as described in the following project, which is best timed for seven or eight weeks before spring's average last frost date.

GROWING SWEET POTATO SLIPS

What you will need

sweet potatoes

a tray or trays with sides at least one inch high
(an aluminum cake pan will accommodate about two large sweet potatoes)

Peat moss or compost, enough to fill the tray or trays

---

1. Obtain as many sweet potatoes as you need for the number of plants you want. One large sweet potato should produce about six slips. Sweet potatoes I've purchased in supermarkets have worked fine, but sometimes sprout-

retarding chemicals have been sprayed on them. If possible, buy them in garden supply shops; if not, wash them very well.

2. Half fill the tray with moist peat moss.

3. Slice the sweet potatoes lengthwise down the middle.

4. Place the sweet potato halves atop the moist peat moss, cut face down, and entirely cover with a shallow layer of peat moss.

5. Cover the whole tray with cellophane.

6. As soon as shoots appear, remove the cellophane and place the tray in a sunny window.

7. After the last frost date, you can snap off each slip with its white roots attached to it, and plant them outside. Sweet potato vines sprawl quite a bit, so give them plenty of room.

TOMATOES

Though American Indians from Mexico to Peru ate tomatoes long before Europeans arrived in the New World, it took a while for people in the Old World to convince themselves that tomatoes were edible. The first Europeans to grow tomatoes from seed brought from the Americas, during the 1500s, regarded them as strictly ornamental. The English called them *love apples*.

Tomatoes are vines and need to be staked or grown inside a wire cage.

For a long time Europeans suspected that tomatoes were poisonous. There was some basis for this; tomatoes are members of the nightshade family, and some nightshades are poisonous, such as tobacco, belladonna, mandrake, and jimsonweed.

GROWING A VERY PRODUCTIVE, SUPER-PAMPERED TOMATO PLANT

What you will need

homegrown or purchased tomato slips

well-digested compost or a small amount of a balanced fertilizer, such as 5–10–10

---

1. Acquire one or more tomato slips. Tomato stems are incredibly fragile, so by no means buy slips bound together with rubber bands or string; each plant should grow snugly in its own little container of soil. The best tomato slips are about eight inches tall. Look for plants with thick, solid stems, and scan each plant for diseases and insects.

2. Before planting the slips, harden them off as described on page 51.

3. If possible, transplant the slips late in the afternoon on a cloudy day. For each slip, dig a good-sized hole at least as deep and wide as the plant is tall. If you are setting more than one plant, place them two to three feet apart. If the soil that comes out is clayey, break it up and mix in two or three hand-fuls of compost or sand to make it crumbly. In the hole's bottom, place a heaping handful of well-digested compost, or a tablespoon of a balanced fer-tilizer, such as 5–10–10, mixed with two or three inches of soil. Do not over-fertilize, or you'll end up with lush foliage but few tomatoes. Add a couple inches of nonenriched, loose soil atop that, and then place upon this the slip with its potting soil in place. Gingerly pull more loose soil around it. If you plan to later water by the bucketful, build a water-holding dike around the plant. To save on water, spread a thick mulch around the plant's base; don't mulch until the ground is warm, however.

4. For protection against cutworms, place a collar around the base of the plant; nearly anything will do, even a sheet of newspaper twisted and folded into a circle. It doesn't take much to discourage a cutworm.

5. Though it be painful to shear your beauties, once they're planted, pinch off the larger leaves, leaving just the top small ones; this reduces the set's trauma from transpiration.

LOOK AT THAT PLANT!

6. Drive a sturdy stake about ten inches from each slip. Stakes should stand at least four feet high.

7. Soak the ground around the plants, and keep the soil moist over the next three or four days. Do what you can to protect the plants from cold and wind. You can keep plastic, gallon-size milk jugs with the bottoms cut out handy for covering the plants in blustery weather.

8. Tomato plants left unpruned produce shoots, or *suckers*, in leaf axils. These suckers produce more stems, leaves, flowers, and more suckers. Most gardeners, therefore, pull off unwanted suckers so that the plants will direct their energy into producing tomatoes rather than suckers. There's no fast rule for "suckering." A good technique is to let two or three side suckers grow to a comfortable height, and thereafter pinch off all growing tips.

9. As they grow, give your plants some kind of support. We tie our tomato plants to stakes and cages with strips cut from discarded nylon pantyhose. As we place the strips around the delicate stems, we spread them so that pressure is distributed over a large surface area; by no means should slender string or wire be used. Staked and caged tomatoes take up less space than sprawling ones, produce cleaner tomatoes with less rotting, have fewer slug problems, and are easier to pick. Erect plants will dry out more quickly, however, as the soil at the base of the plants is exposed, and thus they should be well mulched, or watered frequently.

The fruit of a tomato is, botanically speaking, a berry; its many seeds are encased in a fleshy fruit.

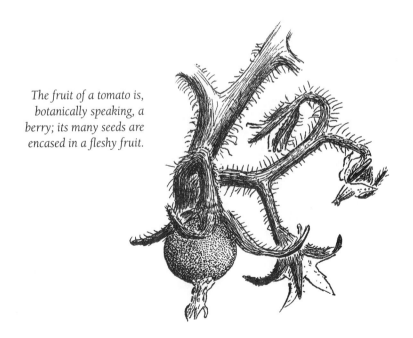

10. Tomato plants can stand a tiny frost, but not much. On the autumn afternoon before the first predicted frost, I pick all immature tomatoes that are at least two-thirds of their mature size; most of them will ripen eventually. If you treat them gently and keep them in a cool, dry place, you can enjoy ripe tomatoes from the garden on Thanksgiving and, with a little luck, even at Christmas!

WATERMELONS

Various schools of thought have developed around figuring out when a watermelon is ripe. My experience is that the thumping strategy works about 80 percent of the time. The problem with thumping is that it takes a while to learn what a good thump sounds like. A ripe watermelon's thump sounds a little muffled and a little hollow, but also a bit tight. It's a *konk* sound. Unripe watermelons sound green. Instead of *konk,* you hear a higher-toned *pumpf.* Rap with one knuckle. Remember that a small, ripe melon may have a higher-sounding knock than a large, unripe one. If you're tone-deaf, forget thumping.

Some use a more technical approach, not necessarily more accurate or more fun to use: the dried-tendril technique. Find the vine's tendril nearest the watermelon. When the melon is ripe, that tendril should be dry and as curly as a pig's tail.

Others look at the melon's skin: A ripe melon's is dull and an unripe melon's is shiny. And still others examine the pale spot that develops where a growing watermelon makes contact with earth. If the spot is white, the melon is unripe; if it's creamy yellow, it's ripe. Finally, there's the holistic approach. Use all the above indicators.

ZUCCHINI

Zucchini belongs to the same genus and species as the pumpkin, the yellow-flowered gourds, and the yellow summer squashes. Just think of the differences between a long, green zucchini and a pumpkin. But then notice how similar the flowers of these two different varieties are.

CHAPTER 6

Flower Bed Portraits

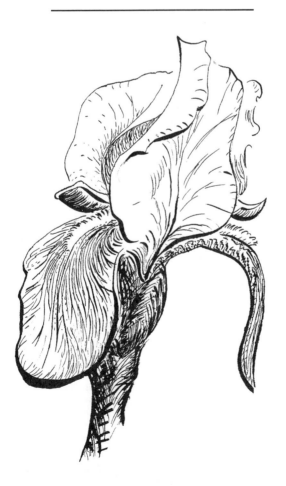

The main reason people grow flowers next to their houses is that they look good. Plants used to prettify our homes are called *ornamentals*. Many ornamentals, such as zinnias, salvias, and amaryllises, are popular because of their big, colorful flowers or flower heads. On the other hand, small-flowered species, like asters, ageratum, and phlox, produce an eye-catching effect through numerous blossoms clustered together. Others, such as ferns, hostas, and caladiums, are valued for their attractive vegetative parts.

Running across a wild plant in its natural habitat with a blossom as large and exotic looking as, say, a spider lily would be extraordinary; most wild plants bear blossoms that may be attractive to a specific pollinator, such as a tiny bee or moth, but that to the human eye generally look scrawny and low-profile.

In other words, from a naturalist's point of view, the ornamentals grown around our homes are usually very special. Moreover, it's unnatural to have in one place so many flowers that are so big, so flashy, or so weird. In nature, you just don't find plants like brightly flowered zinnias, marigolds, and peonies all growing so closely together.

The following are brief looks at a few ornamentals. To learn more about these or other kinds of ornamentals, you can thumb through books at the library, read flowerpot labels, watch garden shows on television, and talk to garden-savvy friends and neighbors.

DAFFODILS

Daffodils are members of the genus *Narcissus,* in the amaryllis family. The original wild species from which our horticultural varieties have been developed are native to the Old World. There are so many horticultural *Narcissuses* varieties that whole catalogs are produced advertising nothing but *Narcissus* bulbs.

As is often the case in the amaryllis family, the daffodil blossom's three petals and three sepals are so similar that they cause the flower to look as if it had six identical petals. However, one feature that distinguishes *Narcissus* flowers from nearly all others is the crown, or corona, which is a frilly topped, cuplike cylinder arising from between the base of the blossom's stamens and the tube formed where the look-alike petals and sepals join together.

There's no hint of a crown in our "standard" blossom; this crown is just a wondrous example of something that nature sometimes endows upon its flowers. In some varieties, the crown is of a color different from the rest of the flower. The blossom of the poet's narcissus is all white, except for the rim, which is frilly and bright red.

LOOK AT THAT PLANT!

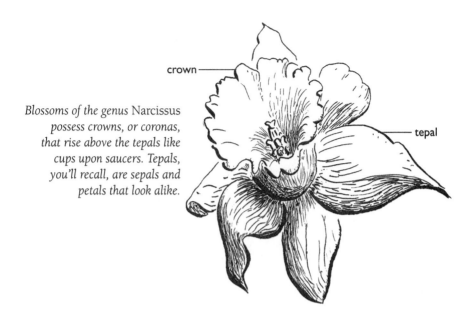

crown

tepal

Blossoms of the genus Narcissus *possess crowns, or coronas, that rise above the tepals like cups upon saucers. Tepals, you'll recall, are sepals and petals that look alike.*

Daffodils are among the best plants to *force,* or "trick," into flowering much earlier than they would if left alone. Hyacinths, tulips, and crocuses also are easily forced. Forcing enables us to have cheery, living bouquets on our window sills while it's still snowy outside. Here's how it works with daffodils:

FORCING DAFFODILS

What you will need
a 6- or 7-inch pot with drainage holes
potting soil
three or four daffodil bulbs

---

1. In the fall, around October 1, dig up some daffodil bulbs, or buy some. The larger, firmer, and more perfectly formed they are, the better. Some daffodil varieties force better than others. For early results, some good varieties include Rembrandt, Orange Queen, Golden Harvest, Forerunner, and February Gold.

2. Fill the pot with potting soil to about half an inch below the pot's rim. Water thoroughly. Throughout the winter, keep the soil moist, but not waterlogged.

3. Bury the bulbs with their necks slightly protruding above the potting soil. It's important for the bulbs to experience winter's cold and moistness, but they should not freeze. One way to provide this environment is to sink the pots in the ground or place them in a cold frame, and then bury them beneath six inches or more of mulch. Another way is to store the pots in a closet, attic, or attached garage, where temperatures never dip below freezing or rise above 50; these will need to be watched closely, to guard against the potting soil drying out.

4. The bulbs should remain in this cool, moist environment for at least six to ten weeks. This is an important time for the plants because this is when the bulbs sprout their roots. Bulbs placed in the cool, moist environment on October 1 can be brought inside the warm house in late November for a flowering date of Christmas, or early January, depending on the variety chosen, house temperature, bulb health, and amount of light. House temperatures between 65 and 75 are best; the colder the temperature, the slower the blooms develop. Also, the closer to spring one brings the bulbs indoors, the more quickly the blooms appear.

5. If the blossoming daffodil's room temperature stays around 70 and is fairly moist, the blossoms may stay pretty for a couple of weeks. Once the blossoms fade, snip off the flower stems and set the pots somewhere cool and moist, so that in the spring the bulbs can be planted. During next year's spring, the bulbs may issue only leaves and no flowers, but by the second spring the bulbs should have recuperated, and will probably blossom. Bulbs don't force well a second time.

FERNS

Ferns are not flowering plants at all, producing spores rather than seeds. The life cycle of a typical fern is an amazing story.

When a spore lands in a place with proper humidity and temperature, it does not develop like a germinating seed. Instead of a radicle emerging, a filament arises from the spore. After a few weeks of growth, this filament has enlarged into a green, usually heart-shaped body that looks more like a green fingernail than a fern. This is called a *prothallus* and is typically about one-fourth inch across. Prothalli grow on the soil's surface, usually in damp, heavily shaded spots, and are easily killed by drying out.

The prothallus, which bears the fern's sex organs, is actually an entirely different, independent plant. In other words, the life cycle of a fern involves two different types of plants that alternate with one another. The thing we think of as a fern is actually just one of two forms that the plant takes.

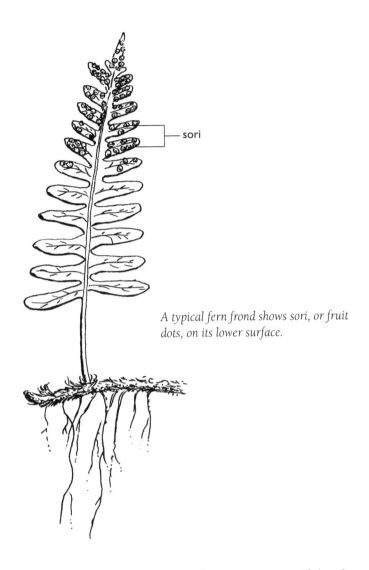

— sori

A typical fern frond shows sori, or fruit dots, on its lower surface.

On the prothallus, which most people never see, even if they have grown ferns all their lives, the female reproductive parts are called *archegonia,* and the male parts *antheridia.* They are both found on the prothallus's undersurface, along with slender *rhizoids,* which serve as roots. When water is present as a film between the prothallus's lower surface and the soil, mature female archegonia produce a secretion that attracts male sperm from the antheridia. If several prothalli are connected by a film of water, sperms from one prothallus may be attracted to the archegonia of other prothalli, and cross-fertilization will occur.

Once fertilization takes place inside the archegonium, the first roots,

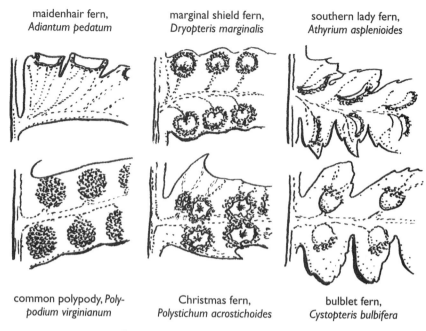

| maidenhair fern, *Adiantum pedatum* | marginal shield fern, *Dryopteris marginalis* | southern lady fern, *Athyrium asplenioides* |

| common polypody, *Polypodium virginianum* | Christmas fern, *Polystichum acrostichoides* | bulblet fern, *Cystopteris bulbifera* |

Sori, or fruit dots, are important identification features.

stems, and leaves of the plant body we think of as the "real" fern emerge from the prothallus. Ferns uncurl as they develop, rising from the ground; at this stage they are called *fiddleheads* because they are shaped like the heads of fiddles.

Mature ferns do not bear sexual parts. They produce spores, and the fern parts that produce these spores come in a tremendous variety of shapes and forms. The cinnamon fern sends up vigorous clusters of spikelike fertile fronds that become brown and produce millions of spores that are released in clouds. Christmas ferns produce little brown dots, called *sori* (singular *sorus*), or *fruit dots,* on the undersides of their frond segments. These sori are clusters of *sporangia,* each of which is about the size of a dust speck and usually contains sixty-four spores. When a sporangium is mature, it opens, the spores escape, and the entire life cycle starts over.

One of the most common ferns sold as a houseplant is *Nephrolepis exaltata bostoniensis,* commonly marketed as sword fern or Boston fern. Most of these ferns have been bred horticulturally to produce no sporangia, because people think that fronds with sporangia are diseased and won't buy them. Such ferns must be propagated vegetatively.

LOOK AT THAT PLANT!

GERANIUMS AND PELARGONIUMS

The names *geranium* and *pelargonium* are fairly confusing. There are indeed two genera called *Geranium* and *Pelargonium,* both of which are members of the geranium family. The confusion arises from the fact that most of the commonly planted, red-blossomed plants gardeners call *geraniums* actually belong to the genus *Pelargonium.* Even if you know that a certain popular plant is *Pelargonium peltatum,* you may call it an *ivy-leaved geranium,* because that's simply what people call it, whether it's scientifically correct or not.

The technical differences between the genera *Geranium* and *Pelargonium* usually can be seen when the flowers are dissected. Blossoms of the genus *Geranium* are radially symmetrical—cut a blossom down the middle, starting with any petal, and one side of the cut will be a mirror image of the other. Also, at least with a magnifying glass, little glands are visible between *Geranium* petals.

In contrast, blossoms of the genus *Pelargonium* are very slightly asymmetrical and bear no glands between their petals. Look at the back side of a *Pelargonium* blossom, and one sepal nearly always is a little broader than the other four. If you were to cut down the middle of the flower through the wide sepal, you would see that this sepal wraps around a deep, nectar-bearing pit descending into the pedicel. A less technical way to distinguish the two genera is that *Pelargonium* is usually sold as an annual (although it is a perennial), while *Geranium* is sold as a perennial. Chances are, however, that everything in your flower bed you call a *geranium* is actually a *Pelargonium.*

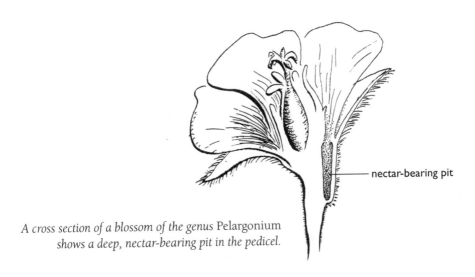

nectar-bearing pit

A cross section of a blossom of the genus Pelargonium
shows a deep, nectar-bearing pit in the pedicel.

IRISES

Irises, members of the iris family and the genus *Iris,* are monocots, so their flower parts, instead of being in sets of five or multiples thereof, appear in sets of three or multiples of three. There are about 150 wild iris species. In North America, naturally growing irises often are found in swampy places and moist forests.

A typical iris blossom consists of three outer segments that are large and colorful, referred to as *falls.* Falls are usually reflexed (curved downward) and frequently bearded, bearing a usually yellow line of hairlike appendages down the middle of their upper faces. Three petal-like segments, called *standards,* rise above the falls. Between the three standards, curving over the falls, are three much smaller, flat, petal-like growths called *style branches,* arising from the style; they form roofs over the three stamens. The blossom's stigma area lies at the base of these style branches.

When a bee lands on a fall, it pulls itself along the fall's line of hairs (the beard) and squeezes between the fall and the overhanging style branches. How does pollen from the anther get onto the bee? How does pollen on the bee get onto the stigma area of the overhanging style branch? You can figure all this out yourself by looking at an iris blossom and poking your finger where a bee would go.

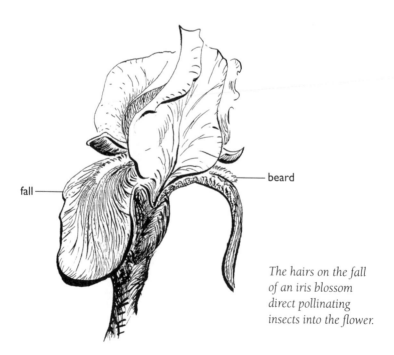

fall

beard

The hairs on the fall of an iris blossom direct pollinating insects into the flower.

LOOK AT THAT PLANT!

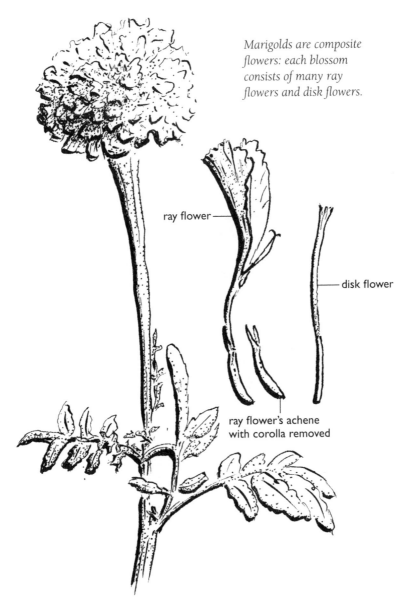

Marigolds are composite flowers: each blossom consists of many ray flowers and disk flowers.

ray flower

disk flower

ray flower's achene with corolla removed

MARIGOLDS

Plants of at least two different genera are called *marigolds*. The pot marigold, of the mostly European genus *Calendula,* bears alternate, simple leaves. Most other marigolds belong to the genus *Tagetes,* native to Mexico, and have usually opposite, pinnately dissected leaves. Both genera are members of the huge composite family.

Marigolds remind us that there is a lot more to do with backyard plants than merely look at them or eat them. Learning more about a plant's uses in other cultures can be a fascinating exercise. For example, I cannot see marigolds without thinking of their use among many of Mexico's native people. In Mexico, our Halloween is a special time with religious meaning; there it is called *el Día de los Difuntos Fieles,* or, the Day of the Faithful Dead. Once I spent Halloween with a family of Nahuatl speakers in central Mexico.

They erected a large altar beautifully adorned with dark green palm fronds, brightly colored crepe ribbons, and orange-yellow marigold blossoms. On the altar they placed burning candles, pictures of deceased family members, and cups of the dead people's favorite beverages—tequila and chocolate, both native Mexican drinks. In front of the altar they began tearing apart marigold blossoms, dropping petals onto the hut's floor, and made an orange trail through the hut, across the yard, and down to the main trail, where their neighbors also had dropped marigold petals, causing the main trail to look like an orange highway snaking across the hillside.

That night, I was told, spirits of dead family members would be wandering about. They would see the orange trail and follow it to the homes of their family, across the yards and through the huts, to the altars, where they would see that the family was remembering and honoring them.

This tradition must have been practiced by Mexico's Indians for many generations. Seeing marigolds causes me to think of all the ways our ancestors used to appreciate plants for reasons other than their just being pretty.

PANSIES

Pansies are members of the violet family and the genus *Viola. Viola* is the same genus that violets belong to. In other words, pansies are violets.

Often people are surprised to hear this. That's because violets usually bear small, unspectacular blossoms, whereas pansies possess two-inch-wide or wider flowers often marked like little faces. If you look at the pansy plant's structure, however, you'll see that it is put together just like the most typical violet. The common garden pansy is *Viola tricolor hortensis.*

ROSES

Wild roses, of the rose family and the genus *Rosa,* are often found in forests and other habitats of North America, Europe, and northern Asia. Just for the northeastern quarter of North America, *Gray's Manual of Botany* lists twenty-four rose species growing without any human help.

Ornamental varieties nearly always have been developed by mankind,

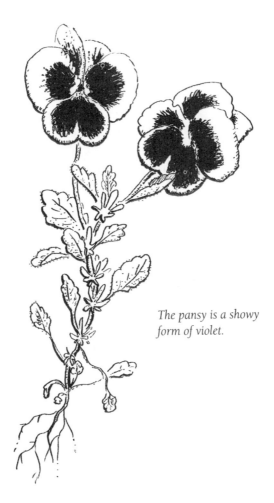

The pansy is a showy form of violet.

using horticultural techniques; in nature, you would never find roses like those sold in stores. Wild roses rarely bear flowers as large and colorful as ornamental varieties, and they possess only five petals. If you look at your ornamental roses, you'll probably see that each flower has many more than five.

These extra petals actually result from some of the blossom's many stamens developing into petals instead of stamens. If you look at the back of an ornamental rose blossom, you'll see that its numerous inner petals rise above five broad, evenly spaced "real" petals that alternate with sepals just the way they do in nature. If you examine those inner, stamen-derived petals, you'll sometimes find remnants of an anther structure along their lower sides. In these cases, a stamen wasn't quite able to make up its mind whether it wanted to be a petal or a stamen.

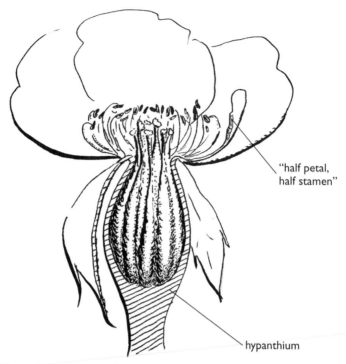

"half petal,
half stamen"

hypanthium

*The rose blossom contains several achene-type fruits, each with its own stigma and style,
inside a cuplike structure called a* hypanthium. *The rose fruit, known as a rose hip,
is actually the ripened hypanthium wrapped around numerous achenes. Note the small
petal on the right with an anther structure along its edges; this is a case where a stamen
"couldn't make up its mind" whether to be a stamen or a petal.*

SALVIA, OR SCARLET SAGE

People plant *Salvia splendens,* or scarlet sage, a species of the mint family,
because its lipstick red flowers are so bright and long-lasting. A native
of Brazil, it was introduced into Britain in 1822 and from Europe came to
America. Several *Salvia* species are cultivated, but only *Salvia splendens* is
properly called scarlet sage.

Some people are surprised to learn that scarlet sage is a member of the
mint family. Mints are generally thought of as having fragrant leaves and
inconspicuous flowers, but scarlet sage has leaves that smell like regular
leaves and flowers that are striking. Nonetheless, it's easy to verify that scarlet
sage is a mint, because it has the identifying characteristics common to the
three thousand members of the mint family: The leaves are opposite or
whorled, the stems are square in cross section, and the ovaries are four-lobed,

with each lobe developing into one *nutlet*. If you'll check, you'll see that scarlet sage fits this description.

HERBS

Now let's look at a whole group of plants that aren't really either vegetables or ornamentals—the herbs. An *herb* can be defined as a plant that is used for its medicinal, savory, or aromatic qualities. Some gardeners with very limited space and with special feelings for plants with heavenly odors and tastes grow only herbs.

My most important herb is spearmint. Some years ago, a sprig was planted at the edge of our house, and now it has spread by underground runners along a twenty-foot foundation. In late summer, I harvest a whole year's supply of leaves—enough for a large, piping-hot mug of mint tea every morning.

Sometimes I pull entire spearmint plants, hang them to slowly dry, and when the leaves are crisp, put the whole plant into a garbage bag, vigorously

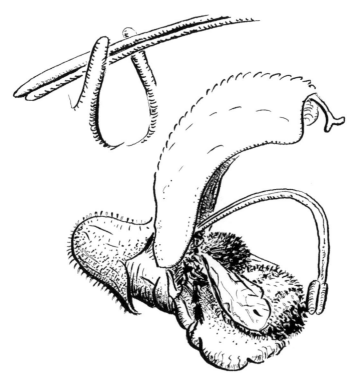

The filaments on a scarlet sage blossom are hinged in such a way that when a bee passes between the pillars, the anthers swing down, daubing the bee's rear with pollen.

knead until all the leaves have crumbled off, and then pour the flaky leaf fragments into jars, where they'll keep for years. If I have enough freezer space, I freeze green leaves and shoots, and when I'm ready for tea, I'll just drop frozen, still-green leaves into boiling water. In the middle of winter, how delicious it is smelling that minty steam billowing up from the kettle!

Most herbs need full sun; among those that can get along in partial shade are catnip, cress, and the mints. Herbs generally do well in poor soil. In fact, in poor soil where they grow slowly and have smaller leaves, their essential oils concentrate in higher levels, causing the vegetative parts to be especially pungent.

Here are some herb favorites:

anise: licorice taste for candies, Chinese food
catnip: a mint that makes cats ecstatic
chamomile: makes a nerve-soothing tea
coriander: nutmeg-citrus flavor for curry mixtures
dill: used for pickling, sauces
lavender: fresh, clean fragrance for sachets
lemon balm: used for lemon-flavored teas
oregano: the familiar flavor in pizza
rosemary: pungent, piney-mint flavor and odor
sage: a favorite herb for stuffing and poultry
sweet basil: used for tomato sauces and salads
tarragon: aniselike flavor for meats, sauces

The Appendix lists several companies that sell herb seeds; write for their free seed catalogs. For an herb lover, a great purchase is Burpee's Herb Garden collection, consisting of seven seed packets, markers, instructions, and a suggested garden plan, all for less than $10.

CHAPTER 7

Weeds

forest ⟶ development ⟶ weeds ⟶ forest

A weed is just a plant living where somebody, for some reason, doesn't want it. In my family's tobacco fields, one of our worst weeds was a morning glory vine that wound itself around the tobacco plants' stalks; they had to be unwound very carefully lest they injure the tobacco's fragile leaves. Back at the house, however, one of the prettiest flowers we had covered a trellis with lovely, pink, funnel-shaped blossoms. It was the very same morning glory we were fighting in the fields.

Thus, in one place this plant was a pernicious weed but in the other an honored guest. Weeds are like that. I find that as I get to know any weed it gradually becomes less of a weed and more of a wildflower. There's an old saying that "A good garden may have some weeds." Here are some reasons why weeds can be welcome in a good garden. When looked at very closely— into their blossoms, underneath their leaves—weeds are truly as interesting and beautiful as the gayest zinnia. Weeds in a garden contribute diversity, and diverse systems in nature are more productive, more sustainable, and much more interesting than simple ones.

Weeds also serve as nature's "first-aid crew." When a natural community is disrupted, it's weeds that start the healing process. For example, when a big tree falls in a forest, at first a ragged hole occupies the space where the tree once stood. Gradually certain plants appear, mostly short-lived ones, forming a kind of plant scab covering the forest's open wound. These are weeds.

As the years pass, weeds give way to other plants, and eventually, perhaps in a hundred years or more, the forest will be healed and it will be hard to see that a tree ever fell there. The process by which one kind of plant replaces another kind, leading to a stable, mostly unchanging environment, is called *plant succession.*

There are many other kinds of plant succession. For example, if a pond is dug and then left to return to nature, over the centuries as it silts up and becomes dry land again a certain well-established succession of plants will characterize each stage of the pond's evolution. Plant succession may even occur on a rock, beginning with a few powdery algae and ending with the rock being occupied by ferns and wildflowers.

From nature's point of view, our gardens are only there temporarily, until prairies and forests can be reestablished. Our garden weeds, therefore, represent nature's efforts to reclaim the soil.

Weeds do several things when Mother Nature sends them into a hole in the forest, or into a garden that's "supposed" to be a forest or a prairie. Weed roots bind soil particles together, reducing the likelihood that the particles will be washed away during the process of *soil erosion.* Living weed bodies

LOOK AT THAT PLANT!

shelter the soil from direct hits by raindrops, and this also cuts down on soil erosion. Weed roots pry apart compacted soil particles, increasing the soil's aeration and workability. Weeds add species diversity to the disturbed ecosystem, thus increasing to the ecosystem's stability and general vigor. When weeds die, their bodies decompose into organic material that earthworms eat, helping earthworms to do their jobs. And decomposing weeds release mineral nutrients into the soil ecosystem.

When soil is disturbed, the natural plant community is destroyed; with the ground left naked, it's amazing to see how quickly weeds invade the disturbed area. How do they know where to go, and how do they get there so fast?

Of course, weed seeds don't really know where to go. It's simply that most weeds produce so many seeds that eventually at least a few of them fall on disturbed ground.

Most weeds have special ways of traveling quickly to where they are needed. Therefore, one interesting question to ask about any weed you encounter is this: What is this weed's special trick for invading disturbed areas fast?

Many weed fruits, especially the kind referred to as *achenes*, are equipped with little parachutes that enable them to hitchhike on the wind; dandelions, thistles, and horseweed belong in this category. The ground cherry's cherrylike fruit is suspended inside a papery bladder; when it falls onto the ground, the wind blows the bladder with its fruit and seed like a balloon across the ground. Fruits of cockleburs and Spanish needles are dispersed by means of spines that stick to the fur of passing animals. Carolina cranesbill fruits are equipped with strange, springlike mechanisms that, when the fruit is mature and ripe, snap so violently that the seeds are catapulted several feet away. Birds also help to spread weeds. When a bird eats a plant's fruit, the seeds pass through the bird's digestive tract and are "planted" in a new location.

A tremendous variety of weed species might conceivably make their way into our gardens. A friend once listed all the weeds he could identify growing along St. Louis's train tracks[1]. He identified 393 species! Those 393 species belonged to 59 plant families, the most common being the grass (74 species), composite (52), and mustard (28) families. Probably the best field guide for beginning weed watchers is *How to Know the Weeds*, listed in the Bibliography.

---

[1]Viktor Mühlenbach. "Contributions to the Synanthropic (Adventive) Flora of the Railroads in St. Louis, Missouri, U.S.A.," *Annals of the Missouri Botanical Garden* 66 (1979): 1.

We can get a taste for weeds' rambunctious diversity by taking a close look at a few randomly chosen species. If these species can prove to be so fascinating, then what must there be to learn about all our other backyard weeds?

HAIRY BITTER CRESS

Cardamine hirsuta, of the mustard family, naturalized in North America from Europe.

Two distinctive features of the hairy bitter cress are it's cold tolerance and extremely early flowering. In the earliest spring, long before the last snow has melted, hairy bitter cress appears on exposed garden soil. As early as Christmas, hairy bitter cress is established in my Kentucky garden as a tiny, stemless rosette of deeply divided, dark green leaves. If the winter is mild, it's even possible to find bitter cress flowering every cold month, especially at the base of south-facing building foundations.

In the heart of cold, dreary January, when you're just bursting for spring to come, finding a little rosette of hairy bitter cress with its promising greenness, and maybe even a tiny white flower or two—its four petals about one-sixteenth inch long—can be immensely cheering. As the flowers mature, the petals and stamens fall away and the stiffly upright, slender ovary elongates to about an inch long.

Hairy bitter cress, a member of the mustard family, possesses a slender ovary that upon fertilization grows tremendously in length, as other flower parts fall away.

LOOK AT THAT PLANT!

There are other bitter cresses, which are similar to hairy bitter cress but are larger and more showy spring wildflowers. Small-flowered bitter cress, *Cardamine parviflora,* grows in open woods, on rocky ledges, and in fields throughout eastern North America. *Cardamine pennsylvanica,* just known as bitter cress, thrives in moist woods and along streams. These species are native, but the hairy bitter cress is an alien, like most weeds, introduced from Europe. Hairy bitter cress is also closely related to the edible spring cress, *Cardamine bulbosa,* of wet woods and meadows.

CHICKWEED

Stellaria media, **of the pink family, naturalized into North America from Europe.**

In February and March, the open areas of my garden acquire a thick mat of chickweed. Like hairy bitter cress, chickweed also may flower during mild winters. Sometimes when I'm desperate for greens, I pick what's available of my stunted turnip greens and kale and add several handfuls of tender chickweed sprouts. Only the growing ends of chickweed sprouts are edible; the main stems are too stringy. Chickweed is basically tasteless, but when you're hungry for greens, it's better than nothing!

In the Appalachian Mountains, some old-timers still use chickweed as a medicinal herb. Supposedly it's a refrigerant (slakes thirst and gives a sensation of coolness to the body), demulcent (protects and soothes mucous membranes), and expectorant (causes mucus to be expelled from the respiratory tract). Usually it's boiled lightly, then it's medicinal-smelling water is used. The soggy plant after boiling also can be applied as a poultice. I've heard of chickweed being used for swellings, rashes, and various skin infirmities.

Many wildlife species, especially small seed-eating birds, find chickweed useful, too. Chickweed produces abundant minute seed, and even its leaves are eaten. Juncos, house sparrows, and finches especially relish chickweed, and cottontail rabbits often are spotted at park edges nibbling contentedly on it.

Chickweed is a member of the pink family. Here, the word *pink* does not refer to color, but to the edges of the flower petals, which appear to have been cut with pinking shears.

The chickweed's petals are deeply notched, making each petal appear to be split in two. Thus, the chickweed blossom looks as though it has twice as many petals as it really has.

Other members of the pink family include carnations, phlox, bouncing Bet, and sweet William, which also appear to have pinked petals. Though the

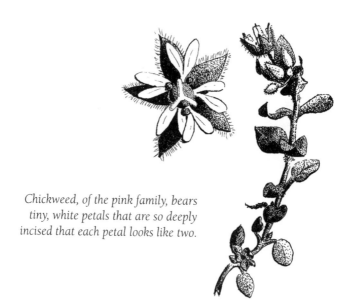

Chickweed, of the pink family, bears tiny, white petals that are so deeply incised that each petal looks like two.

flowers of these species are much more spectacular than the tiny (one-sixth to one-third inch broad), barely noticeable blossoms of the chickweed, the blossoms' structure is fundamentally the same.

If you find a chickweed plant with several blossoms on it, count the number of stamens in each flower. In most species with ten or fewer stamens, stamen number is constant from flower to flower; in chickweed blossoms, however, the number of stamens may range from two to ten, and even the number of petals and other features may vary.

CRABGRASS
Digitaria sanguinalis, **of the grass family, naturalized into North America from the Old World.**

Crabgrass has achieved notoriety as a "serious" weed in lawns. If it's present in a mowed lawn, however, it looks very similar to mowed bluegrass, so why is crabgrass a weed but bluegrass a darling of suburbanites? It's mainly because crabgrass dies back with the first frost but bluegrass doesn't. If a lawn has a large spot of crabgrass, that splotch will become brown and soggy with the first frost.

It's hard to find people who like crabgrass. According to an old botanical text,[2] however, hungry folks living on poor, sandy soil in Poland used to cultivate crabgrass for its seed, as a food crop! In early fall, if you walk through

---

[2]J. C. Loudon. *Arboretum et Fruticetum Britannicum,* 2d ed. (London, 1844), 4 vols.

LOOK AT THAT PLANT!

wet crabgrass bearing mature fruiting heads, you'll find that this grass produces prodigious numbers of tiny seeds, which adhere to wet legs. You'd have to work a long time to collect just a cupful of crabgrass seeds, but if you were starving, I suppose it would be worthwhile. A crabgrass seed isn't much different from a grain of rice, just much smaller.

If most humans lack the patience to collect nourishing crabgrass seeds, the same can't be said about certain small animals. In the winter, if you see house sparrows or juncos hopping and pecking in a large, gray area of crabgrass, they are probably feeding on its seeds. Farther from town, mourning doves, wild turkeys, and all kinds of sparrows seek out crabgrass. Crabgrass seeds may constitute between 10 and 25 percent of the wild turkey's total diet!

Several other species of crabgrass exist. The small crabgrass (*Digitaria ischaemum*) is also weedy and was also introduced from Europe. Others are native American species and, like wildflowers, occupy natural ecological niches occurring over limited geographic areas. One, *Digitaria serotina,* is found only on low, sandy ground from Louisiana to Florida and north to Virginia.

Crabgrass, of the grass family, bears its flowers on one side of a flat rachis, or spine.

PURPLE DEAD NETTLE

Lamium purpureum, **of the mint family, naturalized in North America from Europe.**

This mint doesn't smell minty, but musky and bitter. If you look closely, however, you'll see that purple dead nettle has all the characteristics of a member of the mint family: Its stems are square in cross section; two leaves arise opposite each other at each stem node; its blossoms are bilaterally symmetrical and look like little dog faces; and its ovary has four lobes, which develop into four tiny nutlets.

The name of this plant seems inappropriate, as there's nothing dead about it, and the term *nettle* usually refers to plants with stinging hairs, which this charming little mint just doesn't have.

Dead nettle blossoms possess fairly open throats and supply plenty of nectar, so various small bees pollinate it. The old herbals say that fresh or dried dead nettle plants and flowers can be made into decoctions for controlling bleeding and that the leaves can be applied directly to small cuts and scrapes. Dried dead nettle, made into a tea and sweetened with honey, they declare, makes you sweat, cleanses the kidneys, and ends chills. Linnaeus, the botanist who devised the taxonomic system, reported that Swedish peasants once ate dead nettle as greens, though cattle refused to eat it.

Purple dead nettle, also known as red henbit, is similar to and closely related to another odorless mint, called common henbit, or common dead

Purple dead nettle, of the mint family, has no minty odor, but it does have the bilaterally symmetrical flower, opposite leaves, and square stem characteristic of mint plants.

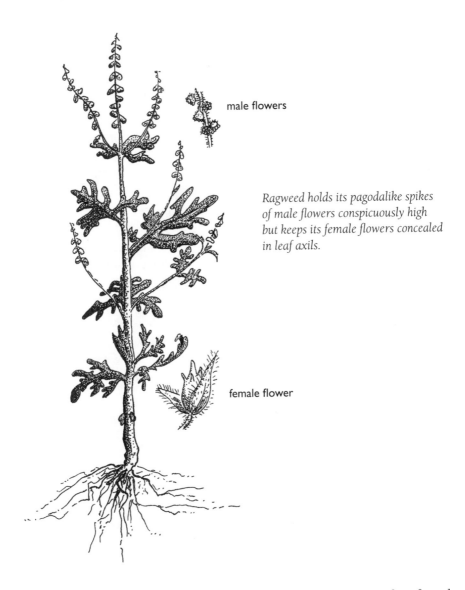

male flowers

*Ragweed holds its pagodalike spikes
of male flowers conspicuously high
but keeps its female flowers concealed
in leaf axils.*

female flower

nettle *(Lamium amplexicaule)*. These two common weeds are often found growing together.

RAGWEED

Ambrosia artemisiifolia, of the composite family, a native North American plant that has become naturalized in Europe and the West Indies.

Few people have anything nice to say about ragweed. Ragweed pollen is notorious for causing hay fever, and ragweed flowers are small and camouflaged by their green color. Even the monumental, supertechnical *Gray's*

Manual of Botany breaks from its usual stodgy, nonjudgmental format to label the ragweed "a polymorphic and despised weed."

Wildlife experts don't agree. Naturalists know that the list of animals benefiting from eating ragweed seeds is a long one. Ragweed seeds are rich in high-calorie oil, and seed production per plant can be enormous. Some seeds remain on plants far into the winter and thus are available when other foods are covered with snow. All ground-feeding birds benefit from ragweed seeds, especially sparrows and finches. One study found that ragweed seeds constitute more than half of the diet of white-crowned sparrows living in the Northeast! Chipmunks and ground squirrels, and sometimes even deer, also eat ragweed seeds.

It's funny that ragweed's genus name is *Ambrosia*, because ambrosia is usually thought of as "the food of the gods," which hay-fever sufferers would sniff at. It's unclear why Linnaeus chose *Ambrosia* as the ragweed genus name. Is it possible that Linnaeus had a sense of humor? Or maybe he thought that something sparrows love to eat also was good enough for the gods.

WILD CARROT, OR QUEEN ANNE'S LACE
Daucus carota, of the parsley family, naturalized into North America from Europe.

If you dig up a wild carrot growing along a weedy roadside, its taproot smells good enough to eat. No matter how good it smells, however, especially if the plant grows in sterile, rocky, compacted soil, you'll find that the root is too woody and slender to be worth eating.

As explained in chapter 5, garden carrots are just domesticated varieties of the wild carrot. Therefore, when you see how small and woody wild carrot taproots are, you'll admire how plant breeders have been able to develop such succulent sustenance from such a scrawny source. On the other hand, if seeds are taken from wild carrots, planted, and cultured with the same care as garden carrot seed, the resulting carrots look much more appetizing. Nevertheless, they are not nearly as large, succulent, and sweet as horticultural varieties.

Wild carrot is a *biennial*—a plant that lives for two years. During the first year of a wild carrot's life, it produces a small, stemless, inconspicuous rosette of leaves. These leaves' main job is to store photosynthesized carbohydrates in the taproot—the carrot.

During the spring of the second year, when all the different weeds begin growing upward, the wild carrot is able to get energy not only from the sun, but also from its starchy taproot, and thus it puts on a spurt of growth that carries it above its neighbors. Just look around; if you find flowering wild carrot

Wild carrot, or Queen Anne's lace, is the wild ancestor of the garden carrot, evidenced by the strong carroty odor of its taproot.

along a roadside, its blossoms probably will overtop the flowers of neighboring weeds that live for just one year.

Take a close look at the wild carrot's flowers. The snow-white, lacy affair known as *Queen Anne's lace* is actually a cluster of tiny flowers called an *inflorescence*. Inside each inflorescence, the individual flowers show surprising diversity. In the inflorescence's very center there's usually a single dark purple blossom. Flowers on the perimeter have longer pedicels, or flower stems, and enlarged corolla limbs. Once you've gotten to know a lot of plants, you'll realize that this is quite a special arrangement.

MAKING A RAINBOW BOUQUET

What you will need

several Queen Anne's lace flower clusters

glasses of water

food coloring

---

1. Snip off a few young, expanding Queen Anne's lace inflorescences.

2. In separate glasses of water, add a few drops of various hues of food coloring.

3. Place the stems of the inflorescences in the colored water, and watch as the white, lacy flowers take on pastel colors over a period of hours.

4. Use the colored inflorescences to make a rainbow bouquet.

PART 2

ANIMALS OF THE GARDEN AND FLOWER BED

If you look around your garden or flower bed, you'll find that there's a lot more to a garden than just plants.

The creatures in our gardens and flower beds are part of wild, untamed nature. The uninvited beetles, slugs, toads, moles, and hummingbirds that invade our gardens are no less wildlife than are zebras in Kenya and whales in the open sea. Our garden animals live and die by the same ecological principles that zoologists observe among creatures in the most isolated jungles. There's nothing domesticated or civilized in the way a garden spider ensnares, immobilizes with poisonous fangs, and then devours a struggling, desperate grasshopper.

Therefore, go into your garden or flower bed knowing that what you learn there about animals is applicable to wildlife the world over. If you learn to recognize the main insect orders in your backyard, you'll be able to pigeonhole most of the insects you find anywhere.

If you become familiar with the living creatures in your garden or flower bed, you'll have gone a good distance toward learning basic facts about the animals of the world.

CHAPTER 8

Insects

THE "STANDARD" INSECT

As I've suggested in the plant section, it's a good idea to keep a "standard" concept of something in mind so that when we find the real thing in nature we'll know what's special about it by seeing how it *differs* from our "standard" model. Well, the same approach works with animals, including insects.

The "standard" insect looks vaguely like a grasshopper, but it's not meant to. It's just the most simple, unspecialized, really boring looking insect I could think up. Now, as we did with our "standard" flowers and "standard" plants, let's take a tour or our "standard" insect by examining some terms of insect anatomy.

First of all, our "standard" insect is divided into three body regions, the *head* (bearing eyes, antennae, and mouthparts), the *thorax* (bearing legs and wings), and the *abdomen* (which in our "standard" insect bears nothing special). Another fundamental feature of insect bodies is that they are *segmented*. The segments, however, are not the three body regions. In fact, an insect's abdomen typically consists of ten complete segments, though often all ten aren't visible. Some may be fused with others, or they may be present but telescoped within one another.

Now let's take a closer look at the various appendages of the head and thorax.

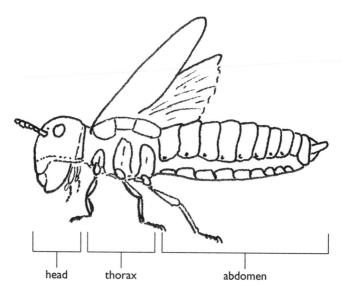

head   thorax   abdomen

The "standard" backyard insect, with six legs, two pairs of wings, a clearly segmented abdomen, and short, simple antennae.

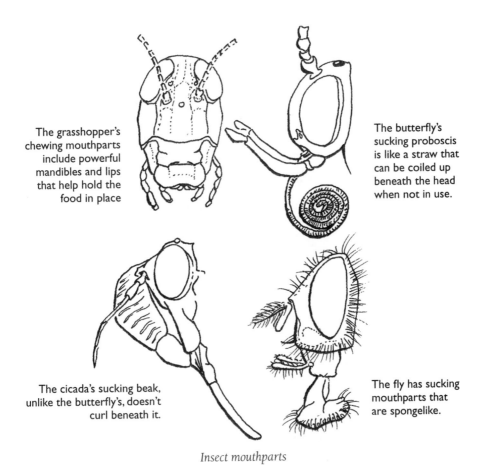

The grasshopper's chewing mouthparts include powerful mandibles and lips that help hold the food in place

The butterfly's sucking proboscis is like a straw that can be coiled up beneath the head when not in use.

The cicada's sucking beak, unlike the butterfly's, doesn't curl beneath it.

The fly has sucking mouthparts that are spongelike.

Insect mouthparts

Insects generally possess two kinds of eyes: simple and compound. *Simple eyes,* technically referred to as *ocelli* (singular *ocellus*), are usually located atop the forehead and typically number three. *Compound eyes* are each composed of many tiny windows—maybe hundreds—called *facets.*

Insect *antennae* vary a great deal among insect groups and serve as important identification characters. The antennae of all fly species, for instance, have three segments; those of thrips, six to nine segments; and those of wasps and bees, more than ten.

Mouthparts are even more diagnostic. All true bugs have mouths designed for chewing. All butterflies and moths have tubelike *proboscises* used for sucking; these can be coiled up beneath the head when not in use. Flies also suck, but their mouthparts are never coiled.

On insect *legs,* the lowest part, the footlike *tarsus* (plural *tarsi*), is of particular interest because the number of tarsus segments remains constant

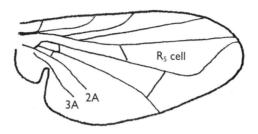

common housefly, *Musca domestica*

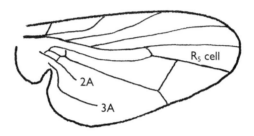

little housefly, *Fannia canicularis*

Subtle differences in wing venation often differentiate species, as here, where the shape of the R_5 cell and the lengths of the 2A and 3A veins mean all the difference.

within an insect group. Thus all flies have tarsi with five segments; all earwigs, three; and all thrips, either one or two.

Often, wings are an insect's most diagnostic feature. The network of veins extending across an insect's wings is not randomly constructed; all members of the same species have the same wing venation. To aid in identification, entomologists are able to label each vein in every insect's wing with a specific name understood by other entomologists.

These "specific names" of very obscure items are very important in all of science, so this is a good place to prove that to yourself by doing the following project.

COMPARING AN INSECT
WITH THE "STANDARD" INSECT

What you will need

a randomly encountered garden insect

magnifying glass (optional)

1. Find an insect that looks as though it will stay still for a while. If it's winter and you can't find an insect (you could if you looked hard enough), use the drawing of the Colorado potato beetle on page 121.

2. Write out ten different ways that it differs from the "standard" insect.

In this project, I'll bet that you had problems describing what you saw. Maybe you used words like "thing," "something," "doohickey," or "thingama-jig." Vague words like these have no place in science. Fortunately, insect field guides, such as those listed in this book's bibliography, usually go into much more detail describing insect anatomy and providing names for obscure body parts, so there is no need for you to be satisfied with having to use inexplicit terms.

If you really want to see the power invested in technically precise terms, find yourself an insect field guide or entomology book, study the terms dealing with mouthparts, wings, legs, antenna, and the rest, and conduct the above project once more, this time making a point to use your new terms. Your second description should be much more clear, concise, and elegant than your first one.

METAMORPHOSIS

Probably no feature of insect life history is as remarkable as the way insects develop from eggs to adults, in the process called *metamorphosis.* Insects metamorphose because their bodies are enclosed by husklike *exoskeletons.* An insect has no internal skeleton, and the exoskeleton gives its body shape. When you look at an insect, you're seeing its exoskeleton. Exoskeletons of immature insects are often thin like cellophane, but on adults they often feel and look like hard, brittle plastic.

If an insect is imprisoned within an exoskeleton, how does it grow from the tiny larva hatched from an egg to a full-sized adult?

Instead of enlarging a little day by day, as we do, insects grow in spurts. When a spurt occurs, typically, in a process called *molting,* or *ecdysis,* the exoskeleton splits, the insect pulls itself from its old shell, and during its first, very vulnerable minutes outside the old exoskeleton, a soft, new, larger exoskeleton expands like a sponge soaking up water. When it finally hardens, the insect finds itself larger than before, but will stay its new size until the next molt occurs.

The stages between molts are referred to as *instars;* most insects experience four to eight instars. Only a few continue molting after becoming adults.

Molting is only one small part of metamorphosis, however. There are two profoundly different kinds of metamorphosis: simple and complete.

Simple metamorphosis mostly takes place in groups that are more primitive, meaning those that evolved first and generally are less specialized in form and habit. Cockroaches, for example, having appeared on earth about 320 million years ago, are primitive and undergo simple metamorphosis. In simple metamorphosis, the immature insect, or *nymph,* that hatches from an egg is very similar to the adult, except that it is much smaller and its wings are less developed. In late summer, you may see grasshopper nymphs in your garden, looking like miniature editions of the grownups.

Complete metamorphosis is a feature of insects that have evolved comparatively recently. Aphids, for instance, first appeared "only" around 135 million years ago.

In complete metamorphosis, what emerges from the egg is a *larva.* Larvae come in all shapes, colors, and sizes and are often more colorful and better known than the adults. Often it's an insect's larval stage that plagues gardeners, because larvae must eat like crazy to fuel the spectacular changes taking place inside them. Some burrowing larvae, such as seed-corn maggots, are legless; others, like cutworms, roam around on tiny legs. Many larvae are called *caterpillars.* Especially for gardeners, identifying insect larvae may be more fun than identifying adults. Most good insect field guides illustrate at least the better-known larvae.

Larvae molt and grow through few to several instars, sometimes changing in color, size, and other characteristics. At the end of the final instar stage, a

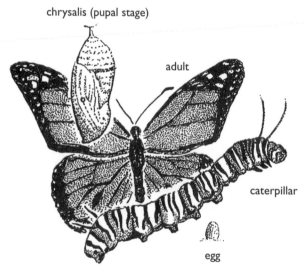

The monarch butterfly goes through four stages of metamorphosis.

ANIMALS OF THE GARDEN AND FLOWER BED

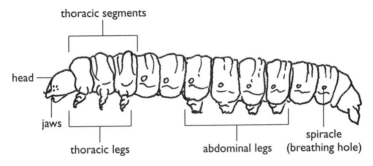

Anatomy of a caterpillar

decisive change occurs: Instead of the larvae simply becoming larger, a *pupa* develops. Pupae are usually inactive and thus don't feed. Sometimes they are enclosed in a protective covering. If the covering is baglike and holds the insect inside, the covering is called a *cocoon*. If the covering is formed of the larva's exoskeleton, it's a *puparium*. In the special case of butterflies, whose pupae are often finely sculptured and sometimes brightly colored, the pupa is referred to as a *chrysalis*. If you look around your garden long enough, usually you will be able to find various kinds of pupae. Being on hand when the adult finally emerges can be exciting stuff.

MONITORING PUPAE

What you will need

pupae
five-inch snippets of bright ribbon
your backyard nature notebook

---

1. Find one or more pupae; the best time to look is from late summer through early fall. Don't restrict your hunt to the garden—also look in surrounding trees and shrubbery. Look under leaves, deep inside vines and bushes, beneath loose tree bark, and among large wood chips. Don't search just once and then give up; as summer proceeds into fall, different species pupate.

2. Tie a brightly colored snippet of ribbon next to each resting pupa you discover.

3. In your notebook, sketch a map of the entire area searched, and mark the location of each pupa. The notebook will cue you to the pupa's general

location, and the ribbon will show you exactly where it is. Note the date of discovery, and later the dates of any changes observed. Sketch the pupae, drawing arrows to important features that might help in future identification. If you can identify either the pupa or the adult that later emerges, cross-reference your sketch with your page on that particular insect species.

4. Each day check on each pupa. If you're lucky, you may witness at least one emergence.

NONSTANDARD INSECT BEHAVIOR

There are some insects whose life histories just don't proceed step by step as outlined above. Aphids, for instance, have their own ways of doing things.

Aphids generally overwinter as eggs. In the spring, they hatch into wingless females that soon give birth (without first having had sex with males!) to more wingless females (not eggs). Two or more generations of such asexual reproduction, called *parthenogenesis,* occur before females with wings are produced. These winged females usually fly onto a food plant different from the one on which they developed, and then on this new food source they too reproduce parthenogenetically. Late in the season, the winged female aphids return to their original food source and again begin giving birth partheno-

Aphids are a favorite food of the syrphid fly larva.

genetically, this time to both males and females. As autumn's chill precedes the season's killing frosts, male and female aphids mate, and the females lay fertilized eggs that overwinter.

Now, knowing all this, can you ever again think of an aphid as just a pesky little green blob?

The entire life cycle of many larger insects, especially in northern areas, can take two or more years. Periodical cicadas need seventeen years and spend most of their lives underground as root-eating nymphs.

CLASSIFYING INSECTS

Insects belong to that great group of animals known as the *arthropods* (phylum Arthropoda). Of all the animals on earth, a good guess is that about 150,000 species are *not* arthropods, but some 900,000 *are*. Think about that. It means that six of every seven kinds of animals on earth are arthropods!

Of these 900,000 arthropod species, about 800,000 are insects. And of these 800,000, about one-tenth are found in North America. Even when plants are included, it can be said that *considerably more than half of all of earth's biological species are insects!*

These are mind-boggling figures, and you should reflect on this diversity and evolutionary success with reverence.

Arthropods include not only insects, but also such diverse creatures as spiders, lobsters, and the barnacles that stick to the sides of ships. Here are the identifying characteristics of an arthropod:

1. The body is segmented, divided into *head, thorax,* and *abdomen.*

2. The legs are jointed. (The word *arthropod* is from the classical Greek words *arthro-,* meaning "joint," and *pod-,* meaning "foot.")

3. Instead of having an interior skeleton composed of individual bones, the way humans do, an arthropod has a hard, caselike *exoskeleton,* or exterior skeleton, that encloses its organs.

4. Blood circulates between veins and a fairly large, open body cavity, called the *hemocoel,* instead of circulating within a network of interconnected arteries and veins as it does in humans.

Insects have some special features that distinguish them from other arthropods.

1. Adult insects have six legs (whereas spiders, for instance, have eight).

2. Adult insects possess one pair of antennae (spiders have none).

All of the world's approximately 800,000 species of insects can be classified into only about twenty-six orders. Learning to put any insect you find into one of these twenty-six orders is something you can do. And doing it makes a jolly good sport.

Figuring out what order an insect belongs to is usually easier than you might think, especially because several of the twenty-six orders are found only in specialized habitats far removed from our gardens. Also, some orders contain only a few extremely rare members. Therefore, most of the insects you find in your garden or flower bed can be placed in one of just eleven orders, which are listed in the accompanying table.

Order	Examples
Orthoptera	grasshoppers, crickets, walkingsticks, cockroaches, mantises
Coleoptera	beetles
Lepidoptera	butterflies, moths
Diptera	flies, mosquitoes
Hymenoptera	ants, wasps, bees, ichneumon flies
Hemiptera	true bugs
Homoptera	cicadas, leafhoppers, treehoppers, aphids, scale insects
Dermaptera	earwigs
Odonata	dragonflies
Thysanoptera	thrips
Neuroptera	ant lions

Making it even simpler, of these eleven common orders, probably 95 percent of the insects you'll find in your garden or flower bed will belong to the first seven. Master those seven common backyard orders, and you'll practically be an expert in the order-placing game! When you find an insect not belonging in one of these seven, you'll just want to sit down and admire your exotic find. With a little experience, you'll come to know the individual characteristics of each of these seven orders.

Common Backyard Insect Orders

Coleoptera. (co-leh-OP-ter-uh; *coleo,* Greek, for "sheath," and *ptera,* Greek, for "wing"; beetles)

The order Coleoptera, which includes all beetles, is the "biggie," holding more species than any other. (In North America alone, there are about 28,600 species.) This is good news for us, because adult beetles are among the most conspicuous, colorful, and recognizable of all insects. Beetle forewings are usually hard, like brittle plastic, forming a protective covering, or *sheath,* over

Coleoptera: A Colorado potato beetle leaves orange eggs on the underside of a leaf.

most of the insect's body. When beetles are not flying, they fold their fragile membranous hind wings like Chinese fans beneath their hard forewings.

Beetle larvae come in a huge array of shapes and sizes; there are thick-bodied grubs, forms that look like worms, some that are flat, and others that look like little silverfish. Metamorphosis is complete. Beetle larvae and adults both chew their food.

Lepidoptera. (le-pi-DOP-ter-uh; *lepido,* Greek, for "scale"; butterflies and moths)

The fact that the order's name is based on a word meaning "scale" makes sense if you look at a butterfly or moth wing under the microscope. The wings are covered with very tiny, often brightly colored scales.

It's not always simple to tell the difference between a butterfly and a moth. In general, butterflies usually fold their wings over their backs verti-cally, like fins rising above a shark's back; are *diurnal* (active during the day); and possess threadlike, unbranched antennae. In contrast, moths hold their wings flush with the ground's surface; are mostly *nocturnal* (active at night); and often bear feathery, branched antennae.

The situation is complicated by the fact that many members of this order are neither butterflies nor moths. Skippers, constituting an intermediate form, hold their wings upward in a V configuration. Their antennae are threadlike, as among the butterflies, but unlike butterflies, they have interesting little hooks at the tips of their antennae.

Lepidoptera: A European cabbage butterfly adult and larva visit a broccoli leaf.

Metamorphosis in the Lepidoptera is complete, and some caterpillars are prettier than the adult forms.

Orthoptera. (or-THOP-ter-uh; *ortho,* Greek, for "straight"; grasshoppers, crickets, walkingsticks, cockroaches, mantises)

Orthopterans make all kinds of clicks, snaps, crackles, and pops by rubbing one body part against another. Crickets and long-horned grasshoppers (including katydids) rasp the sharp-edged *scraper* on one front wing across the *file* on the other wing's underside. Band-winged grasshoppers snap their hind wings as they fly. Slant-faced grasshoppers rub their hind legs against a thickened place on their front wings. Usually males make these sounds to attract females.

The group gets its name from *ortho,* meaning "straight," which refers to the fact that resting adult orthopterans fold their wings straight over their backs, rooflike. When many adults in this order fly, their back wings display striking designs and colors not visible at rest. Metamorphosis here is simple.

Diptera. (DIP-ter-uh; *di,* Greek, for "two"; flies, mosquitoes)

Dipterous insects are easy to identify because winged adults bear only one pair of wings. If you can sneak up on a housefly or mosquito with a hand lens, notice that arising from its body, right behind the wing, there are useless-looking clublike knobs or growths. These are called *halteres,* and they are all that evolution has left of a second pair of wings. Halteres enable flies and mosquitoes to maintain their equilibrium in flight. When entomologists snipped off one of a large fly's halteres and it tried to fly away, it crashed right into the ground. When an appropriate-sized snippet of thread was glued atop the former haltere's stub, the fly could navigate properly.

Metamorphosis in this order is complete. The usually legless and worm-like larvae are often called *maggots;* frequently they burrow inside plant and animal bodies as parasites. Many species in this order are bloodsucking. Others are parasitic or predacious, often on other insects, and still others are of value as scavengers. These insects all have sucking mouthparts.

Hymenoptera. (hi-me-NOP-ter-uh; *hymeno,* Greek, for "membrane"; wasps, bees, ants)

At first glance, hymenopterans are reminiscent of dipterans. There are fundamental differences between these two orders, however. Winged adult wasps, bees, ants, and other hymenopterans have two pairs of wings, not one. Also, most have mouthparts adapted for chewing, not for sucking. Several important hymenopterans are wingless; worker ants and female velvet ants (actually very hairy, brightly colored wasps) are the most common.

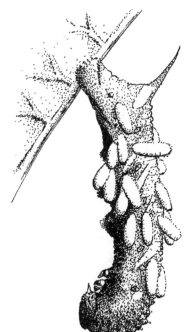

Hymenoptera: Cocoons of a braconid wasp on a tomato hornworm. The female wasp deposits eggs on the caterpillar's skin. Wasp larvae hatch from the eggs and burrow inside the caterpillar, where they feed until their host dies. Then they eat their way through the hornworm's body to the outside, where they pupate in cocoons attached to the hornworm's exterior. When one organism lives in or on another organism, it's known as a parasite.

In many hymenopterans, the ovipositor, a stiff egg-laying appendage at the abdomen's end, has been modified into a stinger. When larvae are plant eaters, the adult may lay its eggs on that plant; when the larvae are parasites, eggs are laid on or inside the host. Metamorphosis is complete.

Hemiptera. (heh-MIP-ter-uh; *hemi,* Greek, for "half"; true bugs)

The term *true bugs* might seem to suggest that there are "fake bugs." What this means, however, is that whereas some indiscriminate folks call any insect a *bug,* to entomologists a bug is only a hemipteran. The group gets its name from *hemi,* meaning "half," which refers to the fact that the bases of most hemipterans' wings are thickened, but the outer tips are membranous; the wing is hemi, or half, hardened. The pair of back wings is entirely membranous.

Hemipterans possess sucking mouthparts, and many spend their time piercing plants with spearlike beaks, sucking out plant juices. This hardly endears them to gardeners. Other species insert their beaks into animals. Ambush bugs and assassin bugs prey on other insects, and bedbugs suck blood from warm-blooded animals, such as man.

Homoptera. (ho-MOP-ter-uh; *homo-,* Greek, for "being the same"; cicadas, aphids, leafhoppers, treehoppers, scale insects)

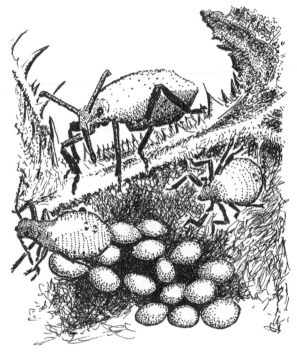

Hemiptera: Immature squash bugs on the underside of a hairy squash leaf gather around a cluster of shiny, brown eggs. As squash bugs feed, they inject toxic substances that cause plant tissue to wilt. The bugs can sometimes be located by their strong musky odor.

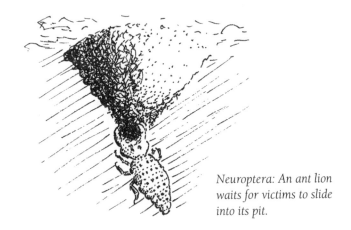

Neuroptera: An ant lion waits for victims to slide into its pit.

Homopterans are similar to hemipterans, except that their front wings are *homogeneously* textured from base to tip—not just halfway. Like hemipterans, however, they also insert beaks into plants and animals.

Other Orders. Occasionally you might spot members of orders other than the above "big seven." If a lake or stream lies nearby, large, fast-moving dragonflies (order Odonata) may sometimes dart among your snapdragons like jet-propelled biplanes. Dragonflies catch other flying insects in midair, then land and eat them.

Earwigs (order Dermaptera), which have pincerlike appendages at the tip of the abdomen, are sometimes found among flower petals—especially on clematises, dahlias, and gladiolus. Usually they do their plant eating during the night, then hide during daylight hours.

Thrips (order Thysanoptera) are easily recognized by the long hairs fringing their four wings. They attack many plants but in the garden show a special fondness for peas. Infestation by thrips can cause gladiolus flowers to become deformed and discolored. Wingless thrip larvae may be more visible than winged adult forms.

Ant lion (order Neuroptera) larvae are more famous than the adults. The larvae, called *doodlebugs* in my part of the country, live at the bottom of conical pits in dry sand or dust and feed on ants and other insects that slide into the pits. The ant lion lies completely buried below the pit, with its sicklelike jaws spread so that they can clamp on anything blundering between them.

As a child I was taught that if you kneel before a doodlebug's pit and say, "Doodlebug, doodlebug, your house is on fire," the doodlebug would knock sand in your face. Sometimes it works! Ant lion adults very much resemble damselflies, which have long, fragile-looking, transparent, net-veined wings.

KEY TO ORDERS OF WINGED, ADULT INSECTS FOUND IN GARDENS

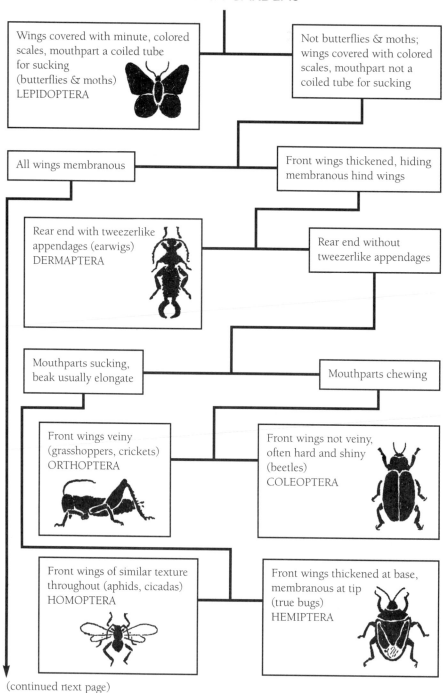

Wings covered with minute, colored scales, mouthpart a coiled tube for sucking (butterflies & moths) LEPIDOPTERA

Not butterflies & moths; wings covered with colored scales, mouthpart not a coiled tube for sucking

All wings membranous

Front wings thickened, hiding membranous hind wings

Rear end with tweezerlike appendages (earwigs) DERMAPTERA

Rear end without tweezerlike appendages

Mouthparts sucking, beak usually elongate

Mouthparts chewing

Front wings veiny (grasshoppers, crickets) ORTHOPTERA

Front wings not veiny, often hard and shiny (beetles) COLEOPTERA

Front wings of similar texture throughout (aphids, cicadas) HOMOPTERA

Front wings thickened at base, membranous at tip (true bugs) HEMIPTERA

(continued next page)

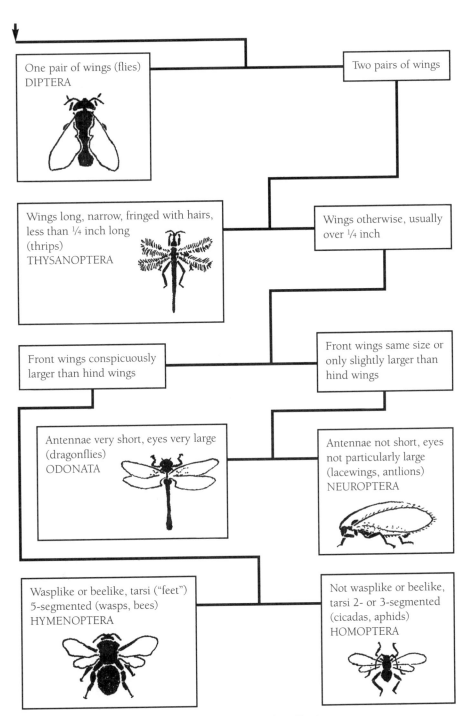

One pair of wings (flies)
DIPTERA

Two pairs of wings

Wings long, narrow, fringed with hairs, less than ¼ inch long (thrips)
THYSANOPTERA

Wings otherwise, usually over ¼ inch

Front wings conspicuously larger than hind wings

Front wings same size or only slightly larger than hind wings

Antennae very short, eyes very large (dragonflies)
ODONATA

Antennae not short, eyes not particularly large (lacewings, antlions)
NEUROPTERA

Wasplike or beelike, tarsi ("feet") 5-segmented (wasps, bees)
HYMENOPTERA

Not wasplike or beelike, tarsi 2- or 3-segmented (cicadas, aphids)
HOMOPTERA

NOTE: "Membranous" means "membranelike"—like cellophane.
        Ants are wingless Hymenoptera.

THE ART OF INSECT WATCHING

Insect watching is a lot like bird watching, and it can become just as habit forming. One important difference is this: With birds, the diligent watcher can usually figure out the exact bird species observed. With insects, however, unless you really get technical and have access to some very scholarly literature, often you're lucky if you can just identify the family the insect belongs to.

Except for very common insects, many species and even many of the genera you find will not appear in the average field guide; there are just too many kinds of insects.

For instance, about fifteen hundred species of crane flies inhabit North America. If a crane fly happens by, you'll probably be able to determine only that it's a crane fly in the crane fly family, Tipulidae, which is in the order Diptera. If you absolutely want to figure out the crane fly's genus and species, you may be able to do so by visiting a university library, going deep into the stacks, and poring over dusty volumes that only specialists use.

Keep track of the insects you come across in your garden or flower bed in your backyard nature notebook. You'll need a good insect field guide, such as *A Field Guide to the Insects* (see Bibliography), to identify the insects you find. For each insect you identify, add a page headed with its name to the insect section of your notebook. Draw a picture of the insect—in each metamorphosis stage, if possible—and write down information about its life cycle, preferred foods, enemies, and so forth. Your own observations should constitute the most important part, but you can also get information from your field guide and from library books. You'll be astonished at how outlandish some of our most common garden insects can be.

Here's a hint about keeping the insect section of your backyard nature notebook organized: Group your pages alphabetically according to orders; within the orders, arrange pages alphabetically by family; within the families, arrange pages alphabetically by genus; and within the genera, arrange pages alphabetically by species. This will ensure that closely related species appear near one another in your notebook—all the butterflies in one place, for instance.

CHAPTER 9

Other Animals

EARTHWORMS

Here is a piece of general wisdom: In life, it is wise not only to know a little about a lot of things, but also a lot about a few things. Being a generalist gives you flexibility in thought and behavior, enables you to see the big picture, and imparts a feeling for trends and an ability to make good guesses. On the other hand, being a specialist provides you with a deeper understanding of complex interrelationships, which sometimes may be found in unexpected places.

This book provides a lot of general information about a broad diversity of things, but here we will look closely at one animal: the earthworm.

Earthworms are among the most common and easy-to-observe animals in the garden and flower bed. Because of their remarkable adaptations, bizarre behavior, and the services they render to mankind and all other living things on earth, they are fun to know and deserve our attention and respect.

The earthworm belongs to the phylum Annelida, the *segmented worms.* Annelids are worms whose bodies are separated into clearly distinguishable compartments or segments. Earthworms look like they're made of numerous strung-together rings or segments. Each segment carries its own collection of organs. Young annelids usually have few segments, but as time passes, new segments are added.

Earthworms, which tunnel below the soil's surface, are the most famous annelids, but other fascinating annelids exist. For example, some annelids are bloodsucking parasites, such as leeches.

Maybe the annelid most likely to be featured on a believe-it-or-not TV show is the palolo worm, which lives in coral reefs in the South Pacific. The bizarre thing about palolo worms is that over 90 percent of the earth's entire population breeds within a single two-hour period of the whole year, and that brief, frenzied moment of mating is determined by the position of the moon.

Many annelids, especially those living in the ocean and along beaches, bear flaps along their segments that serve more or less as legs; tufts of bristles, called *chaetae,* on each flap are analogous to feet. Leeches have suckers at both ends. Earthworms and other members of their class lack both leg flaps and suckers.

Many kinds of earthworms exist; one species in tropical Australia grows eleven feet long! In eastern and central North America, probably the most common two earthworm species are *Lumbricus terrestris,* a reddish worm, and the similar *Allolobophora caliginosa,* a pale pinkish one. Interestingly, *Lumbricus terrestris,* despite its abundance in North America, probably is not native

Lumbricus terrestris, *on the left, bears its clitellum over segments 31 or 32 to 37; the clitellum of Allolobophora caliginosa, on the right, covers segments 27 to 34.*

here. Like house sparrows and dandelions, it was introduced from Europe, and it has flourished on plowed, disturbed American soil.

Earthworm Anatomy. Much of the pleasure of looking discerningly at earthworms derives from noticing what *isn't* there. Some annelids possess eyes, but earthworms, like many creatures living sunless, subterranean lives, have none. Other annelids, especially those living in open water, often bear tentacles, but in the earthworms' tight quarters, tentacles would just be in the way, so earthworms have none. In their cylindrical, underground tunnels, leg-like appendages would be useless, so the body has no appendages from tip to tip. Some annelids bear liplike *palpi,* which help them probe the soil; maybe earthworms are less fussy about what they eat, for they have none.

Another thing that earthworms don't have is lungs. Earthworms "breathe" through their skin. This explains how they can live for months below flooded ground. Any exposure to dry conditions for longer than a few minutes can seriously damage their skin, which is very delicate and specialized to absorb oxygen.

In fact, researchers believe that the reason earthworms are so often found dead on sidewalks after heavy rains is not that they have drowned; rather, the wet ground has invited the earthworms to ramble at night, then when dawn comes, they find themselves unable to burrow back down through concrete, and the sun's ultraviolet rays fry them. Exposure to sunlight for one hour can cause complete paralysis in an earthworm, and several hours of exposure is usually fatal.

Light-sensitive cells, not obvious to anyone just looking at a worm, are widely distributed on an earthworm's skin, especially toward both ends, but absent from the lower surface. Of course, this doesn't mean that with their skin, earthworms see images the way humans do; however, they certainly can sense if the sun is coming up or if an approaching robin is blocking the light. Just try to imagine what it must be like to have your skin "see" light. It's a whole other way of being.

The earthworm has other invisible skin organs thought to be sensitive to touch, chemicals, and temperature. Though earthworms are unresponsive to sound, they can feel vibrations traveling through the ground. Earthworms demonstrate only a feeble sense of smell, but they do show definite taste preferences. For example, they won't eat cabbage scraps if celery is handy, but if carrot leaves are available, they'll pass up both cabbage and celery!

Earthworms, then, are no-frills, no-nonsense, superstreamlined beings, and much of their beauty lies in their simple design. Nonetheless, to exist, they must have *some* features!

Inside their bodies, earthworms do have brains. The earthworm's brain is located right above the pharynx and behind the mouth. Earthworm brains don't look at all like diminutive human brains, and they certainly don't do as many incredible things as our brains do. In fact, earthworm brains seem to pay attention only to light and touch. If an earthworm's brain is removed, the worm's everyday behavior is hardly affected.

The earthworm also has five hearts, one in each segment, from segments 7 to 11.

Each earthworm segment bears four pairs of very minute bristles known as *chaetae*, or *setae*, one pair on each side and two pairs on the lower surface. Special muscles enable the chaetae to angle forward and backward and to be extended and retracted. If you try to pull an earthworm from its burrow, it'll stay stuck, because it thrusts its chaetae into the burrow's wall.

Besides anchoring the worm in place if it's pulled from above, chaetae provide the even more important service of enabling the worm to travel inside its burrow. The earthworm extends the front part of its body, secures that part in place by projecting chaetae into the burrow wall, and then contracts the whole body, pulling the rear end forward. Then the rear end is anchored with extended chaetae, the front end is extended, and the cycle is repeated.

This sounds like a sluggish, inefficient manner of moving around, but if you ever have the fun of watching a mole tunneling beneath the soil, you'll be astounded at how earthworms in front of the mole shoot from the ground in a fraction of a second. Earthworms are obviously capable of very fancy chaetae manipulation.

Each earthworm has a *male pore,* from which sperm are ejaculated during sexual union, and a *female pore,* which produces eggs. Such creatures, equipped with both male and female reproductive parts, are said to be *hermaphroditic.*

Mating usually takes place when the ground is wet. Sometimes earthworms emerge from their burrows and wander around before mating, but their favorite mating strategy seems to be just sticking their front ends from their burrows and mating with a worm in a next-door hole.

During copulation, two worms facing in opposite directions press their bottom surfaces together so that the clitellum of each lies opposite segments 9 through 11 of the other. During mating, sperm are ejaculated from the male pore of one worm into the *sperm receptacles* of the other, located in segments 9 and 10; these receptacles are temporary storage places for the sperm.

The slippery worms are held in place while they are mating by their chaetae, the tiny footlike bristles, and by copious mucus, produced during copulation by the worms' clitellum and skin, which glues them together.

Soon after mating is finished and each worm has sperm stored in its sperm receptacles, the clitellum secretes a membranous *cocoon.* With expert coordination, the worms wiggle and contort in such a way that eggs from the female pore of segment 14 slide into the cocoon. Then the cocoon, with the eggs inside it, is moved forward (or the worm slips backward), and the eggs are fertilized with the stored sperm as they pass the sperm receptacles.

Finally, the membranous cocoon is slipped over the worm's head, and the cocoon's open ends constrict to form a sort of closed, egg-holding capsule. Tiny earthworms eventually develop from the eggs and emerge from the cocoon.

On the earthworm's body, one conspicuous feature is the *clitellum,* a pale, latexlike girdle of skin encircling the body about a third of the distance back from the mouth. Actually, we needn't be so vague about the clitellum's location; as the following project shows, it and several other organs can be accu-

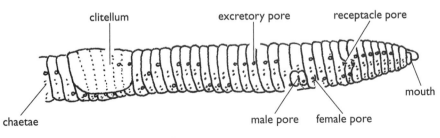

Earthworm exterior anatomy

rately pinpointed by anyone able to methodically count the worm's segments from one end to the other.

EXPLORING THE EARTHWORM

What you will need

large earthworm

wet saucer

magnifying glass (optional)

---

1. Position the earthworm on a wet saucer out of direct sunlight. Notice that the bandlike clitellum divides the worm into two unequal lengths. The short length is the worm's front; the long is its back. The cone-shaped foremost segment is considered segment 1.

2. Notice that the sides of each segment possess tiny, usually hard-to-see indentations. In each segment, the topmost indentation is an *excretory pore* analogous to urinary openings of higher animals.

3. Below most excretory pores, you may see a pair of even less obvious indentations. These mark the lateral chaetae, or setae. If you have an especially large worm, run a moist finger along its side and maybe you'll be able to feel these tiny bristles. Similar ventral chaetae may be observed on the worm's lower surface.

4. Find the earthworm's pointed "nose," or *prostomium,* on the short end. If you can see an opening in the crevice right behind segment 1, that's the *mouth.*

5. On the side of segment 15, you might discover a relatively conspicuous opening, looking like a tiny mouth with thick lips. This is the male pore. A much less conspicuous pore arising on segment 14, immediately before the male pore, is the female pore.

IDENTIFYING YOUR LOCAL EARTHWORMS

What you will need

large earthworm

wet saucer

magnifying lens and a focused mind

---

1. Dig up an earthworm at least large enough for the clitellum to be visible, and place it on the wet saucer out of direct sunlight.

2. Count the segments between your earthworm's clitellum and the pointed "nose" (on the short end of the worm's body). If your earthworm is a *Lumbricus,* counting from the "nose," the last segment before the clitellum will be segment 31; segments 32 through 37 will be sheathed by the clitellum. If your worm is a pale pinkish *Allolobophora,* the last segment before the clitellum will be segment 26.

This isn't nearly as easy as it sounds, unless you're willing to kill your worm and pin it down, which isn't recommended here; doing so would desensitize you to your subject—just the opposite of our intended goal.

Earthworms in Garden Soil. Charles Darwin, who first described the principles of evolution, said of earthworms that "it may be doubted if there are any other animals which have played such an important part in the history of the world."

Yes, history of the *world!* And to think, anyplace in an average garden, a shovel dug into the soil should turn up at least one of these supremely important animals. Earthworms are simply abundant in good soil. The more worms there are, the better off the soil is.

It's been estimated that each year on an acre of typical cultivated land, sixteen thousand pounds of soil pass through earthworm guts and are deposited atop the soil; thirty thousand pounds for really wormy soil. Charles Darwin figured that if all the worm excreta resulting from ten years of worm activity on an acre of soil were spread uniformly over that acre, it would be two inches deep.

If the soil that an earthworm burrows through is loose, then as the worm tunnels along, it shoves soil particles to the side, nibbling as it goes. If the soil is compact and contains little organic matter, however, earthworms simply eat their way through it, minerals, soil particles, and all. Naturally, the richer a soil is in organic matter, and the less dirt the worm has to eat, the better the worm likes it. Decaying plants, tiny seeds, the eggs and larvae of animals, and the live or dead bodies of small animals all are digested, whereas most soil particles simply pass through.

Everything passing through an earthworm gut is subjected to digestive enzymes and to the grinding action of the worm's powerful gizzard. Worms deposit their feces on the ground's surface near the mouths of their burrows. These neat little, mustard-colored coils of worm excreta are properly called *castings.* If organic matter is abundant in the earthworm's recent eatings, cast-

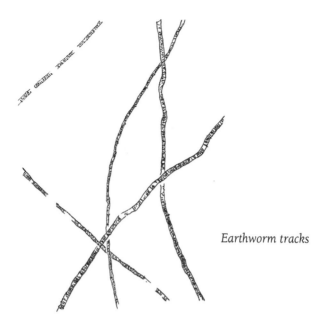

Earthworm tracks

ings around its burrow opening will be at a minimum, but if there's little organic matter, then castings will mount up.

Earthworm castings are great stuff. They are so rich in the chemical elements plants need—usable nitrogen in its nitrate form, calcium, magnesium, and phosphorus—that grass around earthworm burrow openings often grows taller and greener than grass just inches away.

The earthworm prefers to dine at night. At that time, a worm protrudes its front end from its burrow opening and forages for seeds, leaves, and other scraps of organic matter. Sometimes a worm will loop its body so that both ends peep from the burrow opening. One advantage of nighttime explorations, of course, is that robins and other enemies are less likely to spot them; also, the soil's surface is moister, and that's easier on a worm's delicate skin. If the foraging front end finds something like a decaying leaf, it may pull the object into the burrow and eat it there.

The burrows of earthworms also are beneficial. Like living things above ground, soil microorganisms and plant roots need air. If soil is to support lots of life, it needs to have air circulating through it, and earthworm burrows provide superhighways for air. Earthworm burrows also help plant roots grow through the soil; often roots follow the line of least resistance by growing down an old earthworm tunnel.

It's astonishing how, over very short distances in the garden, earthworm populations can change in terms of numbers, size, and even species. Subtle soil changes profoundly affect the well-being of this organism whose naked, moist skin is constantly in contact with the soil.

COMPARING EARTHWORM POPULATIONS

What you will need

shovel

bucket or box about a foot deep

backyard nature notebook

---

1. Designate several sampling locations, each a bit different from the others in terms of how rich the soil looks, how well the soil is drained, and how loose and crumbly it is. For example, one location might be an area of humus-rich garden soil, another the compacted soil along a footpath, and a third the soil of a lawn that's been subjected to heavy doses of insecticides and herbicides.

2. Shovel an equal amount of soil into the box from each sampling location. Try to be consistent with regard to the proportion of upper and lower soil.

3. Count the number of worms, large and small, in each soil sample.

4. Compare your findings, and reflect on the results. Record your findings in your notebook.

A similar sampling technique can be used to see if, as years pass and you improve the soil of your garden or flower bed, your earthworm population increases.

YEARLY SAMPLE OF EARTHWORM POPULATIONS

What you will need

shovel

bucket or box about one foot deep

backyard nature notebook

---

1. Conduct each of the steps described for the previous project, except this time restrict your sampling locations to within the boundaries of your

garden or flower bed, keeping in mind that you will be doing this year after year. Five or six samples should be enough.

2. To cut down on variables affecting your yearly census, sketch a map in your notebook showing exactly where your samples are taken from. Note the date so that each year you can perform the analysis at approximately the same time. For any sampling, be sure that the soil is neither uncommonly wet or dry.

3. Calculate how many worms you estimate to be present in your garden or flower bed, at least to the depth penetrated by your shovel. Determine the size of your garden by multiplying length times width. Let's say that your garden is 20 feet long and 10 feet wide, or 200 square feet. If your soil sample measures, say, 6 by 6 by 6 inches, then each sample you take represents one-quarter, or 0.25, of one square foot of garden surface. Using the basic algebraic ratio-and-proportion formula, you can figure out approximately how many worms are present in 200 square feet. Let's say that your five or six 6 by 6 by 6 samples average 2.32 worms each. Applying basic algebra, if 0.25 square foot of soil has 2.32 worms, then 200 square feet of soil has X worms.

This can also be expressed in the following equation:

$$\frac{0.25}{200} = \frac{2.32}{X}$$

Cross-multiplying, we get 0.25X = 464 (200 times 2.32). To determine X, divide 464 by 0.25. The result shows that there are approximately 1,856 worms in your 200-square-foot garden.

4. On another page of the notebook, draw a graph. Mark the current year's worm count on the vertical axis, positioning your calculated number of worms about one-quarter of the way up the axis. Along the horizontal axis, place about ten evenly spaced marks, designating upcoming years. Next year, your soil should be a little richer and your worms a little more populous, and your graph will start proceeding upward little by little over successive years.

5. Near or on the graph, be sure to note events that may have affected population numbers for a particular year's census. Notes like "last winter was hard, may have killed some worms" or "added two wheelbarrows of Uncle Bob's rabbit manure last fall" may help explain the graph's surprising peaks and dips.

Events such as hard winters and additions of manure can indeed cause your graph line to change erratically. One study of an agricultural field showed that an acre of soil that originally held about thirteen thousand earthworms contained more than a million after being fertilized with farm manure.[3]

When winter comes, young worms are easily killed by freezing. Soon after the first freezes, however, those that survive seem to acquire a cold tolerance; these worms migrate to greater soil depths—up to six feet deep! During the winter, earthworms plug their burrow holes, retreat to deep chambers, and one to several worms roll into cozy balls and pass the winter. They also do this during hot, dry summers.

Part of the enchantment my garden holds for me is the image of multitudes of contented, congenial earthworms always working there below ground as I conduct my everyday business aboveground. Passing by the garden eating a banana, I throw the peel among the beans and walk away picturing the peel gradually turning brown, deliquescing into mush, progressing toward its destiny as garden organic matter.

And then one night, perhaps a bit after midnight, when the garden is pitch dark, crickets chirping and the pregnant odor of rich soil rising with the dew, from a yet unnoticed burrow opening beneath a leaf or a piece of last year's okra stem, a benevolent worm will emerge from its burrow—a worm poetically imbued with the soil's feelings, its tastes and exact degree of acidity, cation-exchange capacity, oxygen diffusion rate, and soil-particle size—bend forward, and take immense pleasure in gnawing on my delectable banana peel.

SPIDERS

From the garden zoology perspective, there's just one large group of animals worthy of coming immediately after the super-rich world of insects and the superimportant world of earthworms: spiders.

Especially in late summer and fall, many interesting and beautiful species occupy our gardens and flower beds. These species display a tremendous variety of hunting strategies, courtship rituals, and other kinds of behavior.

An inexpensive little book called *Spiders and Their Kin,* one of the Golden Nature Guides, can help you identify and learn some basic information about North America's most conspicuous and interesting species.

One reason many people don't appreciate spiders is that they fear being

---

[3]E. J. Russell and F. W. Russell, *Soil Conditions and Plant Growth* (New York: Longmans, Green, 1950), 414.

Spiderlings send out threads of silk into the wind, then hitch a balloon ride to a new territory.

bitten. Of course, the easy way to avoid being bitten is not to touch them. Happily, to be a spider watcher, there is no need for you to ever venture within biting distance. Besides, in North America, fatalities from wasp and bee stings far outnumber those from spider bites. And spiders seldom bite, anyway, even when coaxed; most spiders aren't large enough to bite through a human's skin.

In North America, two spiders that can indeed produce serious bites are the black widow and the brown recluse. Black widows do live in backyards, especially trashy ones; usually they stay beneath objects. Brown recluses are more often found inside homes, especially on the floor behind furniture. Sometimes they are pretty common.

Unlike insects, which have six legs, spiders possess eight. Also unlike insects, spider bodies have two main sections, not three; in spiders, the head and thorax are combined to form what's known as a *cephalothorax.*

If you find a big spider you can study, notice that on its front end, between the jaws and the first pair of legs, there's what looks like a much smaller extra set of legs, or maybe a pair of miniature, fuzzy arms; most of the time they are held below the spider's face. These are *pedipalps,* which are neither arms nor legs, and spiders use them to feel things and hold prey. And male spiders use them to mate.

In male spiders, the pedipalps' tips are much enlarged into special cavities. When the male is ready to mate, he deposits sperm onto a special web, then reaches down with his pedipalps and sucks the sperm into the cavities. Later, if he finds a female, the act of mating is consummated when he reaches below the female with his pedipalps and inserts the sperm into an opening on the female's underside.

Maybe the most appealing thing about spiders is that they are such artists with silk. The silk is produced by tiny spigots called *spinnerets* at the abdomen's rear; usually there are six. Most spiders lay down silk *draglines* as they walk. These can help the spider retrace its steps or, if the spider loses its footing, serve as a safety line.

Immature spiders, called *spiderlings,* climb onto tall plants, fence posts, and other objects projecting above the ground and release long strands of silk into the air. The wind tugs on the silk, and when the tugging grows strong enough, the spiderling releases its grip and the wind carries it attached to its free-floating silk strand into new territory. This method of spiderling transportation is called *ballooning.* In the autumn, often ballooning spiderlings grace the air with silver streaks. When the sun reflects off these silver threads, they are called *gossamers.*

The most fascinating use of silk by spiders is in making webs. Certain kinds of webs are typical for particular families and subfamilies, and it's fascinating to learn how to identify spiders by the webs they produce.

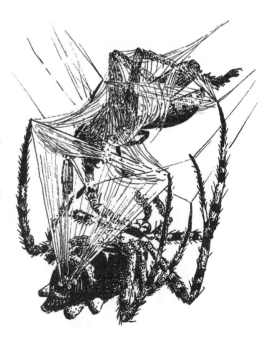

A silver argiope spider, Argiope argentata, *has caught a grasshopper in its web, paralyzed it with its venomous fangs, and now wraps a silk cocoon around the struggling victim by spinning it rapidly with its front legs as it draws silk from its spinnerets with its hind legs.*

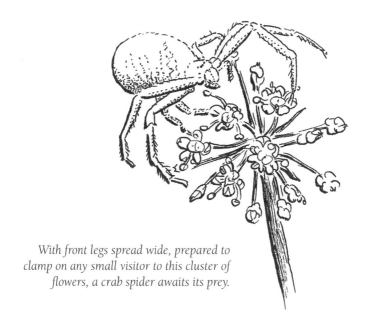

With front legs spread wide, prepared to clamp on any small visitor to this cluster of flowers, a crab spider awaits its prey.

Members of the family Araneidae construct *orb webs,* the flat, vertical sheets we usually think of when we visualize spiderwebs. Members of the family Linyphiidae build *sheet webs,* which are complex, three-dimensional webs with silks running in all directions. Members of the family Agelenidae make *funnel webs,* which look like flat floors erected atop grass blades, except that one end curls up and funnels into a cavelike tunnel. Inside this tunnel, the spider waits to pounce on any tiny critter that rambles across its silken floor.

Not all spiders make webs, however. *Crab spiders,* of the family Thomisidae, wait in ambush for passing insects, often with their front legs spread in anticipation. The larger *wolf spiders,* of the family Lycosidae, are very common, and you may spot one ranging across the garden floor, looking for prey, just as a wolf might prowl for small game.

In short, the world of spiders is as complex, bizarre, and beautiful as any other part of nature, and they are common and easy to observe in your backyard.

BIRDS

Only a few species of birds are likely to visit our gardens, but those few are interesting enough. And with a little effort, things can be done in a garden to make birds feel at home and want to visit frequently.

Especially in late summer and fall, house sparrows look for dusty areas in which to take dust baths; even small open, dusty places are appreciated. Birds need dependable sources of water for drinking and bathing, and a colorful commotion can develop around a simple birdbath placed in or near a garden or flower bed. Bright flowers and feeders that dispense nectar or sugar water can be used to attract hummingbirds during the summer, and sunflowers left standing after frost will attract seed-eating birds such as cardinals, sparrows, and finches.

Birdhouses erected here and there might attract a family or two of sparrows, house wrens, or tree swallows, for example, and few things are as exciting as following the day-to-day development of nestlings and fledglings.

A birdhouse need not be store-bought or expertly made by someone with building plans and lots of hand tools. When my quart-size, plastic coffee mug developed a crack, I used a pocketknife to enlarged the straw hole in the top to about one and a half inches in diameter, hung the mug by its handle ten feet up in a tree, and was rewarded with a family of house wrens! In late summer, after the wrens moved out, a gray tree frog (*Hyla versicolor*) took up resi-

Hummingbirds can be attracted to backyards not only by feeders that dispense nectar or sugar water, but also by ornamental plants with bright flowers.

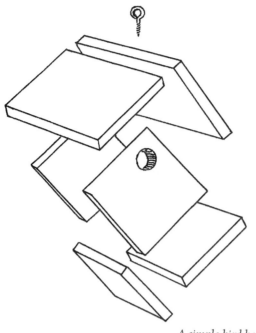

To make a bird box, you need a saw; a hammer; nails; a drill or saw to make a ¾-inch-diameter entrance hole; a 1-inch-long screw eye; and wood cut to the following dimensions:

Ends: two boards ½ × 4 × 4 inches

Sides: one board ½ × 4 × 4 inches
one board ½ × 3½ × 4 inches

Roof: one board ½ × 5½ × 6½ inches
one board ½ × 5 × 6½ inches

A simple bird box

dence in the mug. Before rains, it would call with short, loud trills, which, amplified by the mug's cavity, really sounded unearthly.

It's fascinating to keep an account of which birds visit your garden, and then study the life history of each species. You'll probably see the same four or five species again and again, but occasionally something new will show up, especially during spring and fall migrations.

Several good field guides to bird identification are available in bookstores and libraries; some, such as the little Golden Nature Guide called *Birds*, include only the most common species, but others show all North American birds. When I began my list of garden birds as a child, I got so involved that now my ever-growing life list of species seen in many countries and habitats holds more than eight hundred species!

MOLES

People with manicured lawns as top priorities tend to loathe moles. I've seen a nice old lady, frail and lacy-collared—a smiling woman who bakes ginger-snaps for children—borrow her grandson's pitchfork and watch like a hawk for new mole tunnels being dug, so that she could skewer the poor creature through the sod.

Mole traps tend to be pretty vicious affairs, and mole poisons abound. To control moles, my local agricultural extension agent doesn't blink twice about suggesting fumigating whole lawns with a poison that kills all animals living in the soil, from earthworms to grubs—except the moles. The idea is that if a mole's food supply (worms, beetle larvae, and such) is removed, the mole will go away. This is definitely not the kind of sensitivity to living ecosystems that this book is all about.

Anyone unwilling to follow the live-and-let-live mole philosophy can rid themselves of moles fairly nonviolently. Just keep a shovel and a wide-mouthed gallon jar handy. When you spot a tunnel being dug, softly approach the tunnel, and then very quickly insert the shovel about fifteen inches behind the working area; this should cut off the mole's retreat. Push the blade deep below where the mole should be imprisoned, then pull the handle back, causing the blade to angle upward and pop the mole from the ground. Wearing thick gloves for protection, with luck you can scoop him into the jar.

While you have a chance, take a good look at your prisoner and admire how perfectly he is designed for life underground. The mole's eyes, unimportant in its sunless, subterranean world, have atrophied into tiny slits. But look at those mighty, enlarged front legs, so short and thick that they resemble flippers with hard nails angled backward. Moles are designed to do the breaststroke through the soil.

In choosing a place in which to release your mole, remember that he'll need a food supply and fairly loose soil; a hard-packed, gravelly abandoned lot won't do.

In eastern North America, the main mole is *Scalopus aquaticus,* which favors lawns, golf courses, fields, and gardens. Moles spend most of their time underground, digging and using tunnels, which are linked together in extensive underground networks. Here and there the moles push up mounds of crumbly soil that look like heaps of randomly dumped dirt. The mole eats

The eastern mole, Scalopus aquaticus, *is well suited to its ecological role of foraging underground. In action, he's a champion breaststroker.*

Good field guides often provide distribution maps, such as this one for the eastern mole. Other mole species in the United States are the Pacific, California, Townsend, starnose, and hairytail moles. Looking at the distribution maps in your field guide can help you to identify the species that are found in your area.

mainly earthworms and insects, but if it encounters a soft, starchy tuber or planted corn kernel, it'll eat that too.

But moles are also beneficial. Among the insects they eat are many that consume our garden produce and damage our flower bed plants. Moles aerate the soil as few creatures can. Moles are fun to watch, and they deserve their own spots on earth.

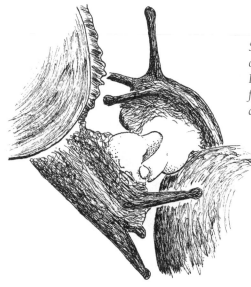

Snails bear both male and female sex organs, so they can fertilize each other. Despite built-in barriers against self-fertilization, sometimes they manage to do so and produce offspring.

In an area where moles are active, if you keep a sharp eye, eventually you'll notice a new tunnel being dug. At the end of a ridge being pushed up, you'll see a plug of soil bobbing up and down. If you approach this area very softly (moles are ultrasensitive to vibrations in the soil), you may see one of the most bizarre sights that ever occur in people's backyards: earthworms fairly *shooting* from the soil, like toothpaste squirting from a tube run over by a steamroller. When earthworms sense a mole coming through the soil, they know to evacuate the area, even if it's into the deadly (to them) sunlight and robin-infested free air.

Interestingly, moles typically dig two distinct levels of interconnected tunnels. One level is the network immediately below the sod that is visible from aboveground as pushed-up ridges. The other level lies as deep as two feet and isn't noticeable from above. Moles are active both day and night, year-round. In grass-lined nests eighteen to twenty-four inches below the ground, each year they raise one litter of four or five naked young that become independent after one month. Birth takes place around March in the South, May in the North.

EXPLORING THE ANIMAL KINGDOM

We've only begun to look at the animal kingdom as it's represented in our gardens and flower beds. For instance, there are slugs, snails, centipedes, mil-

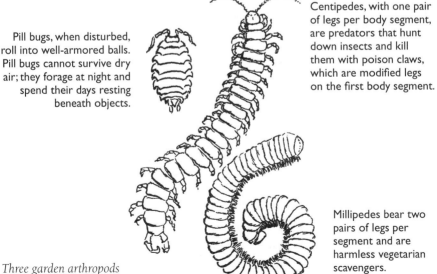

Pill bugs, when disturbed, roll into well-armored balls. Pill bugs cannot survive dry air; they forage at night and spend their days resting beneath objects.

Centipedes, with one pair of legs per body segment, are predators that hunt down insects and kill them with poison claws, which are modified legs on the first body segment.

Millipedes bear two pairs of legs per segment and are harmless vegetarian scavengers.

Three garden arthropods

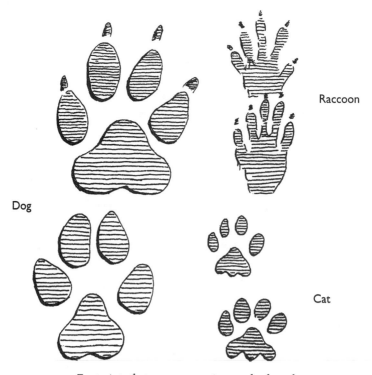

Footprints that may appear in your backyard

lipedes, mites, daddy-longlegs, toads, lizards, and even the occasional skunk, opossum, raccoon, dog, or cat that might wander through.

Maybe by now you see what a pleasure it can be knowing about any kind of animal. If you see a centipede beneath a wood chip next to your petunias, for example, thumb through field guides (see the Bibliography) until you fig-

American toads are mostly nocturnal—active at night. They attach their eggs to vegetation.

snail

slug

Snails and slugs are both mollusks, like clams and octopuses. Snails carry shell houses with them, but slugs don't. Their long "antennae" are actually tentacles used for feeling. Eyes occur at the tips of lower, shorter projections. Reproductive behavior of these animals seems to be controlled by internal clocks. Slugs kept under unchanging conditions of light, temperature, and humidity produce eggs at the proper time, even though they have no cues as to what season it is.

ure out what it is, then insert a page for the creature in your backyard nature notebook and start to gather information about it.

With just about any backyard animal, there is always plenty to be said about at least three different facets of its existence: how the creature is put together—its anatomy—especially with regard to special adaptations that help it exploit its particular ecological niche; what it eats and how it acquires its food; and what its courtship, mating, and production of young are like.

Researching these three areas for any animal spotted in the backyard is sure to lead to entirely new insights into how nature gets things done, how fragile everything is, and how every aspect of nature deserves our awe and respect.

PART 3
BACKYARD ECOLOGY

We have seen that volumes of information exist telling us everything we wish to know about individual plants and animals. We can fill our minds with thoughts about the similarities between potato and tomato blossoms, the aphid's quirky metamorphosis, earthworms shooting from the ground before advancing moles, and a million other things.

This kind of information, however—fascinating as it is—is one-dimensional. It's "postage stamp" information that can be shuffled around and brought out and talked about, but it lacks a certain feature that makes true science and understanding more substantial: a knowledge and appreciation of the *interrelationships* of these various components of nature. Sensitivity to nature's interrelatedness is the hallmark of any good naturalist. Here's an example of the difference between one-dimensional information and sensitivity to interrelatedness.

Let's say you're a boss hiring someone to do a job. You read a potential employee's resume, see his education and employment history, and review his stated goals. This way, you get an idea of what this person is like. This kind of information is one-dimensional. Now let's say you hire this person. As time goes by, you'll see for yourself what he is *really* like.

Yes, this new employee does do the job but, boy, is he grouchy! Moreover, he constantly gossips, complains about everything, stirs up trouble in the office, and yet has accomplished a ton of excellent work. Now you are more sensitive to how this individual relates with coworkers and the job. The understanding you now have regarding this worker's interrelatedness with his working environment is much more relevant—and interesting—than the one-dimensional information you read on the resume.

Well, it's the same way in nature. No matter how much one-dimensional information we collect about plants and animals, we don't develop a feeling for what's *really* happening out there until we focus on how nature's various components interrelate.

In our backyard gardens and flower beds, and in nature in general, the science that deals with the myriad interrelationships between plants and animals and their environment is called *ecology*. The interrelationships that ecology deals with are not only between plants and animals, but also between all living things and their nonliving environment—air, water, soil, rocks, ultraviolet radiation, pollution.

At the very heart of the science of ecology lies the concept of the *ecosystem*. So, on our way to gaining greater sensitivity to the interrelatedness of things, let's begin with that.

CHAPTER 10

Interrelationships in the Garden

THE ECOSYSTEM IDEA

One definition of an *ecosystem* is that it's "any area of nature including living organisms and nonliving substances interacting so that materials are exchanged between the living and nonliving parts."

That's a lot to chew on, but it's worth taking a while to let what's being said sink in. That's because what's being said here is unspeakably beautiful.

The first part of the definition, "any area of nature including living organisms and nonliving substances," is clear; we've already seen that nonliving substances are such things as air, water, and soil. The fact is, nearly every corner of earth's surface falls within the ecosystem definition.

The really mind-expanding part of the definition is its second half. It says that in an ecosystem, the living organisms and nonliving substances must be "interacting so that materials are exchanged between the living and nonliving parts."

In a novel by Alexei Tolstoy, two Russian soldiers are on a battlefield trading bleak thoughts about living and dying.

"Life, my friend," says one to the other, "is a carbon cycle and a nitrogen cycle, and I don't know what other kind of junk. Out of simple molecules, complex ones are formed, and from these, others, which are terribly complex. . . . Then, blam! The carbon and nitrogen and other junk disintegrate back to their most simple state. And that is all."[4]

These gloomy soldiers, facing a big battle, were philosophizing about nothing other than implications of the ecosystem concept—of carbon and nitrogen being exchanged between the living world (the soldiers themselves) and the nonliving (the battlefield's soil).

In fact, all features of man's existence (and the existence of all other living things) depend on the smooth functioning of certain chemical reactions. We've already seen that if for some reason the photosynthesis equation stopped working, before long earth's oxygen-breathing animals would die of suffocation. The photosynthesis process is just one of many upon which all life depends.

Many of these all-important chemical reactions can be observed and worked with in our backyards. For example, without the carbon and nitrogen cycles functioning properly, our garden ecosystems would collapse; our plants just wouldn't grow. Good gardeners, whether they know it or not,

---

[4]Alexei Tolstoy, *Tinieblas y Amanecer 3; Mañana Sombría* (Moscow: Editorial Ráduga, 1976). (In Spanish, translated here by this book's author.)

spend a lot of time managing their gardens' carbon and nitrogen cycles, and a lot more chemical reactions as well.

Clearly it's worth our time to take a deep breath and understand what's going on.

A LITTLE CHEMISTRY FOR THE BACKYARD

First of all, remember that all physical things on earth are made of 105 or so chemical *elements*. The smallest possible particle of an element is its *atom*. Atoms often combine with one another to form *compounds*. The smallest part of a compound that retains the quality of the compound is called a *molecule*. Molecules are made of stuck-together atoms.

Each element has a standardized symbol. The element hydrogen is annotated as H, oxygen as O, carbon as C, and iron as Fe. Elements vary tremendously from one another. Hydrogen is a gas, but the element gold, Au, is a metal.

When elements combine with one another, the resulting compound, which can be described with a chemical formula, often is very different from either of the building-block elements. Water, for example, is composed of two gaseous elements, hydrogen and oxygen. The chemical formula for water is H_2O. This means that a molecule of water is composed of two atoms of hydrogen and one atom of oxygen. A molecule of simple table sugar, $C_6H_{12}O_6$, is composed of six atoms of carbon, twelve atoms of hydrogen, and six atoms of oxygen.

Now, returning to the carbon and nitrogen cycles, we can say that they are similar to one another in that in nature—and this means in our backyard gardens, too—both carbon and nitrogen circulate, or cycle, through many living and nonliving states. Sometimes carbon and nitrogen molecules are suspended in the air, sometimes they adhere to soil particles, sometimes they make up parts of the bodies of living organisms. We haven't space to look at both cycles, so let's just take a brief look at the nitrogen cycle.

The Nitrogen Cycle. A good place to start is with free atmospheric nitrogen, which constitutes about 78 percent of the earth's atmosphere; thus most of the air that we and our garden plants breathe is nitrogen. This superabundance of free nitrogen does not mean that green plants in our backyards have it easy getting the nitrogen they need. The problem is that green plants can't use nitrogen when it's in its free, elemental form.

Our garden plants, for reasons too complex to go into here, must receive their nitrogen in a special form, one in which the element nitrogen is com-

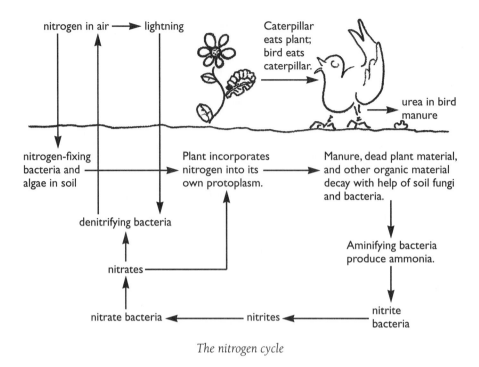

The nitrogen cycle

bined with the element oxygen in a particular way. For nitrogen to be available to green plants, it must be present in a molecule in which each atom of nitrogen is accompanied by three atoms of oxygen, known as NO_3, or *nitrate*.

The process of converting free atmospheric nitrogen into a form usable by green plants is technically known as *nitrogen fixation*. In nature, several things fix abundant elemental nitrogen—combine free nitrogen atoms with three oxygen atoms—so that it can be used by green plants.

Strangely, some nitrogen fixation is accomplished when lightning flashes through the air, but mostly the work is done by several kinds of microscopic bacteria, blue-green algae, and a few fungi. In our backyards, these tiny, unnoticed, unappreciated, unloved little entities live mostly in our soil.

Think of it! Without these organisms that you may never have heard or thought of, nitrogen wouldn't get fixed, our plants wouldn't grow (garden plants just can't live without nitrogen), the whole earth's forests, meadows, swamps, and agricultural fields would stop functioning, and the world's ecosystems would collapse, taking most or maybe *all* humans with them!

Think about these all-important bacteria, blue-green algae, and fungi the next time you hear of someone putting toxic substances into our soils, streams, and lakes.

The many parts of the nitrogen cycle don't all move at the same speed. Some important transitions from one part of the cycle to another are made quickly, but at other times nitrogen becomes immobilized for lengthy periods. Nitrogen can get tied up as part of a living organism's body and not be released back into nature until the organism dies and decays. And when an organism dies, its nitrogen may hang around for years as part of the soil's organic matter. Nitrogen, during its passage from NH_2 to NO_2 (see diagram), may bond with soil clay particles and be released only when the mineral particles themselves break down, and that may take centuries or even millennia.

This just scratches the surface of what's involved in the nitrogen cycle. Plus there are myriad other cycles, each performing a necessary service for life on earth. In other books dealing more exclusively with *biochemistry,* you can learn much, much more. All these interconnecting cycles join together and harmonize in a sort of earth song. Our backyard tomatoes, zinnias, hummingbirds, grasshoppers, you, and I are all tones in that song.

COMPOSTING

Maybe the most simple "chemical engineering" a gardener does is to make sure that his or her plants have adequate H_2O—water. Plant nutrition also is a matter of properly managing chemicals. To get a better feeling for backyard chemistry, let's take a look at the chemical events in just one aspect of good gardening, the earth-friendly process known as *composting.*

Composting is the process of turning biodegradable waste into a very useful material of a special kind. Something that is *biodegradable* is something that can be degraded, or decomposed, or turned back to the soil by regular biological processes such as rotting or decaying.

For example, if you put a dead fish on the garden, and a cat doesn't eat it, eventually the fish will decompose and sort of melt into the soil; therefore, that fish is biodegradable. Tree leaves and dead weeds are biodegradable, as is wood, barnyard manure, and even paper that is not treated with toxic chemicals. Glass, aluminum cans, Styrofoam, and most plastics are not considered biodegradable; bury them in the soil, and a hundred years later they'll still be there.

In the backyard, biodegradable things are nearly always forms of *organic matter.* Organic matter is simply matter that is or once was alive. You and I are organic, but stones, water, and air are not. All biodegradable material is not necessarily organic matter, but all organic matter is biodegradable if toxic chemicals haven't been added.

Partially enclosed compost bins like this one need their sides open enough to allow air to freely enter. If composting material acquires a powdery, gray coating, add more water; if it turns black and stinks like a sewer, spade it more frequently and don't keep it as moist.

Some biodegrading processes look and smell bad, such as rotting and some forms of decaying, but the decomposition process that goes on during the process of composting is a "clean" form of decay, one that doesn't smell bad or look at all like putrefaction. When you dig into a heap of organic matter that has been composting for a while, it feels warm and moist and smells musty in a wholesome, natural kind of way.

Usually biodegradable organic matter to be composted is piled into a *compost heap* near the garden. That's because much of the organic matter that goes into a heap—overripe tomatoes, cantaloupe rinds, bean plants no longer producing—comes from the garden. Also, the material that remains after a compost heap is finished composting is especially useful in and around the garden. This finished material is a dark, loose, moist, spongy, earthy-smelling matter that can be mixed into the soil to improve its quality and spread around plant bases to keep the soil from drying out. This is *compost.*

In a properly functioning compost heap, *microorganisms*—bacteria and fungi so small they can be seen only with a microscope—are what decompose the biodegradable material. These tiny living things have no mouths, and they'd be too small to eat the material with mouths even if they did.

Instead, most of them exude chemicals that dissolve the organic matter, like water dissolves table sugar, and then absorb or soak up the resulting chemical solution through the surfaces of their bodies.

If a compost heap works well and the microorganisms in the heap are given enough time to decompose everything just about as much as it can be decomposed, the resulting dark, powdery material is something wonderful called *humus*. Other than plenty of air, water, and nutrients, humus is the most desirable thing you can have in your garden soil. The main reason humus is so desirable is that it improves a soil's ability to hold water and nutrients and to be worked.

Gardeners usually interrupt the compost heap's march toward humus, however, using the moist, loose, spongy material constituting the middle stage between the raw organic matter put into the compost heap and powdery humus. Holding this loose, spongy material in your hands, you can usually recognize remnants of what were once stems or straw, now disintegrated into tiny, moist, spongy, dark-stained particles. It's truly amazing to think that living organisms so small that they can't be seen can so quickly decompose organic matter in a compost heap.

Because composting converts waste material into something useful, nowadays many ecology-minded people do it. Composting is an *in* thing to do. Compost heaps can be established next to any garden. When you finish eating a slice of watermelon and the big, green rind remains, it feels a lot better to compost it than to throw it into the garbage to be shipped to a too-full landfill, or maybe to be disposed of in the already-polluted ocean.

Nonetheless, despite all the TV programs, magazine articles, and composting paraphernalia sold in garden stores, it's astonishing just how often ventures into composting turn out as complete failures. People heap up their organic matter, but instead of producing good-smelling, humusy material for spreading around their pansies, they create fly-infested, smelly eyesores.

That's because most inexperienced composters don't understand that what they are actually trying to do is to help microorganisms eat organic matter. Maintaining a compost heap is more like keeping a barn full of hungry chickens happy than just letting nature take its course. Moreover, since microorganisms don't have mouths and essentially use chemistry to do their eating, good compost heap managers would do well to know a little chemistry.

First of all, not all kinds of organic matter should be added to a compost heap. Some of the most common items that can be added include tree leaves, lawn clippings, raw kitchen wastes of plant origin, coffee grounds, sawdust, even well-soaked newspapers. Actually, the list of compostable material is so long that it makes more sense to list what *shouldn't* be composted. Therefore, *don't* compost the following:

- any meat or fish, and vegetables prepared with grease (these attract animals and decompose too slowly)
- diseased garden plants or produce (their diseases can spread into your garden)
- roots of perennial weeds and grasses (they might sprout and grow)
- weeds with viable seeds (they might germinate in your garden)
- nonorganic material, such as Styrofoam, ceramic, glass, plastic, and metal
- items containing toxic substances, such as slick, colorful pages from magazines and catalogs, flakes of lead-based paint, petroleum products, wood soaked with preservatives or oil, and medicines
- citrus rinds (take too long to break down)
- onions (if you don't want a smelly heap during hot weather)

Carbon and Nitrogen in the Compost. In biology, there are not only carbon and nitrogen cycles, but also a concept referred to as the *carbon-nitrogen ratio*, or *C:N ratio*. In any well-functioning biological system, whether it's the soil in a garden, a whole forest with all its living things, or a compost heap, there is a certain ratio between carbon atoms and nitrogen atoms that is most favorable for life.

In the soil of a typical agricultural field, the ratio averages between 10:1 and 12:1.[5] That's ten to twelve atoms of carbon to each atom of nitrogen. In a heap of bean vines pulled up to make way for something new in your garden and piled onto your compost heap, the ratio may range between 20:1 to 30:1. If you're composting a pile of barnyard manure mixed with lots of dry straw, the ratio will be higher than 90:1—ninety atoms of carbon for every atom of nitrogen.

These numbers begin to have meaning once you realize the following fact: In the bodies of the microorganisms that decompose organic matter, the C:N ratio is *much lower* than the ratios just described. In microorganism bodies, the C:N ratio ordinarily ranges between 4:1 and 9:1. Therefore, effectively, microorganisms are tiny concentrations of nitrogen in a compost heap's nitrogen desert.

Now let's think about this situation from the microorganisms' point of view. Let's say that you've just piled up a big heap of grass clippings and

---

[5]Harry O. Buckman and Nyle C. Brady, *The Nature and Properties of Soils,* 7th ed. (New York: The Macmillan Company, 1969), 147–51.

kitchen scraps and want the microorganisms inside the heap to turn all that organic matter into something you can put around your petunias. The *microbes* (another name for microorganisms) are faced with a problem: They must undergo a tremendous population explosion in order to produce the number of organisms needed to break down all that material. But first, since microorganism bodies contain so much more nitrogen than the organic matter around them, before they can undergo their population explosion, they must somehow acquire nitrogen from someplace. And we've seen that our compost heaps are nitrogen deserts.

When we ask the nitrogen-rich microorganisms to multiply and break down our nitrogen-poor compost heaps, even if we provide them with the right kind of organic matter and plenty of air and water, we are simply asking the impossible. Microorganisms are nearly everywhere in nature, especially in soil, and the small number already in place will do a little composting, but usually their efforts are overtaken by other organisms that require less nitrogen but that cause the organic matter in the compost heap to rot and putrefy.

Therefore, successful composting is very much a matter of managing nitrogen, and there are ways that we composters can deal with this problem.

For example, most garden-supply stores and gardening catalogs offer compost activators—usually powdered mixtures of dried microorganisms themselves, along with the nitrogen they need once they start multiplying.

People who understand chemistry often save a little money by buying a bag of agricultural fertilizer, such as ammonium sulfate or sodium nitrate, and "supercharging" their heaps with nitrogen. These chemical fertilizers make sense when you look at their chemical formulas: ammonium sulfate is $(NH_4)_2SO_4$, and sodium nitrate is $NaNO_3$. (Remember that N is the symbol for nitrogen.)

Barnyard manure is a fine natural source of nitrogen because usually it is mixed with hay that has absorbed a good bit of livestock urine. Urine contains a lot of the chemical called urea, which is $CO(NH_2)_2$. Since the urea molecule has one carbon atom (C) for each two N atoms, the urea molecule has a C:N ratio of 1:2, which would make most microbes lick their lips—if they had lips.

Doing Some Composting. The first step any potential composter should take is to do a little thinking, because several different compost strategies can be followed. The approach you choose should depend on your answers to the following three questions:

1. What do you plan to compost? Are you dealing with huge piles of leaves or just occasional scraps from the kitchen and waste from the garden?

2. What do you plan to do with the resulting composted material? Do you want high-grade humus worthy of using in seed trays, or a less-digested material appropriate for spreading around the base of your tomato plants? Or is your goal simply to recycle nutrients into your garden or to get rid of organic waste?

3. Do you really have the time, energy, and interest not only to build a compost heap but also to maintain it once the novelty has worn off? Keeping a smoothly functioning, large heap operating is hard work, and you have to do the work according to the heap's schedule, not your own.

To help you answer these questions, let's look at what must be done to operate a rather large, easygoing, open-type compost heap. An open-type heap is one that is not enclosed within some kind of container; it's just a big mound of organic material lying on the ground.

BUILDING A LARGE, SLOW-COOKING, OPEN-TYPE COMPOST HEAP

What you will need

*about a pickup truck load of organic matter, such as
tree leaves or grass clippings*

pitchfork and shovel

activator (described below)

---

1. Choose a spot for the heap near your garden but out of the way, preferably in a shady place. Loosen the soil atop which the heap will stand by tilling it or spading it up; this will encourage water soaking through the heap (carrying nutrients in solution) to soak into the soil instead of draining away.

2. Establish the heap's base with a well-trampled, one-foot-thick layer of organic matter; make it five to seven feet square. Drench the entire heap with water.

3. Add an activator. If you're lucky enough to have barnyard manure, spread an inch or so, then a couple of inches of soil atop that. Otherwise just spread an inch of rich soil and use a commercial, nitrogen-rich activator.

Just about anything with lots of nitrogen, other than meat, can serve as an activator—high-protein, dry, crumbly dog food will work, or bone meal, blood meal, cottonseed meal, or a one-third-inch layer of alfalfa meal (certain commercial kitty litters are composed of alfalfa meal). Obviously, this can become expensive. If you're not one of the lucky minority who has an uncle with a horse stable or a cousin who owns a grain mill, you might do well just to forget about building a big heap; having a nitrogen source is essential!

4. Repeat the above two steps, constructing another layer atop the first; make its horizontal dimensions a little smaller than the one below it. Keep adding such layers until you have a steep-sided, flat-topped, four-cornered, five-to seven-foot-high pyramid. Keep the heap's interior as loose as possible so that microorganisms there will have access to oxygen.

5. Wet the finished pile thoroughly, but don't make it soggy. Top the finished pile with about half a foot of rich soil; make it concave so that rainwater collects.

6. Throughout the heap's life, keep it moist but not soggy. Being too wet is as bad as being too dry. From time to time during the heap's existence, to get a feeling for what's going on inside the heap, stick your arm shoulder-deep into it. Two feet inside, it should feel fairly hot and moist. During a dry summer, hose down the heap every week or so. If you must use city water, this can be another major expense.

7. After about a month, dig into the heap's interior and look at what's happening. If the material is gray and fungusy, you're keeping it too dry; if it's black and smells like a sewer, you're keeping it so wet that the microbes don't have enough oxygen. If the material seems to have properly decomposed, and if you have the back for it, move the whole pile, a shovelful at a time, to a space beside it, making sure that material previously at the heap's exterior now gets placed inside. The idea is to aerate the whole pile and give it a new start.

One very common type of compost heap failure is for the outer layers to settle into a kind of impervious "skin" that sheds water and prevents air from circulating through the heap; this absolutely must be kept from occurring. The more frequently you perform this last step, the better the pile should turn out. Stop when you have what looks like the compost you want.

This kind of heap should be ready in about three months during warm weather, longer during winters. On winter days, you may be gratified seeing steam rising from the heap as it "cooks," indicating that billions of microorganisms are busy at work for you.

Now that you're probably discouraged from building a very large heap, let's look at a smaller system that is much more appropriate for most of us.

1. If you want the nutrient-rich water that seeps from the future heap to soak in where the heap is standing, loosen the soil below the future heap by tilling or spading it up.

2. Connect the ends of the wire fence, forming an upright cylinder.

3. At the bottom of the wire cylinder, arrange a layer of organic material. If the organic material is mostly dense, moist matter, such as overly mature garden produce and kitchen trimmings, a loose layer of about two inches will do. If it is mostly dry material, such as straw or dry leaves, make a layer three to four inches deep.

4. Add the activator. If employing a concentrated form of nitrogen, such as alfalfa meal, bone meal, or dry, high-protein dog food, sprinkle on a large handful; if using barnyard manure, scatter about a shovelful, with a shovelful of rich dirt atop that; if using store-bought activator, follow directions on the box.

5. Repeat the above two steps until you reach the top of the fence or run out of organic material.

6. Moisten the pile thoroughly, but don't soak it. During the heap's entire life, keep it moist; during hot, dry summers, you may need to hose it down every three or four days.

7. If there's room, add organic material as it becomes available, repeating steps 3 and 4. Be sure to keep the center loose so that air can circulate.

8. In a week, remove the wire. Lift it over the heap if you can, or else detach the wire ends and unwrap it from around the heap. Next to the free-standing heap, reerect the wire cylinder, and fork all the material back into it. Try to place the outside, drier material inside the new pile. This is the time to appraise how your heap has been doing. If it looks dry and uncooked, you'll need to become more conscientious with your watering. You may need to sprinkle in more activator.

9. In two more weeks, you should have a fairly coarse mulch appropriate

for spreading around tomatoes or mixing into the soil. If you want a finer, richer material, repeat the above step until the compost is the way you want it.

Garden shops and seed catalogs often sell composting paraphernalia that can be useful with the above two projects. For example, the compost aerator is a metal, T-shaped item with hinged wings at the tip of its thirty-inch stem. When the stem is inserted into the heap and withdrawn, the hinged wings flare out, snagging on and rearranging the organic matter as they are withdrawn. This creates air channels into the heap. The tool works, but so do pitchforks and sturdy, jiggled-around sticks.

Compost thermometers are fun. Usually they have shafts about twenty inches long and measure temperatures up to 220 degrees Fahrenheit. When microbes decompose organic matter and large molecules are reduced to smaller ones, energy in the form of heat is released as the atomic bonds break. Earlier, this sunlight energy was captured among the atomic bonds making up the plant's photosynthesized carbohydrate; now the stored energy is being released. The result is that the compost heaps heats up, or cooks. A good compost heap should cook around 140 to 150 degrees Fahrenheit.

As another alternative, you can buy polyethylene compost bins, which look like belly-high rubber thimbles perforated with holes. Such bins are capable of holding about twenty cubic feet of compost. Adequate aeration is promised, though the holes look a bit too few and far apart for my taste. I've learned that air is important!

I find that most people who do battle with compost heaps don't really generate enough organic matter to bother making real heaps. These next two techniques require only a fraction of the time and expense, even though they accomplish the main function of composting, which is to recycle unwanted organic matter into the garden ecosystem.

TRENCH COMPOSTING

What you will need

*a digging tool with which to make a trench
(in really loose soil, a human heel should do)*

---

1. Make a four-inch-deep trench across your garden.
2. As kitchen garbage is generated, dump it into the trench and rake dirt over it.

3. When the trench is filled and covered, till or spade it, mixing the organic material well with surrounding soil.

4. Dig another trench and repeat the above steps.

That's all. It's simplicity itself. It's not as simple as the next technique, however.

SHEET COMPOSTING

What you will need

rotary tiller

---

1. Spread organic material rather loosely atop the garden soil. Cover only about two-thirds of the ground's surface area, leaving one-third showing open soil.

2. Till the organic material into the soil.

And that's it! You have a dishpan full of apple peelings, so you simply walk into the garden, toss them someplace other than onto your lettuce patch, and the next time you till, till them in. Just think how surprised and glad your earthworms will be that night when they poke their heads from their burrows and find all those juicy, luscious peelings waiting for them!

ECOLOGICAL PYRAMIDS

When I was in college back in the sixties, ecology was a biology course dealing with such topics as food chains, population sampling techniques, community trophic levels, and indicator species. Ecology almost felt like mathematics. Nonetheless, it was fascinating stuff. One way my former ecology professors taught me to look at a backyard garden was by looking at nature's *ecological pyramids.*

In a pond, for instance, water lilies and free-floating algae use sunlight energy to photosynthesize the carbohydrates they need; water lilies and algae, then, form the base of an ecological pyramid. Snails and certain vegetarian insects, turtles, and fish, which eat water lilies and algae, form the next level of the pyramid.

Carnivorous fish such as bass and gar, which eat the insects, turtles, and fish that ate the water lilies and algae, make up the pyramid's third level. When an animal such as a human or a raccoon catches and eats a bass or a gar, then it assumes the position at the pyramid's top, since humans and raccoons usually are not eaten by anything else.

Now, in this ecological pyramid, the vegetarian insects, turtles, and fish that eat water lilies and algae are said to be "eating low on the pyramid," whereas humans and raccoons are "eating high." When we eat hamburgers derived from cows that ate grain and other vegetable matter, once again we're "eating high," but when we eat directly from our gardens, we're "eating low."

This is an important insight for anyone concerned about efficient land use, the environmental effects of human overpopulation, and the general trashing of earth's limited natural resources, because with each step up the ecological pyramid, a great deal of wastage occurs.

Let's look at the energetics involved. If we examine a very simple ecological pyramid consisting of a field of alfalfa, cattle grazing on that field, and a boy who eats the beef from the cattle, it's been calculated that during the course of a year, 20,000,000 alfalfa plants weighing 17,850 pounds are needed to fuel 4.5 cows weighing 2,250 pounds to satisfy the energy needs of one 105-pound boy.[6]

But what if the boy becomes a vegetarian and uses that same field to grow spinach instead? It's calculated that he can get up to twenty-six times more protein per acre by eating spinach than he could by eating beef.[7] Another way of saying this is that as a vegetarian, the boy uses one-twenty-sixth the amount of soil for food growing than he would if he ate hamburgers.

When humans replace any natural ecological pyramid with an agricultural system—which is a simplified pyramid with humans at the top—inevitably the new pyramid is inefficient and one way or another translates into severe environmental degradation. For example, the grass and corn that hamburger-destined cattle eat nearly always is grown on land that, if nature had its way, would be species-rich forest or prairie. Maintaining unnatural monocultures such as the cattle pastures and cornfields results in soil erosion, and pesticides and fertilizers run off these lands into our streams and rivers.

Therefore, when a human gains enough intelligence, sensitivity, and compassion to treasure the wisdom in eating low on the food pyramid, and does so, it's nothing less than beautiful.

One of the more dramatic ways to eat low on the food chain is to eat leaf concentrate. Someday, leaf concentrate factories may efficiently and cheaply produce concentrate for us all, and leafburgers will be as common as Big Macs, but today big business still follows the hamburger track.

The following project for making leaf concentrate is more interesting for

---

[6]Eugene p. Odem, *Fundamentals of Ecology*, 2nd ed. (Philadephia: W. B. Saunders Company, 1959).

[7]F. Wokes, "Proteins," *Plant Foods for Human Nutrition*, 1 (1968): 32.

the promise it holds for the future, and for its novelty, than for its usefulness to individuals as a frequent food; a lot of work yields just a couple of leafburger patties. If someone wants to eat low on the food chain, it's much easier and just as tasty to eat greens as greens.

Nonetheless, it's fascinating to see how a green, tasty, cheesy, high-protein material can be manufactured from simple, abundant, extremely inexpensive, bottom-of-the-pyramid green leaves. Leafburgers as prepared here taste like fried onions with a slight grassy taste.

MAKING LEAFBURGERS
What you will need
plenty of greens

blender or food processor

stove, pots, skillet, and spatula

strainer

I cup chopped onion

I cup rolled oats

dollop of crunchy peanut butter

cooking oil

---

1. Pick greens. Any greens will work—kale, chard, collards, turnip greens, mustard greens. Even weeds such as chickweed, dandelion, curled dock, and lamb's-quarter are good when the leaves are young and succulent. Newly sprouted, green shoots of alfalfa and wheat similarly do. Don't pick anything the identity of which you are unsure, because many wild plants contain bitter and even toxic chemicals. Pick at least a paper grocery bag full of fairly tamped-down greens; this should make two leafburgers.

2. Fill the blender or food processor with loosely packed washed greens, add water until the bowl is about one-quarter full, and then liquefy the greens. The idea is to rupture as many plant-cell walls as possible, liberating the cells' contents. Continue until a smooth, yellowish green emulsion with green froth forms on top. Juicers usually clog up with leaf fiber, but old-fashioned meat grinders do well.

3. Squeeze the juice from the emulsion, saving the juice but sending the pulp to the compost heap. One way to separate out the juice is to filter the emulsion through clean nylon stockings or cheesecloth. Gardeners who make tomato juice can use the apparatus that separates tomato pulp and seeds

from juice. A loose-knit towel might do. Whatever material you use, be prepared to have it stained eternally green.

4. Heat the juice rapidly to boiling, stirring frequently to prevent burning. Remove from heat as soon as the juice boils. Watch closely, because the juice is capped with froth at this stage, and bubbling is hard to observe. Microwaving works. During this step, plant proteins coagulate just like heated-up egg protein.

5. Once again filter out the juice, but this time discard the juice and keep the solid part. Now it's appropriate to call the juice *whey* and the hard part *curd*. The curd, which now constitutes the leaf concentrate, should be squeezed so dry that it crumbles.

6. Mix together 1 cup crumbly leaf concentrate, 1 cup chopped onion, 1 cup rolled oats, and a dollop of crunchy peanut butter. The patties should stick together. If they don't, add just enough water so that they do. The amount of water needed depends on how thoroughly the whey was separated from the curd.

7. Fry the patties in oil as you would hamburgers.

CHAPTER 11

Plant and Animal Names

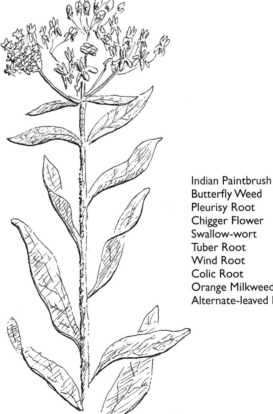

Asclepias tuberosa

Indian Paintbrush
Butterfly Weed
Pleurisy Root
Chigger Flower
Swallow-wort
Tuber Root
Wind Root
Colic Root
Orange Milkweed
Alternate-leaved Milkweed

I magine this: You're walking through your garden, paying special attention to weeds. As you saunter along, a little voice in your head narrates: "That jimsonweed at the edge of the compost pile is *Datura;* its seeds are poisonous, but certain Indian cultures have mixed them with other things for magical purposes. That lamb's-quarter coming up between the bean rows gets its funny name because it tastes like lamb. That bindweed twining into the okra stems is listed in Grieve's *A Modern Herbal* as having 'purgative properties' and was used back when doctors believed that vomiting purged the body of impurities. That crabgrass along the garden's edge produces seeds that house sparrows love to eat. That henbit coming up through the mulch has purple little flowers that look like goofy dog faces. . . ."

Well, such a little voice with all its interesting facts would make anyone's backyard garden pretty interesting. The point is that if you make a real effort to learn about the plants and animals in your backyard garden or flower bed, someday you'll be able to really hear that little voice in your head. It will just keep recalling facts about weeds, insects, spiders, fungi, crop plants, flower bed plants, the compost heap, the soil—just about anything you encounter. Of course, for this to happen, lots of information must be stored in your head, ready to be retrieved.

Happily for the backyard naturalist, there is a simple way to acquire this information: Find out the name of the thing in which you are interested, and look up that name in books and other reference sources.

But how do you find out the name of the plant or animal? The easiest way is simply to ask someone. There may, however, be no one available who can tell you the name. In this case, books called *field guides* come to the rescue.

FIELD GUIDES

Many kinds of field guides are available at regular bookstores. Most help identify birds, insects, wildflowers, and similar conspicuous, easy-to-observe, popularly loved organisms; you may have to look awhile before finding a field guide to weeds, grasses, or immature insects.

The field guide approach to plant and animal identification is very simple. Just look in the field guide for a picture of the organism you wish to identify. Guides usually are organized in such a way that there's no need to thumb from one end to the other. For example, plant field guides typically group their species by flower color.

The best thing about the field guide approach is that it obliges you to look closely at plants and animals and to learn about them. For example, the

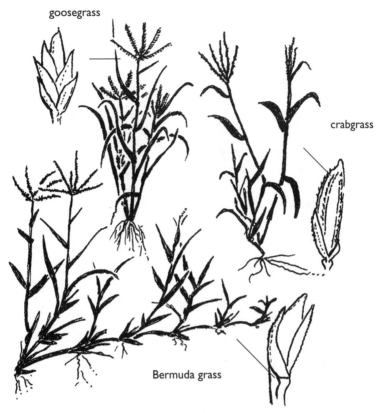

goosegrass

crabgrass

Bermuda grass

At first glance, these weeds—all of which invade gardens—look alike. A close examina-
tion of their spikelets, however, reveals profound differences in basic structure. Goosegrass
spikelets each consist of several florets; crabgrass and Bermuda grass blossoms have just
one floret per spikelet. In Bermuda grass, the glumes nearly equal the floret; in crabgrass,
they are much shorter.

little weed called *white clover* is common in lawns throughout North America.
To prove to yourself that what you have is a species of clover instead of, say, a
mint, you'd need to notice that the blossoms are shaped like pea blossoms
and that the leaf is divided into three wedge-shaped sections called *leaflets*. To
confirm that your clover is white clover and not the look-alike alsike clover,
you'd have to verify that each leaflet bears a pale, triangular design and that
the stem creeps along the ground rather than standing upright. If not for the
field guide requiring you to examine these features, you'd probably never
even think to notice that clover leaves have three parts or that their stems can
creep as well as stand or lean.

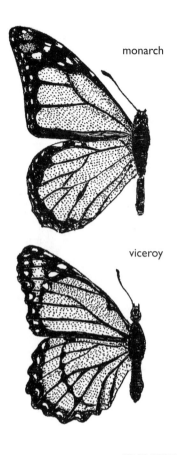

monarch

viceroy

The monarch butterfly tastes disagreeable to birds because monarch larvae eat bitter milkweeds; thus birds avoid eating them. The mimicry of the unrelated viceroy butterfly, which looks very much like the monarch, is so successful that birds avoid eating it too, although, experts assure us, viceroys aren't bitter at all.

IDENTIFICATION KEYS

Field guides do have their limitations. For bird identification, because the number of species in a given area is very relatively small, field guides work great. There simply cannot, however, be a handy, pocket-size guide to North American insects; in North America, there are approximately 88,600 insect species!

When working with large groups of plants or animals, often identification is impossible without looking at rather technical details—characteristics, such as the number of carpels—that don't show up in a field guide's illustrations. For those of us who enjoy being technical and really getting into the nuts and bolts of nature, there's a whole field of plant and animal identification beyond using illustration-based field guides.

This involves using *identification keys.* This kind of key is something you write out, so it's easy to present one here. You can figure out how to use it yourself.

IDENTIFICATION KEY TO COMMON GARDEN ONIONS AND ONION RELATIVES

1   Leaves (not flower stalk) flat 2

1   Leaves (not flower stalk) cylindrical. 3

    2   Bulb consisting of 6–10 bulblets, or cloves, enclosed in a white, papery membrane, leaves without creases . . . . GARLIC

    2   Bulb solid, leaves creased down middle, along midrib . . . . LEEK

3   Leaves many, wiry, in a dense tuft . . . . CHIVES

3   Leaves few, softer, not densely tufted 4

    4   Leaves numerous, slender, tapering from base to sharp point . . . . SHALLOT

    4   Leaves few, large, thickest near midlength 5

5   Bulb large and rounded . . . . ONION

5   Bulb hardly larger than stem above it. . . . . SPRING ONION

The fact is, biologists who must identify poorly known plants and animals seldom use the illustration-matching field guide approach. They use technical publications with identification keys of the above kind. Also, more and more, they use computer programs, which are essentially keys that have been adapted to computer use.

The above key is easier to use than most keys, because it uses familiar terms such as *bulb, leaves, rounded,* and *papery*. Real keys usually must use a much more technical language to refer to very special characteristics. For instance, here is a typical line from *Gray's Manual of Botany*, which can be used to identify any flowering plant, from grass to tree, as well as ferns and gymnosperms, growing naturally in northeastern North America:

> Annual; leaves not harsh above; staminate involucres glabrous or pilose; fruits with 4-7 acute teeth or small tubercles.

Well, maybe you can figure out "leaves not harsh above," and maybe you recall from chapter 1 what an annual is. But what about the rest? "Staminate involucres"? "Glabrous or pilose"? "Tubercles"? The above lines from *Gray's* are the final ones in a key identifying the common ragweed. Did you recognize anything "ragweedy" about it?

Actually, these esoteric words are part of what makes using keys so much fun. Because, in any key, or field guide for that matter, when you run across a word you don't understand, like *involucres*, you can look it up. Nearly all field guides and manuals using keys have glossaries where such terms are defined.

Gray's says that an involucre is "a circle or collection of bracts surrounding a flower-cluster or head or a single flower." If you don't know what a *bract* is, the same glossary tells you that it is "a more or less modified leaf subtending a flower or belonging to an inflorescence, or sometimes cauline." If you don't understand *inflorescence, cauline,* or any other terms, then look them up.

Leapfrogging through a key like this, it may take you a week or two before you identify a single plant. But think of all the extraordinary facets of botany you'll learn.

At the end of any key, whether it's for weeds or bugs or anything else, your mind will feel stretched, images of regions of life never even dreamed of will hang suspended in your imagination, and you will feel a certain smugness every time a bug flies past or a pansy nods at you from the corner of the house.

Several technical keys are listed in the Bibliography. The How to Know series is specially designed for beginners.

COMMON AND SCIENTIFIC NAMES

You already know that the plants and animals in our backyards possess two kinds of names: *common names* and *scientific names.*

When I was a kid on the Kentucky farm, each summer a pretty weed about knee-high and with bright orange-red flowers blossomed on the banks of a drainage ditch next to our house. My parents told me that the weed was called *Indian paintbrush.*

One day my parents bought me a little wildflower identification book called *A Field Guide to Wildflowers,* and the first thing I looked up was Indian paintbrush. To my surprise, the Indian paintbrush shown in that book didn't look at all like our ditch plant. Thumbing through all the field guide's pages, eventually I did find our ditch plant, but it was called *butterfly weed.*

Like any good teenager, convinced I'd caught my parents in an error, I confronted them with my discovery. They wouldn't budge. They said that they knew our ditch plant, and that everyone they'd ever known had always called it *Indian paintbrush.* And my grandparents, cousins, neighbors, friends, and teachers all agreed: That ditch plant was Indian paintbrush, and nothing else.

Years passed. In college, the first chance I got, I looked up that ditch plant in the biggest, most expert-looking botany book I could find, *Gray's Manual of Botany*. It gave three names for our ditch plant: butterfly weed, pleurisy root, and chigger flower. The two-volume work called *A Modern Herbal* mentioned the further names of swallow-wort, tuber root, wind root, colic root, and orange milkweed. To top it off, my college botany teacher insisted that the best name of all was alternate-leaved milkweed! Nobody except my family and neighbors seemed to call the plant *Indian paintbrush*.

But though the books didn't always agree on the ditch plant's common names, all agreed that its scientific name was *Asclepias tuberosa*.

When you're learning the names of plants and animals, don't forget to take a look at the names themselves. Every name of every plant and animal comes from somewhere, and the story of how it made its way into English is often an interesting one. You may want to collect name stories in your back-yard nature notebook as you learn them.

A good first step in doing the detective work needed to discover the secrets behind names is simply to look in a good dictionary that provides word derivations. As an example of what name stories can be like, here's what I've found out about the word *tomato:*

Tomato comes to us by way of the Spanish word *tomate;* this is what Spanish conquistadores thought they heard when the Nahuatl-speaking Indians in Mexico called the plant *tomatl.* Thus our *tomato* comes pretty close to being the name used by the American Indians who first domesticated wild tomatoes.

Tomato's scientific name is *Lycopersicon esculentum. Lyco* is from classical Greek and refers to "wolf," and *persicum* is classical Latin for "peach." Thus *Lycopersicon* translates to "wolf peach," probably in reference to an early European belief that tomatoes were poisonous. The species name *esculentum,* however, is based on the Latin *esculus,* meaning "edible."

Scientific names are much more than merely handles we can use to look up information; they also can help us understand how organisms are related to one another. The study of how plants and animals are related and how they should be categorized is called *taxonomy.*

For the basic rules of modern taxonomy used today, we can thank the Swedish naturalist and taxonomist Carolus Linnaeus, who developed the system during the 1700s. When we speak of "the oak family," "a frog species," or "a variety of rose," we're using Linnaeus's taxonomic system. If we should use his system to write out a comprehensive classification of a particular variety of garden bean, here's one way it could be done:

KINGDOM: Plantae (plants)
SUBKINGDOM: Embryophyta (multicellular embryo)
DIVISION: Tracheophyta (vascular plants)
SUBDIVISION: Pteropsida (large, complex leaves)
CLASS: Angiospermae (flowering)
SUBCLASS: Dicotyledones (two cotyledons)
FAMILY: Leguminosae (beans)
GENUS: *Phaseolus* (beans)
SPECIES: *vulgaris* (common)
VARIETY: Kentucky Wonder

Similarly, here's a taxonomic breakdown for the firefly, which on summer nights may grace your backyard:

KINGDOM: Animalia (animals)
SUBKINGDOM: Metazoa (multicellular animals)
PHYLUM: Arthropoda (arthropods)
SUBPHYLUM: Mandibulata (mandibles present)
CLASS: Insecta (the insects)
ORDER: Coleoptera (the beetles)
FAMILY: Lampyridae (fireflies)
GENUS: *Photuris* ("light-tail")
SPECIES: *pennsylvanica* (of Pennsylvania)

You'll notice that the taxonomic subdivisions of the two breakdowns sometimes go by different names. Nevertheless, they generally serve the same purpose. Real taxonomists might add more subdivisions than the ones listed above, but these are enough for us.

Linnaeus's system is just wonderful to think about. For one thing, it's simply illuminating to know that so many definable relationships interconnect all of earth's living things. The classification of an oak tree, for instance, would be exactly the same as the above bean classification all the way down through subclass. But then oaks are placed in different families from beans. Just think of all the fundamental similarities that unite snap beans and oak trees at the kingdom, subkingdom, division, subdivision, class, and subclass levels.

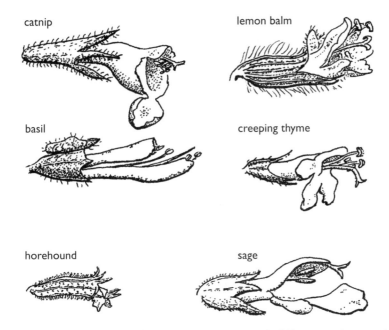

These six herb blossoms, all in the mint family, are obviously different, yet because they are all mints, they share important features: symmetrically irregular blossoms, opposite leaves, and stems that are square in cross section. All except sage bear four stamens; sage's second pair are rudimentary or lacking. Not all mints smell minty, however.

One of the handiest things about Linnaeus's classification system is that the lower levels, those of genus, species, and variety, are not only taxonomic subdivisions, but also names. Referring to the bottom part of the breakdown for Kentucky Wonder snap beans presented above, note that *Phaseolus vulgaris* is Kentucky Wonder snap bean's scientific name. Lima beans, *Phaseolus limensis*, belong in the same genus as snap beans, but they're a different species. Peas are also members of the bean family, but they are so unlike snap beans and lima beans that they belong to a different genus; the garden pea's scientific name is *Pisum sativum*.

GATHERING INFORMATION

Merely knowing the names of the plants and animals in your backyard isn't your final goal; you want to know those names so that you can look them up in a variety of places to learn more about the living things they belong to.

Let's say, for example, that you want to learn more about the white clover plant. At the library, a book on edible plants reports that American Indians used to eat young white clover plants cooked and as a kind of salad. A nutritious bread can be made from the clover's ground-up seed and dried flowers. And early European settlers in North America brewed tea and made a medicinal drink from the dried flower heads. A book on wildlife food tells you that many seed-eating birds, such as quail, grouse, and various sparrows, as well as woodchucks and marmots, relish clover's tiny, hard seed. A wildflower book reminds you that white clover is the species supplying "lucky" four-leaf clovers. Finally, a general high-school biology book mentions that white clover, a member of the bean family, has roots with nodules inhabited by a special kind of bacterium that changes unusable atmospheric nitrogen into a form of nitrogen more accessible to plants.

In short, the more places you look, the more information you'll turn up, and the more interesting white clover becomes.

As you gather information about the various species you identify, write it down in your backyard nature notebook. Make sketches of what you find, with arrows pointing to important identification features, such as the pale V on the white clover leaflet,

As time goes by and you continue to browse in books and magazines, watch nature shows, and talk to people who know about plants and animals, you'll be surprised at how much fascinating information turns up and how interesting your notebook becomes!

CHAPTER 12

Soil

The soil is that part of the garden ecosystem where the subtle and not-so-subtle workings of chemistry are most manifest. Soil scientists often refer to *the soil solution,* because much more than dirt, soil is a solution of living things and chemical compounds interacting in intimate and significant ways.

To begin with, let's consider the following very simple but exceedingly profound energy flowchart;

$$\text{sun} \longrightarrow \text{plants} \longrightarrow \text{animals}$$

With regard to life on earth, this may be the most fundamental of all formulas. It says that energy from the sun is captured in plants; we animals, unable to derive the energy that keeps us going from other sources, take our energy from the plants we eat, or from eating other animals or their products, which are full of energy that also, originally, came from the sun via plants.

Since the energy that powers animals must at one time or another pass through plants, and nearly all of the green plants that we, cattle, and other animals eat are rooted in *soil,* soil is unspeakably important to nearly all life on earth.

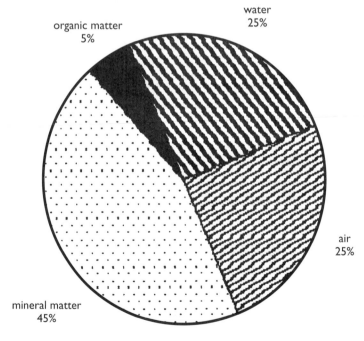

Composition of a good garden soil by volume

"Nearly all" must be said because sometimes we humans eat fancy dishes made from free-floating sea algae, and sometimes the fish, oysters, and other aquatic organisms we eat have also derived their energy by grazing on free-floating algae. Also, some humans someplace are bound to be eating fungus scraped from the walls of geothermal springs, or fish raised on plants cultivated in warm water issuing from nuclear-fueled power plants. But these are tiny exceptions.

So think about it: Without the unappreciated, abused, and often despised soil, the earth's terrestrial ecosystems just couldn't exist; all the jungles and prairies and fields of the world—and the great masses of human life—would simply die.

Because soil is so important and beautiful, you'd think that the teaching of soil conservation would begin in the first grade. Sadly, however, most of us think of soil as something equivalent to dirt, which must be washed from jeans with powerful, polluting detergents.

If a gardener is an artist, then seeds are the paint, and the very canvas on which the art is developed is majestic, benevolent, usually abused and unloved soil.

THE MINERAL NATURE OF SOIL

You already know (although you probably haven't thought too much about it) that the size of a soil's mineral particles varies tremendously. Soil scientists have thought about this fact a great deal, because the size of a soil's individual mineral particles profoundly affects a soil's fundamental nature. There is a standard system of classification of soil particles based strictly on particle size; this is presented in the accompanying table.

CLASSIFICATION OF SOIL PARTICLES
ACCORDING TO DIAMETER IN MILLIMETERS

very coarse sand	2.00–1.00
coarse sand	1.00–0.50
medium sand	0.50–0.25
fine sand	0.25–0.10
very fine sand	0.10–0.05
silt	0.50–0.002
clay	below 0.002

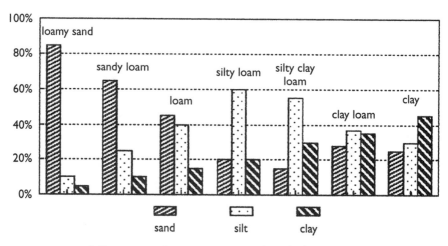

Soil types according to proportions of sand, silt, and clay

A soil's character—its workability, its richness, its ability to hold water, and many other features—depends very much on the relative amounts of sand, silt, and clay present in it. Here's a project exploring one of those aspects.

SEEING EFFECTS OF PARTICLE SIZE ON SOIL WATER-HOLDING CAPACITY

What you will need

two pots with drainage holes

two or three cups of dry sand

two or three cups of dry silt or clay soil

water

---

1. Fill one pot with dry sand and the other with an equal amount of dry silt or clay. Dust is fine clay; look for it where the soil is sheltered from rain. You'll know it's dust if it feels soapy, not gritty, between your fingers. If you can't find dry dust, just use any dry dirt you can find composed of very small mineral particles.

2. Slowly pour water into each pot, keeping track of how much water you're using, until it begins to run through the drainage hole; if water pools atop the silt or clay, stir it into the soil.

3. Much, much less water should have been needed in the sand-filled pot than in the silt- or clay-filled pot before it began draining out. From the results of your experiment, do you agree with the statement that the smaller the average grain size of a particular soil, the more water it holds?

If your garden plants are wilting too soon after watering because of a problem with soil particle size, is the situation caused by soil particles being too large (sandy soil) or too small (clayey soil)?

SOIL CHEMISTRY

Besides water-holding capacity, soil particle size also very much affects a soil's nutrient-holding capacity. *Nutrients* are chemical elements, such as nitrogen, phosphorus, potassium, calcium, iron, and magnesium, that the plants in our lawns and gardens absolutely must have in order to live.

The surfaces of mineral soil particles are very slightly *negatively* charged electrically, whereas most of the particles comprising plant nutrients are *positively* charged. Therefore, since unlike charges attract one another, soil particles are like tiny magnets holding nutrients in place until plants can use them.

Look at the accompanying graph. It says that the smaller a soil's average particle size, the greater the total particle surface area per unit volume of soil. Now, keeping in mind that the surfaces of mineral soil particles are very slightly negatively charged, we can deduce the following: The smaller a soil's average particle size, the more total particle surface area will be present; thus

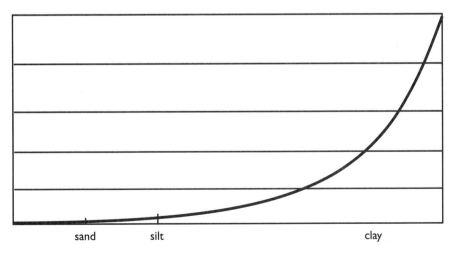

Soil particle surface area increases as particle size decreases.

the more negative charge the soil will have and the more positively charged nutrient entities the soil will be able to hold, so the more nutrient rich the soil will be.

In other words, small-particled soils hold more plant nutrients than large-particled ones. Silt not only holds water better than sand, but, other things being equal, also holds more calcium, phosphorus, magnesium, and other nutrients!

Unfortunately, soil nutrition isn't as simple as that. If it were, garden stores would be selling bags of clay to serve as potting soil, not the dark, crumbly stuff that they do sell.

One problem with soils composed of just very tiny particles—clay soils—is that the tiny particles pack together so closely that not much room is left for air or water. What air and water there is in clay soil can't freely circulate. This may seem to conflict with what you learned in the last project, but things will be clarified below. Another problem with clay soils is that when they dry out, they solidify into hard, unworkable clods; clay pottery, after all, is made from baked, very fine clay. Soils with too much fine clay are said to be *heavy*.

SOIL AIR

Microbes inhabiting the soil, just like microorganisms in compost heaps, need air like we do. This is important for soil ecology because soil microorganisms do important jobs, such as breaking down organic matter and fixing atmospheric nitrogen so that plants can use it.

Like humans, most soil microorganisms breathe in oxygen and breathe out toxic gases such as carbon dioxide, methane, and hydrogen sulfide. If a soil is so clogged with tiny clay particles or water that air can't circulate, the microorganisms' oxygen level plummets and toxic gases build up. In such soil, the microorganisms smother just like we would with plastic bags over our heads. Soil with bad air circulation is said to be *poorly aerated*.

Plants' growing roots also need oxygen, and plants differ widely in their ability to deal with poorly aerated soil. For example, tomato roots need lots of air, but rice normally grows submerged in water, with very little soil aeration.

SOIL WATER

Although it's true that the small-particled clays hold more water than the large-particled sands, in soils with really tiny particles the grains mass together so closely that little room for water is left. How can we reconcile these facts?

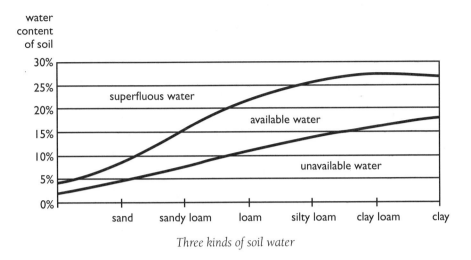

Three kinds of soil water

First of all, we need to understand that in reality there are three kinds of soil water, not one. When too much water is poured into a flowerpot, as done in the project above, the excess water that dribbles out of the bottom hole is called *superfluous water*. In real soil, where there is no drain hole, superfluous, or excess, water can drive out soil air, thereby causing problems to plants. And when superflous water finally drains away, it carries with it dissolved nutrients.

After all superfluous water has drained from a soil, the soil is still moist and each soil particle is covered with a film of water that is available for plant use—plant roots can soak it up. This second kind of water is known as *available water*.

As time passes, plant roots, gravity, and evaporation of water from the soil's surface remove more and more water from the soil, and the film of available water on individual soil particles becomes thinner. The thinner the film of water is, the more tenaciously it sticks to soil particles and the harder it becomes for plants to pry it off. Eventually the film becomes so thin and tightly bound that plant roots can't wrest away what they need, and plants wilt, even though a little water remains in the soil. This remaining soil water is referred to as *unavailable water*.

It's good for a gardener to know about these three kinds of water. For example, if a plant very badly needs to be watered, there is no guarantee that providing it with a single glass of water would be of much benefit. Before any water makes its way to a plant root, it might attach itself to soil particles and become held there so tightly that it remains unavailable—and therefore useless—to the plant.

PLANT NUTRIENTS

The universe is made up of 105 or more distinct varieties of matter, called *elements*. All the chemical plant nutrients, such as calcium, magnesium, and iron, are elements. When plants use sunlight energy to manufacture carbohydrates for their own food, those carbohydrates, which make up most of the nonwater bulk of plants, are composed of just three elements: carbon, hydrogen, and oxygen. If a plant is like a house, then in terms of weight, these three elements are like the house's bricks, wood, and mortar. All other elements found in the plant are present in relatively tiny amounts, as, in the house, wiring, window glass, and plumbing make up just a tiny fraction of weight.

These three elements found in carbohydrate—carbon, hydrogen, and oxygen—are foremost among our backyard plants' essential elements. Fortunately for our plants, these three elements, being basic components of plain air and water, are abundant and freely available in nature.

If we were to burn a corn plant so that nothing was left but its ashes, over 94 percent of the dry ashes would be composed of hydrogen, oxygen, and carbon. The high percentage of these three elements in plants becomes even more astonishing when we consider that something like a fresh apple is about 84 percent water, and that water is, after all, just hydrogen and oxygen. And when we burn something, the resulting carbon dioxide that escapes is departing carbon and oxygen. Life, it seems, is little more than an essay in carbon, hydrogen, and oxygen!

This is not to say that other elements are unimportant. In fact, besides these three elements, scientists have designated fourteen other elements as essential to plant growth. Without them, plants just won't grow, and death or disease results if all fourteen, called the *essential elements,* are not present.

If we analyzed the elements in the ashes of the burned corn plant, we'd find that the most prevalent of the fourteen essential elements are nitrogen, constituting about 1.5 percent of the ash's weight, and silicon, about 1.2 percent. Elements we hear a lot about as being important in plant nutrition are present in much smaller amounts. Potassium contributes less than 1 percent of weight, phosphorus only about 0.2 percent, and others even less.

Despite the tiny amounts of these fourteen elements present in plant bodies, they are all absolutely necessary for growth of green plant. For example, at the heart of the photosynthesis-enabling, green-color-giving chlorophyll molecule, nestled among fifty-five atoms of carbon, seventy-odd atoms of hydrogen, and five or six atoms of oxygen, are four atoms of nitrogen and one lonely but absolutely essential atom of manganese.

Without that single atom of manganese, green plants such as those in our gardens and flower beds, as well as those in earth's forests, fields, and prairies, simply could not photosynthesize. All major ecosystems depend on that one atom of manganese being in place in every single chlorophyll molecule!

Calcium is just as critical in the material called *pectate,* which cements plant cells together. Potassium is necessary for the synthesis of proteins, from which are made the chromosomes carrying the information that makes every living thing what it is. And many of a plant's most important chemical reactions can't occur without iron, copper, and zinc. All of the reasons why these essential elements are needed are not known. It's just certain that without them, green plants don't survive.

SEVENTEEN ESSENTIAL NUTRIENT ELEMENTS

Air and Water	all used in relatively very large amounts	carbon (C) hydrogen (H) oxygen (O)
Soil	Macronutrients used in relatively large amounts	nitrogen (N) calcium (Ca) phosphorus (P) magnesium (Mg) potassium (K) sulfur (S)
	Micronutrients used in relatively small amounts	iron (Fe) copper (Cu) manganese (Mn) zinc (Zn) boron (B) chlorine (Cl) molybdenum (Mo) cobalt (Co)

By convention, plant nutrients are often grouped according to whether they are *macronutrients,* needed by the plant in relatively large amounts (still tiny quantities in comparison with those of carbon, hydrogen, and oxygen), or *micronutrients,* also known as *trace elements,* needed in truly minuscule amounts.

Fertilizer Analysis. My mother often wins our family's first-tomato-of-the-year contest, and one trick she's willing to tell me (probably she's withholding her main secrets) is that each year she doctors her contestant with a kind of liquid fertilizer bought at the local garden center. On this fertilizer's label, there is a lot of mysterious gobbledygook, among which is the following:

4–10–3
GUARANTEED ANALYSIS

Total nitrogen (N)	4.0%
Available phosphoric acid (P_2O_5)	10.0%
Soluble potash (K_2O)	3.0%
Diammonium phosphate, Muriate of potash, chlorine, not more than	2.5%

This is fascinating stuff. There's a code here that needs to be deciphered, and numbers that need to be thought about.

The heart of this information is the 4–10–3. These numbers—there are always three of them, separated by dashes—are so important that they must grace the labels of all commercially sold fertilizers. That's because these numbers reveal what's being bought.

These three numbers are often referred to as a fertilizer's N–P–K. The N stands for nitrogen, the P for phosphorus, and the K for potassium. (Well, codes aren't supposed to be easy to crack; the K actually stands for *Kalium*, the German word for *potassium*, because Germans did a lot of pioneer work in plant nutrition.) A fertilizer's N, P, and K are always listed in that order. One way to remember the order is that you need the right N–P–K for "Nice, Pretty Kohlrabi."

The 4–10–3 reveals that my mother's "secret weapon" fertilizer consists of 4 percent total nitrogen; 10 percent available phosphoric acid (P_2O_5), which provides the phosphorus; and 3 percent soluble potash (K_2O), which provides the potassium. In short, maybe my mother's secret is that she uses a high phosphorus fertilizer. In comparing prices, remember that a 20–20–20 that is supposed to be diluted half-and-half in water is essentially the same as a 10–10–10 that you don't have to dilute.

Let's practice using these N–P–K numbers, just to get a feel for them. Sometimes blood meal is sold as a fertilizer; a typical blood-meal analysis is 6–1–0, which means 6 percent nitrogen, 1 percent phosphorus, and no potassium. Thus blood meal is actually more nitrogen-rich than my mother's 4–10–3 secret-weapon tomato grower, but it has much less phosphorus and potassium. Bone meal can have an analysis of 3–6–0.

An expensive, "specially designed raspberry food" advertised in a seed catalog carries an analysis of 20–20–20, but it must be diluted before applying. In the same catalog, a "high-potassium asparagus food," with an N–P–K of 17–16–28, emphasizes potassium, which asparagus does need in high amounts. Compared with a general-purpose fertilizer with a 5–10–10 rating, the expensive Squanto's Secret Fish Fertilizer, based on liquefied fish protein, looks like pretty weak stuff at 2–4–2.

Most fertilizers contain more than just N, P, and K. For example, my mother's secret-weapon tomato grower also lists indole-3-butyric acid and thiamine hydrochloride. And there's no telling what extraordinary substances are present in Squanto's Secret Fish Fertilizer. My own experience is, however, that if your soil is of more or less average fertility and you're not trying for some special condition, such as an acid soil for blueberries or azaleas, these other ingredients don't amount to much. Just master the "secret" of N–P–K, and quit paying big bucks for slickly marketed but watered-down fertilizer!

Now let's take a closer look at these three major essential elements.

Nitrogen. One year, right before my family began its annual contest to see who could grow the earliest ripe tomato, my grandmother heard someone on TV say that nitrogen made lawns lush and green. Therefore, she reasoned, why wouldn't a superdose of nitrogen cause her tomato plant to produce tomatoes like crazy?

Well, using some high-nitrogen fertilizer, Grandma did indeed produce one of the fastest-growing, most robust-looking tomato plants this town had ever seen; however, her plant was all vine, no tomatoes. Actually, it did produce a few tomatoes, but they matured hilariously late and were watery, tasteless things.

Each nutrient, you see, is good at some specific job or range of jobs, and it is necessary to know what each essential nutrient does best. Grandma learned the hard way that nitrogen encourages aboveground *vegetative* growth—leaves and stems, but not flowers and fruits. Nitrogen is great for golf courses and lawns, and for leafy garden crops, such as spinach, lettuce, chard, and green onions. But too much nitrogen for any plant meant to bear fruit, such as tomatoes, peppers, or beans, may result in a beautiful, robust plant with little produce.

Nitrogen deficiency limits general plant growth more than a lack of any other nutrient. That's why N is the first letter in the fertilizer analysis, N–P–K.

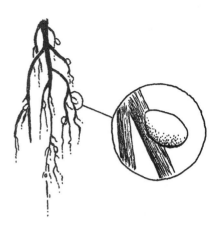

Nodules on roots of white clover, about the size of a pinhead, hold bacteria that convert free nitrogen, unusable to plants, to ammonia (NH$_3$). This then is converted by soil bacteria and fungi to nitrate, which garden plants need.

It's curious that nitrogen deficiency can be such a problem, because by volume about 80 percent of earth's atmosphere is nitrogen.

The problem is that free atmospheric nitrogen isn't usable by green plants, nor is the nitrogen present in soil organic matter such as decaying leaves and stems, where it's stored in the form of proteins and related compounds. Unusable nitrogen must be fixed before it becomes usable nitrogen.

Around 300 B.C., the Greek philosopher Theophrastus, successor to Aristotle, wrote that the Greeks planted broad beans, *Vicia faba,* to enrich soil. Nearly four hundred years later, Pliny, a Roman naturalist, reported that Romans plowed bean crops under to improve the soil. In 1888, two German botanists, Hellriegell and Wilfarth, explained Theophrastus's and Pliny's observations. They found that bean plants have bumplike *nodules* on their roots, and in these nodules there live microorganisms that can fix atmospheric nitrogen so that it's usable to higher plants. Though most plants don't have nitrogen-fixing nodules, you can probably walk into your backyard right now and see the kind of nodules Hellriegell and Wilfarth were talking about.

OBSERVING NODULES ON CLOVER ROOTS

What you will need

clover plant
small penknife or garden trowel

---

1. Look for a grassy area that is a little weedy and uneven, as along a sidewalk.

2. Among the grass blades, look for clover plants. Clover is easy to iden-

tify because its leaves are divided into three wedge-shaped leaflets (it's *trifoliate*), just like an Irish shamrock.

3. Remove a plug of soil containing the clover's roots.

4. Thump the plug until the soil falls away, exposing the roots. If the soil is too compacted to come undone, wash it away with water.

5. Among the clover's pale, much-branched, threadlike roots, look for little bumps. These are the nitrogen-fixing nodules.

A clover plant's first rootlets don't have nodules. As these young roots grow through the soil, however, they encounter certain kinds of microscopic bacteria that stimulate the roots' cells to divide, and then the bacteria take up residence in the resulting bumps, or nodules.

Farmers and ranchers often sow clover and other nitrogen-fixing plants of the bean family as winter cover crops or livestock pasture. Before they sow their clover seeds, they often mix them with a special formulation composed of nitrogen-fixing bacteria. This process is referred to as *inoculating* seeds. Later, when the seeds germinate, nodule-inducing bacteria will be waiting on the seed coats to infect the first rootlets that emerge.

Inside nodules, the bacteria use sugar or other compounds from the bean-family plant to fix soil air's free nitrogen, N_2 (unusable to garden plants), to ammonia, NH_3. And it's not just a little ammonia; ammonia suffuses the soil around the plant's roots, causing not only this plant, but also neighboring ones, to become rooted in a diffuse ammonia bubble.

Ammonia isn't itself usable by garden plants, but quite a few different kinds of garden bacteria and fungi work together to transform ammonia to the chemical nitrate, NO_3, which is the form of nitrogen garden plants use.

In our gardens, the roots of various kinds of beans and peas, which are also members of the bean family, possess nitrogen-fixing nodules. Thus by planting beans and peas, we actually fertilize our gardens with nitrogen. Good gardeners try to alternate crops of beans and peas with other crops that can't produce their own nitrogen.

Barnyard manure is a fine source of ammonia, which can quickly be decomposed by soil microorganisms into the nitrate form usable by garden plants. Ammonia comes from livestock urine. It's funny to think of barnyard manure in terms of chemical formulas, but it can be done:

Step 1

$$CO(NH_2)_2 \quad + \quad 2H_2O \quad \longrightarrow \quad (NH_4)_2CO_3$$

urea in urine + water $\longrightarrow$ ammonium carbonate

$$\text{Step 2}$$

$$(NH_4)_2CO_3 \longrightarrow 2NH_3 + CO_2 + H_2O$$

ammonium carbonate $\longrightarrow$ ammonia + carbon dioxide + water

Of course, gardeners also can add nitrogen with commercial fertilizers. Early-spring crops, such as greens and onions, especially benefit from commercial nitrogen, because nitrogen-fixing bacteria in the soil don't really get to work until the soil warms up.

Phosphorus (P). Phosphorus accounts for the second letter in a fertilizer's N–P–K analysis. Phosphorus helps plant cells divide; is critical in fat formation; is necessary for flower, fruit, and seed formation; strengthens stems; improves resistance to certain diseases; and helps crops mature and roots develop. If a corn crop is poor and the leaves bear purple edges, it's probably a sign of phosphorus deficiency.

Because of the importance of phosphorus to root development, root crops, such as potatoes, sweet potatoes, carrots, beets, and turnips, often benefit from a special high-phosphorus fertilizer such as a 0–20–0. A much-advertised root-stimulator fertilizer not surprisingly has an N–P–K analysis of 4–10–3.

Writer Isaac Asimov refers to phosphorus deficiency in soils as "life's bottleneck." He points out that in earth's biosystem, organisms use up phosphorus before other critical nutrients; thus phosphorus becomes a weak link in the chain of life.

Plants in acid soils sometimes show phosphorus deficiency even if plenty of phosphorus is present in the soil. In acid soils, phosphorus forms complex compounds with iron, aluminum, and manganese and thus is not available to plants. On the other hand, in basic soils, phosphorus combines with calcium, again becoming unavailable to plants. Thus phosphorus is a fussy element. Typically two-thirds of a soil's phosphorus is unavailable to plants.

Potassium (K). Potassium, the K in N–P–K, is also referred to as *potash*. In the past, potassium was obtained from ashes left from wood that was burned in pots, hence "potash." Wood ashes are still a fine source of potassium. Do not, however, use more than one or two buckets of ashes per one thousand square feet of garden space.

Potassium deficiencies in garden plants are often hard to spot. Things grow sluggishly, corn ears don't fill out, tomato plants don't set fruit, beets end up looking like purple carrots.

If you ask someone at the garden shop for a fertilizer especially for your tomatoes, you may end up buying one with an N–P–K of 18–18–21. One seed company sells a specially formulated high-potassium asparagus food, with an N–P–K of 17–16–38, for "stronger stems, healthier growth, and larger yields." Fertilizer manufacturers certainly do know the importance of potassium for fruit setting and strong stems.

THE MYSTERY OF PH

Soil pH is a measure describing how acid (sour) or alkaline (sweet) a soil is. Though gardens rich in humus and other organic matter seldom have severe pH problems, in humid areas, such as most of eastern North America, soils do tend to drift toward acidity over the years. If you're beginning a garden in poor soil or city soil, you should have its pH tested.

An important feature of the pH concept is that it is logarithmic, not linear. In other words, a pH of 5 is ten times more acidic than a pH of 6, a hundred times more acidic than a pH of 7, and a thousand times more acidic than a pH of 8. Thus when we say that the pH of garden soils ranges between 5 and 9, that may not sound like much variation, but in fact a soil with a pH of 5 is ten thousand times more acidic than one with a pH of 9!

The pH of a soil profoundly affects many critical chemical reactions taking place. We've already seen how it can tie up phosphorus. A too-alkaline soil can do the same thing to iron. In very acid soils, aluminum, iron, and manganese dissolve and become toxic to certain plants, and the availability of nitrogen, phosphorus, potassium, sulfur, calcium, and magnesium is diminished, even if they are abundant.

Both nitrogen-fixing bacteria and bacteria that digest organic matter such as decaying leaves and stems to humus have problems functioning at a pH below 5.5. Clubroot fungus, which afflicts cabbage plants, thrives on acid soil, so cabbage growers often keep their cabbage patches slightly alkaline. In contrast, azaleas and blueberries require acidic soils. Though most garden

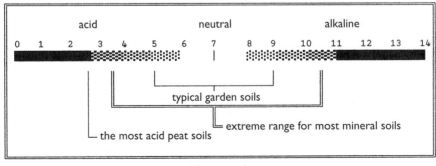

The pH scale

plants are happy with a very slightly acidic soil (pH 6 to 7), potatoes find acidic soil between 5 and 6.5 optimum, and watermelons and eggplants thrive between 5.5 and 6.5. Peas, spinach, and summer squash do well at 6 but are adaptable enough to flourish at 7.5. Compliant asparagus can grow well from pH 6 to 8.

One way that soils in humid areas drift toward acidity is that natural rainfall is slightly acidic. This is because carbon dioxide (CO_2) combines with water (H_2O) to form carbonic acid (H_2CO_3). In some areas, especially downwind from tall industrial smokestacks, rain can become exceedingly acid because of pollutants.

Acid soils abound in positively charged hydrogen atoms—the more acid the soil, the more H+ atoms we have. And hydrogen is *not* a nutrient that gardeners worry about having too little of. Because most important nutrients are also slightly positively charged and are held in the soil by humus and clay particles that are slightly negatively charged, a problem can develop when soil pH drops and positively charged hydrogen atoms flood the soil. The abundant hydrogen atoms push aside the positively charged nutrients plants need—particles such as calcium, potassium, and manganese. These desirable nutrients then may be carried away dissolved in water, in a process called *leaching*, and be lost from our garden plants forever. The end result is a nutrient-poor soil. This is one way that letting a soil become too acid causes serious, long-term harm to the soil's fertility. Naturally, the more rainfall an area receives, the greater the leaching problem becomes.

Leaching and becoming acid aren't the only ways a garden can drift toward sterility. Rainwater running over unvegetated slopes carries away tiny humus and clay particles, which are precisely where many nutrients are stored. A cornfield in Missouri on a slight, 3.7 percent slope was found to lose nearly twenty tons of topsoil per acre per year. A similar plot protected by a bluegrass sod cover lost only a third of a ton.

In areas where rainfall is scant, rather than seeping underground, water full of dissolved nutrients will evaporate from the soil's surface. During the evaporation process, the heavier nutrients are left behind on the surface. These nutrients crystallize, forming white salts atop the ground, and also cause the soil's pH to soar, becoming alkaline. Many of the alkali flats in the West, if not too sandy, turn out to be very fertile when irrigated.

Lime. The time-honored way of battling acidity in garden soil is to add a white, powdery material called *lime*. If you walk into a garden-supply shop and ask for lime, you'll probably be sold a box of hydrated lime, with an analysis of approximately 60 percent calcium oxide, CaO, and 1 percent magnesium oxide, MgO. CaO and MgO are produced by kiln-burning limestone, $CaCO_3$, and dolomite, $CaMg(CO_3)_2$.

The calcium in lime's calcium oxide and the magnesium in its magnesium oxide are among our most beloved nutrient cations. Therefore, if we add lime, we're flooding the soil with positively charged nutrients that, simply because of their numbers, will nudge useless hydrogen cations from humus and clay particles. And once the H+ atoms are out of the picture, our soil's pH and fertility both rise.

Gardeners in humid areas may need to add lime every four or five years on loam or clay soils, or every three or four years on sandy soils. It's possible to overlime, especially on sandy soils with little humus. And too high a pH can cripple a garden plant's uptake and use of iron, as well as phosphorus, boron, manganese, copper, and zinc. The nutrients may be there, but they can't be used.

Testing the Soil. Soil-testing procedures vary from place to place. To find out how it works in your area, call your local Agricultural Extension Service, which is present in most counties throughout the United States. Look for it under the name of your county in the county pages of your telephone book. Ask if a soil-testing service is offered and, if so, what the procedure is.

My county's Agricultural Extension Service office supplies me with a bag for the sample, detailed instructions, and a cost list. Though your costs will surely be different from mine, just to give you an idea, here is what soil testing in McLean County, Kentucky, costs in 1995: for the routine soil test (phosphorus, potassium, pH, and buffer pH), $5; for the above plus calcium and magnesium, $6; for all of the above plus an analysis for zinc, $7; for an assay of organic matter only, $5; and for a test for boron only, $5.50.

HAVING YOUR GARDEN SOIL TESTED

What you will need
trowel or shovel
bucket

---

1. Dig a hole in your garden about six inches deep.

2. Scoop half-inch-thick soil sections from the hole's side, being sure to take representative amounts from the top, middle, and bottom. Avoid including larger rocks and other debris.

3. Take four or five more samples at various spots in the garden, combin-

ing them all together in a bucket, and mix thoroughly without touching the soil with your hands.

4. Place about a quart of the mixed soil in a clean, sealed plastic bag, and send the sample off.

Kits to test your own soil are available at garden-supply stores and through seed catalogs. One such kit, for example, calls for mixing a small sample of soil with water, pouring this mixture into the supplied comparison chamber, dissolving a tablet, and checking against the kit's color chart. This kit is good for forty tests and costs $20.

The best time to test soils is in the fall. If fertilizer must be added to correct deficiencies, it may take a few months for the nutrients to become available. By adding fertilizer in the fall, you will ensure that the nutrients are available for spring growth.

ORGANIC MATTER

Maybe you know someone who always worries about getting enough of this or that obscure vitamin, pays big money for exotic nutritional supplements, and tries one weird diet after another. Yet this person may not be any healthier than the rest of us. Gardeners can fall into the same kind of molecule-counting trap.

With all the complex talk about nitrates and pH, positively charged this and negatively charged that, please don't get the idea that gardeners must be chemists. In gardening, there is a simple equivalent to the well-balanced meal of human nutrition.

As humans can remain healthy just by eating a variety of foods from the main food groups, so can gardens be kept healthy by paying attention to the fundamentals. And probably no fundamental is as important at this one: Gardens need organic matter. The term *organic matter* refers to material that once was living, such as grass clippings, kitchen scraps, garden refuse, and so on.

When organic matter is mixed into garden soil, it eventually is decomposed by soil microorganisms, fungi, and earthworms into a dark, moist material resembling powdered charcoal. This material, called humus, is dispersed throughout the soil. Humus is a gardener's secret weapon, part of the magic of gardening, and it is important all out of proportion to its limited presence. Here's why: In soil, humus particles behave like clay particles in their ability to hold nutrients and water; they also improve the soil texture and make it more workable.

For example, a mineral soil under humid conditions with only 1 percent humus typically would hold about *four times* the amount of macronutrients and micronutrients as a similar mineral soil without any humus at all. The soil's water-holding capacity is similarly increased. Moreover, humus makes soil a lot easier to work; it improves the soil's structure by encouraging it to fall apart, to be granular instead of blocky. A tiny bit of humus just works wonders for a soil!

SEEING EFFECTS OF ORGANIC MATTER ON SOIL STRUCTURE

What you will need

two small clay pots

one and a half potfuls of dry clay soil (dust)

*a half pot of dry, humus-rich soil, dry potting soil, dry peat soil,
or dry, well-digested compost (these all are sources of organic matter)*

---

1. Fill one pot and half fill the other with dry clay soil or dust.
2. Add the half pot of dry humus-rich soil, potting soil, peat, or well-digested compost to the half pot of dry clay soil, and thoroughly mix.
3. Pour a cup of water into each pot.
4. Place the pots in a warm or hot dry place with good ventilation, and wait until the soils dry out. (This may take a week or more.)
5. Compare the dried-out contents. The soil composed of nothing but tiny clay particles should dry into a very hard, bricklike substance; the soil into which organic matter has been mixed should be much more granular and workable—it should have a better *soil texture.*

If clay soils low in organic matter are too wet when they are plowed, rock-hard clumps of soil called *clods* form atop the drying ground. Clods are awful because if a hoe or tiller blade strikes one, it will glance off and likely will slice down a good plant. And once a clod is formed, it's a permanent feature in the landscape until a soaking rain melts it or the gardener expends considerable energy pulverizing it.

Humus and larger particles of organic matter loosen up soils and keep clods from forming by creating lines of weakness in the soil mixture. Plant roots follow these "lines of least resistance" and pry apart clay particles. Particles of humus and other organic matter are food to many kinds of soil organisms that produce chemicals and slimes that lubricate soil particles, causing them to slip past one another. Water on organic particles expands when frozen and retracts when melted, also prying clay aggregates apart.

Therefore, there is simply nothing you can do that's better for your soil than adding organic matter. If you do so, chances are that all the problems regarding nutrition, pH, water-holding capacity, and workability will simply take care of themselves. Your soil's general health will be vastly improved.

CHAPTER 13

Plant Diseases

Diseases are important facets of ecology because they have very much to say about the success with which plants and animals relate with their environment. Also, most diseases are themselves organisms with an environment, that environment being the plant or animal in which the organism lives.

The study of diseases, called *pathology,* is so large and complex—even if we restrict our observations only to our backyard gardens and flower beds—that we need to approach it systematically. One way of doing that is to think like a detective, using deduction.

NUTRIENT DEFICIENCIES

Let's imagine that you have a sick plant. Pathologists refer to the set of symptoms produced by a specific illness as the disease's *syndrome.* Let's say that this plant's syndrome includes leaves that are yellow or even completely white, except for the veins, which are green. Plant parts that have lost their green color are termed *chlorotic.* Now let's use some deduction to figure out what's wrong with your plant.

First, because a plant's greenness is caused by the green pigment chlorophyll in its leaves, chlorotic leaves must have leaves with too little chlorophyll. The complex chlorophyll molecule is composed of fifty-five atoms of carbon, seventy-odd atoms of hydrogen, five or six atoms of oxygen, four atoms of nitrogen, and one lonely but absolutely essential atom of manganese.

Now, carbon, hydrogen, and oxygen are abundantly available in air and water, but manganese and usable nitrogen are not; they must be present in the soil. Therefore, if a plant does not have enough nitrogen and manganese, it simply may not be able to manufacture enough green chlorophyll molecules to give its leaves an appropriately green color. And, indeed, plant pathologists have discovered that too little manganese or nitrogen in the soil are among the main causes of plants losing their green color.

One piece of information we can deduce from the above reasoning is this: Some plant diseases are not caused by germs; a large number of them are caused by a deficiency of nutrients in the soil.

It's not enough, however, to know that too little manganese or nitrogen in the soil are among the main causes of plants becoming chlorotic. Besides soil deficiencies of manganese and nitrogen, deficiencies of magnesium, iron, and other nutrients can also cause chlorosis. So how do you determine which of the several nutrient deficiencies is causing the problem?

Within plant bodies, certain nutrients are easily transportable from one site to another, but others are not. If leaf yellowing is being caused by the deficiency of a nutrient that is easily transportable, the leaf will lose its green color everywhere at the same time, but if the deficiency is caused by a nutrient that is hard to transport from one cell to another, areas away from leaf veins will suffer more than areas around the veins themselves. The veins may remain green while the blade areas between them turn pale.

And this is exactly the problem we are talking about. Knowing which of the nutrients causing chlorosis are transportable, or *mobile,* and which are not will help us determine which nutrient is lacking.

The most important nutrients that are easily transportable from cell to cell, or mobile, are nitrogen, potassium, phosphorus, and magnesium.

The most important nutrients that are immobile, or not easily transportable, are sulfur, calcium, iron, manganese, boron, copper, and zinc.

Therefore, a soil deficiency of one of the seven hard-to-transport, immobile nutrients probably is causing your sick plant to be chlorotic. If we were real plant pathologists, we would have had enough education and experience to know that this set of symptoms usually results from iron deficiency.

In fact, it's possible just to memorize syndromes without learning background information of the kind mentioned above, but it's not nearly so much fun.

When you find a sick plant in your garden, you can determine whether the problem is a nutrient deficiency by seeing if any of the following syndromes seem to apply.

Symptoms	Diagnosis	Treatment
Leaves yellow-green, later turning yellow or completely white, but with veins remaining green; newest leaves show symptoms most.	Iron deficiency in soil. Sometimes too much calcium in the soil keeps iron from being available, even if the soil has plenty of iron.	Apply high-iron fertilizer; over a period of years, work into the soil lots of compost or fresh lawn cuttings.
Leaves yellow-green between veins, starting from outside edge and running inward; older leaves show symptoms most.	Manganese deficiency in soil. Sometimes too much calcium in the soil keeps manganese from being available.	Add manganese sulfate to soil; use plenty of compost and keep soil moist.

Symptoms	Diagnosis	Treatment
Leaf edges turn brown, dry, and curl inward, maybe even fall off.	Potassium (potash) deficiency in soil.	Apply sulfate of potash or nitrate of potash to soil.
Red-violet color along leaf edges, or sometimes yellow or white leaf edges, or sometimes brown, dead sections of leaf appear, then leaf falls off.	Magnesium deficiency in soil.	Usually occurs in acid soil, so application of magnesium-rich lime helps; spraying on 2 percent magnesium sulfate solution provides fast relief.

There are other syndromes caused by deficiencies or overabundances of certain chemical elements in the soil, and there are books with many pages of color pictures showing the symptoms. The above four deficiencies are the most common, however, and give you a feel for how diagnosing nutrient problems works.

OTHER SOIL PROBLEMS

Unfortunately, nutrient deficiencies are not the only soil problems that can make plants sick. Clayey soils containing too little organic matter often become so compact that air and water cannot circulate properly, and plants become stunted. A too-sandy soil, on the other hand, dries out quickly, stunting and killing thirsty plants.

VIRUSES

Now we come to that great body of diseases caused by plants being attacked by other living things. Or, have we? Scientists still aren't sure whether viruses are something alive or dead. Viruses are among the most interesting and hard-to-deal with of all disease organisms—if they really are organisms at all.

Viruses are much smaller than bacteria, which are what we usually think of when we speak of *germs*. Though most bacteria are visible with regular microscopes using light, electron microscopes capable of magnifying objects seven thousand times must be used to see viruses. About one hundred thousand typical viruses all clumped together still would be hardly visible to the naked eye.

When a virus is in nature—maybe floating in the air or adhering to a soil particle—even to scientists who study them, they appear as dead as specks of dust. They are tiny, inert globs of matter encased in protein, and by themselves, they can't move, eat, or reproduce. They just sit, waiting.

When they come into contact with the right kind of living organism, however—maybe the virus is breathed into a human nose or absorbed into a plant along with water and nutrients—the glob begins doing things. And what the glob does is like something from a science-fiction novel.

The main part of a virus is hardly more than a complex molecule structured like the DNA or RNA molecules that in the cells of living things carry the genetic information that makes each organism what it is. Because of this, viruses are able to insert their own information into a living cell's genetic code.

And that information, from the infected organism's point of view, is the wrong information. Maybe, for example, the information the DNA or RNA molecules are supposed to carry is something like this: "Send a hormone to the root tip to cause it to grow." But the information the virus slips into the DNA or RNA strand says, "Make more viruses."

Naturally, if enough viruses are created by infected cells, problems happen. Cells fill with viruses and stop functioning, die, or even explode. If enough cells on an infected leaf die, a dead splotch appears. Then the whole leaf may die. If enough leaves die, the whole plant dies.

Among humans, viruses cause the common cold, measles, rabies, smallpox, polio, AIDS, and many other diseases. Among garden plants, viruses cause aster yellows, potato leaf roll, beet curly top, and the mosaic diseases, which affect tomato, potato, cucumber, bean, sugar beet, sweet pea, tobacco, rose, delphinium, bleeding heart, pelargonium, and many other important backyard plants.

In English, the word *mosaic* describes a kind of design made of various colored pieces of a material arranged so that they form patterns. Therefore, it is appropriate that what are termed *mosaic diseases* in plants show up as patterns of mottling or splotchiness, mostly as irregular areas of light green or yellow alternating with the leaf's basic darker green color.

Many plant viruses are extremely infectious. They can be transmitted from one plant to another in various ways, including rubbing sap of diseased plants onto the leaves of healthy plants. Probably the most common way viruses are spread among plants is by insects that have fed on diseased plants. This is especially true for insects with sucking mouthparts, such as aphids, leaf hoppers, mealy bugs, and thrips. And when humans handle cigarettes made from tobacco plants that were infected with tobacco mosaic, the virus can be transmitted to tomato plants, which tobacco mosaic also infects!

Since viruses are so tiny and simple, they can be very hard to destroy. Therefore, a common "treatment" when a plant seems to be dying from a mosaic or some other kind of viral disease is to pull up the plant and burn it. Happily, not all plant viral infections kill their hosts; thus all viral infections should not automatically be treated with such drastic measures.

For instance, poplar trees sometimes become infected with a mosaic that causes its leaves to become splotchy. The tree itself seldom seems to be hurt, however, so it would be a shame to cut down a whole poplar tree just because its leaves become splotchy.

Sometimes the decision as to whether to burn is harder to make. A whole group of mosaic viruses infects the colorful petals of tulips, crocuses, hyacinths, gladiolus, and other plants with bright flowers, causing the usually one-colored blossoms to be striped, or *variegated*. At first these striped flowers may impress a gardener as prettier than the unstriped ones. But unless the plant is marketed as a striped variety, the plant usually will weaken, so horticulture books often prescribe "dig up and burn."

There is one excellent defense against mosaic diseases. Mosaic is such a serious disease that many resistant varieties of tomato and other plants have been developed. If your garden is contaminated with tomato-killing tobacco mosaic, just plant a resistant variety. Some varieties are resistant to other diseases as well, such as verticillium and fusarium wilts.

BACTERIAL DISEASES

Bacterial diseases are among the most dreaded of humankind, including leprosy, plague, tuberculosis, whooping cough, cholera, and diphtheria. Just in the United States, more than one hundred species of bacteria cause plant diseases. Among garden plants, the most serious bacterial diseases are rots, leaf spots, and galls.

One of the most serious rots is soft rot, which may kill a seedling before it even emerges from the ground. If the seedling does emerge, it may have yellow-brown stripes lengthwise on the leaves, which gradually become limp and rot. This is a terrible disease for hyacinths. Infected plants should be dug and burned, and hyacinths should not be planted in the soil for several years. In hyacinth bulbs, the disease can be positively diagnosed if, a few minutes after being cut, a cross section of a bulb reveals small, yellow, shining spots.

Although we usually think of galls as being produced by insects, an interesting bacterial disease called *crown gall disease* causes pelargoniums to produce masses of small shoots that sprout in groups, either at or near the stalk's base; these are the galls. They are light in color and sometimes produce very small leaves, while normal growth ceases. This doesn't kill the plant, but infected pelargoniums are not very pretty, so the plants need to be pulled and burned.

Other bacterial diseases include bacterial bean blight, fire blight on apples and pears, citrus canker, and wildfire on tobacco. In cucumber wilt, the bacteria invade leaf vessels and cause the plant to wilt suddenly.

The most common route of invasion of plants by bacteria is through wounds, but they also enter through stomata and flowers. They can be transmitted by insects, rainwater, gardeners moving from one plant to another, or planting infected seeds, bulbs, or tubers.

FUNGAL DISEASES

Most plant diseases are caused by fungi. In some ways, fungal diseases are the most fun to observe, because at some point in a fungus's life cycle, it usually produces a visible structure for the production of spores. Therefore, with fungal diseases, sometimes we can see the disease itself, not just the symptoms it causes.

The world of fungi is incredibly large and interesting, and not all fungi are disease causing. In the soil, fungi are absolutely necessary for breaking down organic matter, such as fallen leaves and dead animals. The yeast form of some fungi is used for making bread and for brewing beer and other liquors. Many mushrooms, which are fungi, are edible, but many are poisonous, too.

One major disease is late blight of potatoes. From 1845 to 1847, this disease ravaged Europe's potato crops, causing a great famine. In Ireland alone, half a million people died or emigrated—many of them coming to North America. The fungus causing late blight of potatoes also causes late blight of tomatoes. This is not surprising, since tomatoes and potatoes are in the same family.

When the spore of the fungus causing late blight of potatoes lands on a potato or tomato leaf, if moisture and temperature conditions are appropriate, it germinates, issuing a *germ tube*. The germ tube penetrates the leaf, perhaps through a break in the leaf or via a stomata. Inside the leaf, the tube branches into a network of threadlike *hyphae* that grow between leaf cells. The hyphae sprout slender side branches called *haustoria* that stab into leaf cells, absorbing the cells' contents. In this way, the fungus's hyphae wander through the leaf's interior, "robbing and killing" as they go. Eventually the killed cells show up as large brown spots on the leaves.

Once the late blight fungus is well established, its hyphae grow out through stomata on the lower side of the leaves and develop very slenderly

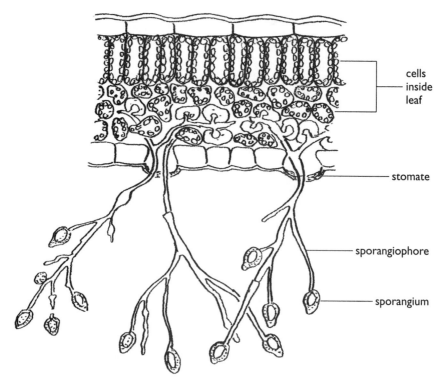

cells
inside
leaf

stomate

sporangiophore

sporangium

Sporangia on sporangiophores of the late blight fungus exiting stomata on the lower surface of a potato leaf.

branched "fruiting bodies" called *sporangiophores*. These sporangiophores, which massed together give the leaf surface a moldy look, bear very tiny, oval bodies called *sporangia*. When rain or wind transfers these sporangia to other plants, it begins the most remarkable part of its life cycle.

If the temperature is around 77 degrees Fahrenheit, the sporangium behaves like a spore and sprouts, sending out new hyphae that penetrate the new host. But if the temperature is only about 54 degrees, the sporangium becomes divided into many extremely tiny entities called *zoospores,* each propelled by two little tails called *flagella.* Wiggling their flagella to propel them, the zoospores escape through a pore in the sporangium wall, swim about in rainwater or dew, and finally settle down and germinate. Then the zoospore's hyphae penetrate the host leaf, and the cycle begins again.

The downy mildews have a life cycle similar to that of late blight fungus. They cover young leaves and shoots, as well as flower stalks, bud bracts, and even sepals, usually producing a grayish white covering, with the tissue underneath turning dark. Plant parts attacked by downy mildews typically cease growing and become deformed. Cabbage, lettuce, onion, cucumber, pea, and grape are commonly affected.

Powdery mildews appear white and powdery on the same kinds of places as downy mildews. The hyphae of powdery mildews do not penetrate plant tissue themselves, however; they wander the plant's surface, sending down short haustoria into living cells.

At the end of the host plant's growing season, powdery mildews form *fruiting bodies* on the leaf surfaces. They look like black dots just large enough to be visible to the naked eye. These fruiting bodies remain on the fallen leaf all winter. In the spring, they absorb water, swell, and crack open, and special kinds of spores called *ascospores* escape into the environment, where they will fall onto new hosts, germinate, and start the life cycle over. Powdery mildews particularly infect wheat and other cereals, members of the bean family, grapes, roses, and lilacs.

If one day you walk into your corn patch and are shocked to see that an ear on one of your corn plants has a baseball-size, white growth bursting through the shucks, you have one of the most interesting of all fungal diseases, corn smut. Wheat and other cereals, onion, spinach, ragweed, and knotweed are among our backyard plants that have their own kinds of smuts.

Corn smut begins its life when a special kind of spore called a *teliospore* germinates in the soil. It produces a short, tubelike item called a *basidium,* which is typically only four cells long. Each of the four basidium cells may generate armlike appendages called *basidiospores,* and these appendages may bud new basidiospores as the whole organisms lives in the soil, deriving its energy from dead organic matter.

Eventually wind tears a basidiospore from the ground's surface and deposits it onto a young corn plant. Infections can take place not only on the developing ears, but almost anyplace on the plant, even among the tassels— the male flower inflorescences. The basidiospores germinate hyphae that invade the corn's tissue and grow through it. And here is where this life cycle really gets bizarre.

It happens that basidiospores come in two different kinds of strains. They are not exactly male and female strains, or positive and negative strains, but just different. A basidiospore by itself produces just small, weak hyphae that migrate listlessly through the corn tissue. But if wandering hyphae of opposite strains meet, they combine and become much stronger, more aggressive hyphae.

As these hyphae grow through the corn plant's tissue, the tissue begins growing cancerlike; a single grain of infected corn may grow as large as a

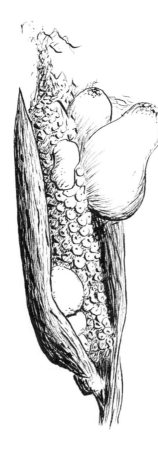

Corn smut fungus turns the kernels on an ear of corn into large masses. Inside are spores that when released can germinate in soil and begin the fungus's life cycle anew.

baseball. When the big mass is mature, it is composed of a mixture of hyphae and corn-plant tissue. Eventually the hyphae produce teliospores. Then the big "smut ball" breaks open and millions of teliospores are released onto the ground, where, if it's the end of the growing season, they overwinter and will germinate in the spring to start the life cycle over.

Smut may be interesting and spectacular, but the rust fungi are the most serious disease-causing, or *pathogenic,* fungi. More than two thousand species of rusts are known, and all infect seed plants or ferns. If you thought that the smut life cycle was complex because it involves two kinds of spores, then hear this: Many rust species produce up to five different kinds of spores at different stages of the life cycle.

The rust fungi are divided into two large subgroups. One kind of rust, the *autoecious* species, spends its entire life on just one species of plant; important autoecious rusts infect beans and hollyhocks. The other big subgroup of rust fungus, the *heteroecious* species, requires two unrelated kinds of plants for the completion of its life cycle. For example, one heteroecious rust fungus, the cedar-apple rust, must alternate between apple trees and red cedar trees. If you want to see how complex and fascinating a fungus life cycle can be, in the library look up the biology of stem rust of wheat, caused by the fungus *Puccinia graminis*.

OTHER CAUSES OF DISEASES

Plants can become sick for many other reasons. For instance, most flowering plants, even healthy-looking ones, are to some degree infected with wormlike *nematodes, or eelworms.* Nematodes spend at least part of their life cycle embedded in plant roots, stems, or leaves; each species has its particular place for living. Most nematodes are so small that they can hardly be seen by the naked eye. Nevertheless, they are almost unbelievably numerous in soil. It's been estimated that in a single acre of soil there could be forty-five billion nematodes!

In our gardens, one kind of nematode, *Ditylenchus*, attacks daffodils and other bulb plants, causing them to grow stunted and making them so weak

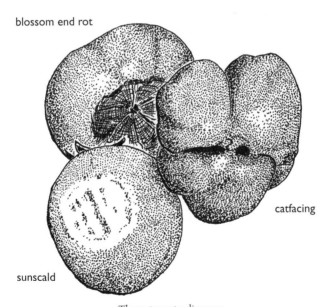

blossom end rot

catfacing

sunscald

Three tomato diseases
Diseases are often caused by environmental factors. Blossom end rot appears after hot, dry spells or periods of heavy rain and can be prevented by watering regularly and using mulch. Catfacing results from abnormal flower development, and usually after cool weather. Sunscald, which appears as a white blister, results from overexposure to sunlight and can be avoided by providing shade; overpruning overarching branches encourages sunscald.

that their blossoms hardly open; bulbs develop black rings that later rot, causing the bulbs to become soft. This same nematode species attacks phlox, causing the leaves to become almost threadlike. Nematodes can develop hard cases, becoming *cysts,* and survive in soil for years. Nematodes are such serious pests on tomatoes that resistant strains have been bred.

Climatic factors can also harm plants. These include too much sunlight if the plant hasn't been hardened off, too much heat, and too much or too little rain. Dogs and cats can also cause problems for garden plants. Dogs tend to urinate on conspicuous landmarks, whether it's a fire hydrant or a favored tomato plant. The urea in dog urine is a source of nitrogen and can burn leaves, causing them to look as though they had been singed by a blowtorch. Cats preparing their toilet often disturb roots. Most garden stores and seed catalogs sell dog and cat repellent.

People also do their share of accidentally making their plants sick. If a neighbor goes after dandelions with the wrong kind of herbicide, or the right kind but on a windy day, serious damage can be done to garden plants. A common weed killer, 2,4-D (short for 2,4 dichlorophenoxyacetic acid), is actually a synthetic, hormonelike chemical that causes herbs to grow themselves to death. In weak concentrations, it causes leaf and stem distortion that might be misdiagnosed as being caused by a fungus.

In short, diagnosing plant diseases is something of an art. A lot of background knowledge is needed, and even then sometimes the best gardener can't figure out why his or her plants are sick. A few common syndromes can be memorized, such as the symptoms of iron deficiency, but being able to memorize isn't nearly as important to plant pathologists as cultivating a snoopy, wide-eyed attitude.

If you find a sick plant, remember what's written in this chapter, look in plant pathology books, talk with experienced gardeners, and use your own eyes and mind to try to figure out what is going on.

CHAPTER 14

Thought Gardens

By now it should be clear that a main goal of this book is to get you thinking every time you step into the garden. More than just vegetable or flower gardens, our fussed-over plots of soil should be "thought gardens." Let's examine a few arenas of thought we've only touched on lightly until now.

For example, we've spoken of how vegetables and ornamental plants are developed from wild ancestors. Here the word *developed* refers to both gradual and not-so-gradual genetic change—in other words, evolution. To my way of thinking, nothing in nature is as wonderful and thought provoking as evolution. Thinking about how species change to adapt to perpetually altering climates, geography, and other features of nature fills me with awe and respect. So how does evolution work?

If you look around at your fellow humans, and any other population of living things at hand, you'll see that the members of every population are different from one another, at least a little. This *natural variation* in all populations is the basis for evolution. Here's an example of how evolution could work:

Let's say that today mankind decides that the longer one's nose is, the more children that person should father or mother. People with really short noses don't get to have any babies at all. Well, in a few thousand years, simply because for a long time long-nosed people will have been producing more babies than short-nosed ones, and because babies tend to inherit many features of their parents, people *on the average* will have longer noses than they do today. There still may be some short-nosed folks around, but there won't be nearly as many as today.

This same process works in nature, except that nature selects for such things as an ability to survive hard winters or to outsmart enemies. Those individuals that can't survive hard winters die and therefore produce no babies; thus their inability to endure hard winters is not passed on. The same is true of those individuals that can't outsmart, or at least outrun, their enemies.

Through this same process, mankind has developed many of the plants found in our gardens and flower beds. Maybe one day a human many hundreds or thousands of years ago saw a naturally growing sunflower with flowers larger than usual, though of course not nearly as large as today's sunflower blossoms. This prehistoric person planted seeds of this large-flowered sunflower. A crop of sunflowers resulted the next year, and then that fall this individual once again collected planting seeds only from the largest heads. The next year, the same process was repeated, and year after year the same thing happened, always collecting the next year's seeds only from the largest heads. Maybe it went on like this for thousands of years. Eventually, sunflower heads become very large indeed, as large as they are today. But, maybe not as large as they will be someday in the future . . .

Most variations in a natural population are subtle, but sometimes *mutations* occur—something happens at the genetic level that causes the offspring to be very different from either parent. Usually mutants die, but sometimes they live and can be propagated. Natural dogwood blossoms are white, but years ago a mutant red-blossomed plant appeared, horticulturists propagated it, and today suburban gardeners love having red dogwoods in their backyards.

Hybridization is something completely different that plant and animal breeders do. Hybrids often are larger and more robust than either parent (this is termed *hybrid vigor*) and frequently are sterile. If the seed produced in a hybrid tomato can be coaxed to germinate, it's likely that the resulting plant will look like one of the runty parents, not the hybrid plant the tomato came from, and its fruits won't be as desirable as the hybrid fruit was. Nonetheless, planting seed from hybrids makes an interesting experiment.

Seeds for hybrid plants usually cost much more than regular seeds, because hybrids are relatively hard to make. Creating hybrid plants usually involves taking the pollen of one variety of plant and, by hand, putting this pollen onto the stigma of the flower of another variety. To produce a hybrid, the two parent plants must be of the same genus. For example, you can't make a hybrid between an oak tree and a pumpkin, but often you can hybridize between two rose varieties or two corn varieties.

All the plants we've talked about in this book are specialists at something, whether it's surviving in a particular corner of nature or growing a large, bright flower. It makes an eye-opening project just to walk around your backyard, looking at every plant species and determining each one's specialty.

THE GARDEN AS A PLANT ZOO

Sometimes a plant's specialty is simply that it's so seldom grown that it's a curiosity. Visiting gardens harboring such plants is no less fun than visiting a zoo populated with exotic animals. What makes a plant exotic?

Seed catalogs often introduce new plant varieties being sold for the very first time in the history of gardening. Seldom are such new varieties freshly discovered species found by explorers in isolated and exotic places. Rather, they result from years of painstaking, systematic horticultural breeding. It's always fun to see what plant breeders have come up with, for each new variety presents a fresh face of nature hitherto unseen.

In one recent issue of Henry Field's seed catalog, there's a new Snow Belle radish with round, pure white roots instead of the usual red; these radishes look like big mothballs. A new Lumina pumpkin is white, not orange, and the Sunspot sunflower grows ten-inch heads on two-foot stems—much shorter stems than seen before. A Rose wisteria is being offered with blossoms of a color not expected of wisterias, and the Sonia variety of hybrid tea rose is being marketed for the first time.

The attraction of new varieties is obvious. Nevertheless, many people find that it's more fun to grow crops that were planted long ago but then for one reason or another went out of style and today are seldom seen. These may be varieties pioneers planted or American Indians grew before Europeans arrived.

Nowadays certain seed companies specialize in selling such antique seed varieties. Some of these companies are listed in the Appendix, identified as marketing *heirloom* seed. Typically, heirloom varieties of plants are smaller, don't preserve as well, and are less flashy than newer kinds, but often their taste and general toughness are superior to those of modern-day varieties.

Wood Prairie Farm in Maine, for example, sells a Russian Banana heirloom potato that's banana shaped, waxy yellow, and fingerlike in size and shape; this was first grown in America by early Russian settlers. The farm's Ozette potato was grown by the Makah Indians, a tiny tribe living in northwest Washington State. Though this potato is too runty to be sold in supermarkets, it has a wonderfully nutty flavor and dry texture, making it perfect for roasting and baking. Wood Prairie also sells blue potatoes: the Caribé strain, with purple skin but snow white flesh, and the All-Blue, with deep blue skin and purple flesh.

Heirloom varieties are also worth growing because their chromosomes carry information developed through millions of years of evolution and centuries of mankind's horticultural breeding—genetic information that must never be lost. With potatoes, by the way, growing heirloom varieties is especially interesting because each potato, having developed vegetatively by asexual reproduction, is an exact genetic replica of the parent potato. Therefore, we can plant the same potatoes as the early Russian settlers and the indigenous Makahs.

THE BACKYARD AS A PART OF NATURE

Maybe the most important way of thinking about gardens is the way that Mother Nature does. Here's how I'd describe her attitude:

Before humans came into being, the whole earth was a kind of lush garden, a lovely patchwork of forests, meadows, deserts, and hundreds of other kinds of specialized environments. Every environment had its own unique community of plants and animals that interacted with one another in complex and beautiful ways. When people tilled fields and built cities, most of these plants and animals were pushed out of the way, but not all. Even today, earthworms remain in the soil, and certain butterflies, deprived of their favorite blossoms of forest and meadow, take nectar from our garden weeds.

Moreover, nature always does something that is very important to know about. It's always trying to take back land. We all see this process of returning to nature every day. Leave a disturbed piece of ground alone long enough, and weeds arise, bugs come to gnaw on the weeds, toads come to snatch up the bugs, skunks come nosing after the toads, tree seedlings sprout in the feces left by the nosy skunks, and so on.

This is what would happen to our gardens and flower beds if we abandoned them for years. Abandon them for even a few days during the summer, and you'll see how fast weeds make an appearance. Essentially, nature sees our gardens as temporary conditions. Our fun as gardeners comes when we recognize nature's way of doing things and we find ways to work in harmony with these natural strategies.

PEST CONTROL

Perhaps no challenge to our wish to garden in harmony with nature is more daunting than the one we as gardeners face every time we find ourselves in competition with other animals. The truth is that often there is no elegant way to protect our tomatoes or any other garden plant from the myriad insects and other animals that want to eat them before we get a chance. At some point, every gardener must decide where on the pest control spectrum he or she resides.

At one end of the spectrum lies doing nothing, and at the other end lies hitting bugs (and everything else in and around the garden ecosystem) with all the hard-hearted mole traps and synthetic chemicals a gardener can buy. In the middle of the pest control spectrum lies the practice of using organic-based chemicals such as rotenone and pyrethrin, which do their killing and then decompose into harmless, organic residues. Where on this spectrum you will fall has very much to do with how you end up feeling about your garden's life forms and systems.

Organic gardeners eschew using synthetic chemicals. Probably most organic gardeners "go organic" for health and environmental reasons. If you want to explore the world of organic gardening in depth, take advantage of

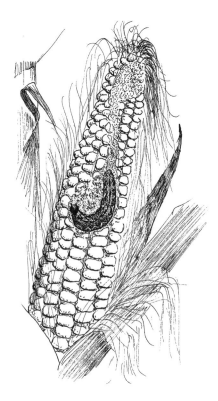

Finding a worm in an ear of corn will spur you to examine your priorities. Do you want flawless produce, or are you willing to share your corn with creatures that feel at home in your garden? Does finding a compromise between these two extreme points of view mean using just a little chemical pesticide, letting corn earworms take over your corn, or picking out the worm, cutting out the ruined area, and then cooking and eating what's left?

Organic Gardening magazine, and send for catalogs of seed and garden-supply companies specializing in nonchemical gardening (listed in the Appendix). Most seeds from catalogs and garden-supply stores, unless specifically marked as untreated, are coated with chemicals, especially those meant to ward off fungi upon planting.

I find I can't maintain the level of sensitivity and intimacy with my garden I want if I drift far from the "doing nothing" end of the spectrum. I'm quite happy watching aphids and flea beetles. As Albert Schweitzer wrote, "It is in reverence for life that knowledge passes over into experience."

Even gardeners filled with reverence for life have certain tricks for dealing with garden pests, however. For instance, nowadays gardeners can actually give natural diseases to certain insects regarded as pests by spraying or dusting them with *Bacillus thuringiensis* (BT), a disease-causing bacterium that causes leaf-chewing caterpillars to become ill and die. It is perfectly harmless to humans and other higher animals and to all plants. Spray or dust BT onto tomatoes, cabbage, broccoli—anything bothered by such leaf-chewing caterpillars as hornworms and cabbage loopers—and the caterpillars will become diseased and die when the BT organisms establish themselves in the worms' guts. BT can work fast too, often overnight.

BT isn't just an experimental item. Nowadays it's produced and sold by long-established, no-nonsense businesses. On the insecticide page of a seed catalog, you'll likely find BT sold under the trade names of Thuricide or Dipel. A pint of Thuricide costs about $10, and a tablespoon of the product makes one gallon of spray. Using a biologically based agent such as BT to control pests in gardens is an example of *biological control,* and to my way of thinking, biological control is infinitely preferable to spraying and dusting toxic chemicals into our backyards, which some gardeners still do.

BT isn't the only biological control agent on the market. In many garden shops, you can find packaged grasshopper plague sold under the name of Semaspore Bait—a real disease concocted just for grasshoppers. Bioquest is a package of parasitic nematodes—tiny wormlike creatures that bore into the living tissue of cutworms, grubs, borers, and other crop-munching caterpillars. One vial of nematodes treats 450 square feet and costs about $25.

Bug-eating bugs can be bought in catalogs and other places. Green lacewing larvae specialize in dining on aphids, mites, and mealybugs; a thousand eggs for five hundred square feet of garden cost about $11. Tiny Trichogramma wasps, which parasitize the eggs of more than two hundred

Praying mantises deposit eggs in these hard, crusty, overwintering cases. Mantis egg cases can be purchased from some seed companies for about $9; often they can be found for free on weed stems. Each case contains about three hundred eggs. Praying mantises eat beetles, moths, cutworms, and many other garden pests.

Beneath a bean leaf, a ladybird beetle well fed on aphids may lay ten to fifty eggs every day for a month.

species of insect pests, cost about $5 for four thousand. Praying mantises, which consume everything from small flies and aphids to beetles, moths, and cutworms, cost about $9 for nearly one thousand eggs. A half pint of ladybird beetles will take care of 2,500 square feet of garden space and cost about $12.

Do these forms of control work? Well, they seldom kill with the speed and thoroughness of the toxic chemical pesticides some gardeners use, and often they are not even as effective as the middle-of-the-road insecticides made from plant-derived substances, such as pyrethrum. You must pay close attention to directions and coordinate your usage with weather conditions. Nonetheless, you certainly can keep pest populations from soaring, and there's no worry about spraying substances that may be hazardous to your family's health or damaging to the ecosystem.

As an example of how a biological control agent might work, let's look at ladybird beetles.

Ladybird beetles usually lay small clusters of orange eggs on the under-surfaces of leaves, very often in the neighborhood of aphids. When the eggs hatch, little blackish creatures with voracious appetites emerge, and their favorite foods are aphids, scale insects, mealy bugs, and other soft-bodied beings. As the ladybird larva matures, its body grows, develops spines, and becomes variegated with red, blue, and yellow spots, the precise pattern depending on the species. When grown, the little larval monster ceases its depredations, glues its rear end to a leaf, sheds its skin, and becomes a resting pupa. Before long, a perfect ladybird beetle emerges.

You can see from all this that ladybirds have their own agenda, and it might be a bit tricky to get them or their offspring to devour the exact pests that are bothering your garden. Sometimes the ladybirds' and the gardener's interests overlap, however, and then what a pleasure it is to see biological control working!

Much less iffy than hoping that ladybirds will eat your enemies is this simpler and more certain approach to pest control: Just watch your plants closely, and when you find a worm or bug on it you don't like, snip its head off. Large aphid concentrations can be wiped out—if you have the stomach for it—by lightly rubbing a thumb or handkerchief across an infested area, smashing the little critters as you go.

This is not an absurd idea. You can actually get on your knees and examine each plant weekly, looking on both sides of every leaf, to keep pest populations from exploding. After a while, your eyes become habituated to spotting the enemy, and you can develop speedy search-and-destroy routines.

Certain insecticides are classified as *biodegradable* because they decompose into supposedly harmless residues after being released into nature. Insecticidal soaps based on organic formulas can kill specific pests without harm to plants or people. Many other biodegradable insecticides are derived from plants. Sabadilla, made from the seeds of a Mexican plant, kills harlequin bugs, striped cucumber beetles, Colorado potato beetles, and more. Natural pyrethrum is manufactured from dried flowers of certain chrysanthemum species; rotenone likewise is extracted from natural plant products. Though biodegradable pesticides are much preferable to toxic chemicals, those that are sprayed or dusted onto garden plants often kill many beneficial insects in addition to the pests listed on their labels.

Another nature-friendly form of pest control entraps just one pest species, and this is excellent. One such type of trap uses a sexual attractant that draws only Japanese beetles.

Certain other bug-control techniques may not be as "ecofriendly" as they claim. For example, yellow boards sold as aphid-whitefly traps attract and trap not only aphids and whiteflies, but also any other small creature that happens to blunder onto their sticky surfaces. A yellow jacket and wasp trap may indeed trap yellow jackets and wasps, but also all other small critters attracted by the decaying meat, fruit, or fish scraps suggested as bait.

Every year, new pest-control products advertised as "earth-friendly" appear on the market; nowadays these items are becoming big business, and some of them really are worth taking a look at. For example, as this book goes to press, Stokes Seed Company is introducing what it calls "the world's first bug-catching tomato plant," the Allure variety. Colorado potato beetles are said to prefer Allure's leaves to all other crops. Plant one row of Allure amid three to five rows of plants infested by Colorado potato beetles, and the beetles flock to eat Allure, not the desired crops. Then the beetles concentrated on Allure plants can be picked off by hand. If any Allure plants remain at season's end, you'll get an extra crop of tomatoes.

It is often said that marigolds and garlic keep insects off nearby plants. To find out if this is true, conduct your own experiment.

TESTING INSECT AVERSION TO MARIGOLDS AND GARLIC

What you will need

marigold seeds and garlic bulbs

---

1. Early in the spring, choose a type of plant in your garden that usually is vigorously attacked by insects (snap beans and potatoes are good candidates). Thickly plant marigolds and garlic in and around part of this year's crop. If you have pole-bean tepees, plant marigolds and garlic inside and around some tepees but not others; if you have rows, plant around one end but not the other.

2. At the peak of bug season in late summer, choose five plants far from any marigolds and garlic, and count the number of bugs on them. Make a breakdown of bug species if you can. Then calculate the average number of bugs per plant by dividing the number of bugs by the number of plants.

3. Now do the same thing for five plants in a part of the garden thickly planted with marigolds and garlic. Try to examine garden plants of similar size in each sample, because larger plants would probably harbor more insects, and that would throw off your calculations.

4. Write your results in your backyard nature notebook, and if your experimental technique has been good and your results are dramatic, let people know what you found out. Write to the local newspaper and even contact local radio and TV crews, for people like to know about these things.

In addition to biological controls, there are several devices available. Several companies offer plastic great horned owls and falcons; perched in gardens, these are meant to frighten away birds that might pluck up germinating corn sprouts. The Scareaway Birdline is a ribbon strung between two poles; it makes a noise that people can't hear but that terribly upsets birds. The Guard-N-Eyes Balloon is an inflatable globe with reflective stickers that are said to look to a bird like the eyes of a predator. And there are nonviolent traps for larger animals such as raccoons.

OLD OLD-TIME GARDENING

It's funny, but nowadays young people are often more interested in nontoxic pest control than older people; now old-time gardening often means dousing with any chemical the garden center will sell you. Before toxic chemicals became popular, however, people had gardens without them. This *old* old-time gardening is worth thinking about.

In many foreign countries, *old* old-time gardening still can be seen. In the tiny, terraced vegetable gardens on the volcanic slopes of the Madeira Islands, nearly all garden soil is sheltered beneath productive, protective herbage. In a Madeiran garden, one is expected to step carefully and find footing beneath arching plants or upon wandering, three-inch-wide trails kept weedless by constant use.

In the New World tropics, American Indians garden among trees and shrubs, creating a congenial form of agroforestry. Manioc may grow next to a hut's door, serving as a pretty shrub until its tapioca root is dug up and eaten. Herbs grow here and there in the family's outdoor living space, wild yam vines spread luxuriantly anywhere plenty of sunlight gathers, and if the vines begin shading something important or crowding onto a trail, someone simply bends over and directs their growing tips elsewhere. When crops are harvested and open spaces result, new crops are immediately planted in their place.

If a cutworm or leafhopper is brazen enough to appear, a wandering hen or turkey gobbles it down. A few weeds are simply tolerated, but if a weedy spot grows out of control, several machete swipes restore discipline. Corn is planted in clumps, and in the corn patch, bean and squash vines range among the stalks, helping keep down weeds. When a plant looks thirsty, it is watered. If chewed holes appear on a plant's leaves, a child is set to work looking for the offending bugs, and the bugs are picked off and thumped toward the nearest hen.

If there is any one particular hallmark for most of the world's highly productive, traditional gardens, it is that those gardeners watch their gardens closely, get to know the individual plants and animals in them, and keep track of everyday happenings as closely as they can.

I call this "keeping eye contact" with the garden. Gardeners keeping eye contact are likely to be found sometimes just sitting inside or beside their gardens, looking, listening, smelling, thinking, feeling. They are doing something good for their garden, and their garden is doing something good for them.

Gardeners who keep eye contact tend to notice not only if aphids are starting to get established, but also the occasion of their first open sweet-pea blossom. Maybe they'll mark the occasion on the calendar, not so much because the information will be useful later as that it's simply a happy event, worthy of being chronicled. Around the supper table of such a gardener, the day of the first ripe tomato is marked with appropriate ceremony, maybe with oohs and aahs as it's brought in on its own saucer.

In some important ways, we North Americans can become even more intimate with our gardens than our foreign, *old,* old-time gardening counterparts can. For one thing, we have the resources to learn about such aspects of gardening as our plants' and animals' life cycles, the carbon and nitrogen cycles, soil microbes, root-hair absorption, and micro-and macronutrients. Knowing about these things, and being able to visualize them in our gardens, can make us feel good in a way that gardeners who are ignorant of such technicalities never can.

We members of Western technological society also can keep up our spirits by networking with like-minded gardeners. This networking may include really absorbing a beautiful book like David Farrelly's *The Book of Bamboo* (see Bibliography), which dwells nearly as much on oriental philosophy, the joy of building with bamboo, and bamboolike elements of the human spirit as on bamboo itself. And on the computerized "information highway," we can find electronic bulletin boards on which gardeners exchange messages and recipes and download gardening files.

BUTTERFLY GARDENS

I can think of no better way to end this book than by considering the concept of the butterfly garden—doing things to make a garden or flower bed even more attractive to butterflies than it already is.

First, someplace in the sun but out of the wind, add a few flat stones butterflies can rest on, and provide them with a source of water. The water can be in a shallow plate or some other vessel providing sloping access large enough for the insects to rest on as they drink.

Keep in mind that in general, butterflies like sweet-scented flowers with plenty of nectar. They seem to be attracted to white flowers in the spring (alyssum), lavender in the summer (perennial buddleia, or butterfly bush), and yellow in the fall (marigolds). Other good butterfly species include rock cress, honeysuckle, columbine, sweet pea, phlox, cosmos, impatiens, aster, bachelor's button (cornflower), dianthus, fennel, dill, nasturtium, and zinnia.

It's as simple and brief as that. In nature, and in our backyards, most of what is really beautiful is, essentially, simple and brief—like the image of butterflies flooding into a nontoxic garden friendly with diversity.

Selected Bibliography

GARDENING HOW-TO

Coleman, Eliot. *The New Organic Grower's Four-Season Harvest.* Post Mills, VT: Chelsea Green Publishing Company, 1992.

Ernst, Ruth. *The Movable Garden.* Old Saybrook, CT: The Globe Pequot Press, 1992.

———*The Naturalist's Garden.* Old Saybrook, CT: The Globe Pequot Press, 1993.

Farrelly, David. *The Book of Bamboo.* San Francisco: Sierra Club Books, 1984.

Freeman, John A. *Survival Gardening.* Brevard, NC: John's Press, 1984.

Growing Vegetables in the Home Garden. Washington, DC: U.S. Department of Agriculture, 1986.

Harker, Donald, et al. *Landscape Restoration Handbook.* Boca Raton, FL: CRC Press, 1993.

Joyce, David. *Windowbox Gardening.* Old Saybrook, CT: The Globe Pequot Press, 1993.

Martin, Laura C. *The Wildflower Meadow Book.* Old Saybrook, CT: The Globe Pequot Press, 1990.

Raymond, Dick. *Garden Way's Joy of Gardening.* Charlotte, VT: Garden Way Publishing, 1982.

Reader's Digest Illustrated Guide to Gardening. Pleasantville, NY: The Reader's Digest Association, 1978.

Sombke, Laurence. *Beautiful Easy Lawns and Landscapes: A Year-Round Guide to a Low Maintenance, Environmentally Safe Yard.* Old Saybrook, CT: The Globe Pequot Press, 1994.

Williamson, John. *Perennial Gardens.* Old Saybrook, CT: The Globe Pequot Press, 1992.

GENERAL NATURE REFERENCES

Bailey, L. H. *Manual of Cultivated Plants,* rev. ed. New York: Macmillan Publishing Co., 1949.

Buckman, Harry O., and Nyle C. Brady. *The Nature and Properties of Soils.* New York: The Macmillan Company, 1969.

Crompton, John. *The Way of the Ant.* New York: Nick Lyons Books, 1989.

Fabre, J. Henri. *The Life of the Spider.* New York: Dodd, Mead, 1913.

Fernald, M. L., et al. *Edible Wild Plants of Eastern North America.* New York: Harper & Row, Publishers, 1958.

Grieve, M. *A Modern Herbal.* 1931. Reprint. Dover Publications, 1971.

Milne, Lorus, and Margery Milne. *Insect Worlds.* New York: Charles Scribner's Sons, 1980.

Schaller, Friedrich. *Soil Animals.* Ann Arbor: University of Michigan Press, 1968.

Shorthouse, J. D., and O. Rohfritsch. *The Biology of Insect-Induced Galls.* New York: Oxford University Press, 1992.

Snodgrass, Robert Evans. *Insects: Their Ways and Means of Living.* Washington, DC: The Smithsonian Institution Series, 1930. Reprint. New York: Dover Publications, 1967.

Stokes, Donald W. *A Guide to the Behavior of Common Birds.* Boston: Little, Brown and Company, 1979.

Went, Frits W. *The Plants.* New York: Time Inc., 1963.

FIELD GUIDES

Arnett, Ross H., Jr., N. M. Downie, and H. E. Jaques. *How to Know the Beetles,* 2nd ed. Dubuque, IA: Wm. C. Brown Company Publishers, 1980.

Bland, Roger G., and H. E. Jaques. *How to Know the Insects,* 3rd ed. Dubuque, IA: Wm. C. Brown Company Publishers, 1978.

Borror, Donald J., and Richard E. White. *A Field Guide to the Insects of America North of Mexico.* Boston: Houghton Mifflin Company, 1970.

Chu, H. F. *How to Know the Immature Insects*. Dubuque, IA: Wm. C. Brown Company Publishers, 1949.

Kaston, B. J. *How to Know the Spiders,* 3rd ed. Dubuque, IA: Wm. C. Brown Company Publishers, 1978.

Pohl, R. W. *How to Know the Grasses*. Dubuque, IA: Wm. C. Brown Company Publishers, 1968.

Pyle, Robert Michael. *The Audubon Society Field Guide to North American Butterflies*. New York: Alfred A. Knopf, 1981.

Robbins, Chandler S., B. Bruun, and H. Zim. *Birds of North America*. New York: Golden Press, 1966.

Zim, Herbert W., and Lorna R. Levi. *Spiders and Their Kin*. New York: Golden Press, 1968.

GARDENING PHILOSOPHY

Cesaretti, C. A. *Let the Earth Bless the Lord: A Christian Perspective on Land Use*. New York: Paulist Press, 1984.

Clark, W. C., and R. E. Munn. *Sustainable Development in the Biosphere*. New York: Cambridge University Press, 1987.

Devall, Bill, and George Sessions. *Deep Ecology*. Salt Lake City: Peregine Smith, 1985.

Granberg-Michaelson, Wesley. *A Worldly Spirituality: A Call to Take Care of the Earth*. New York: Harper & Row, 1984.

Keswick, Maggie. *The Chinese Garden*. New York: Rizzoli International, 1978.

Taylor, Paul W. *Respect for Nature: A Theory of Environmental Ethics*. Princeton, NJ: Princeton University Press, 1986.

Tze-chiang, Chao. "Discourses on Vegetable Roots." In *A Chinese Garden of Serenity: Epigrams from the Ming Dynasty*. Mount Vernon, NY: Peter Pauper Press, 1959.

Yoshida, Tetsuro. *Gardens of Japan*. New York: Praeger, 1957.

APPENDIX

FREE SEED CATALOGS

Bluestone Perennials
7235 Middle Ridge Road
Madison, OH 44057
    perennial flowers

Brittingham Plant Farms
P.O. Box 2538
Salisbury, MD 21802
    berries, asparagus, rhubarb

Brudy's Exotics
P.O. Box 820874
Houston, TX 77282
    exotic tropical plants

Burgess Seed & Plant Co.
905 Four Seasons Road
Bloomington, IL 61701
    vegetables, bulbs, herbs, house-
    plants, supplies

Burpee
300 Park Avenue
Warminster, PA 18974
    vegetables, ornamentals, herbs

D. V. Burrel Seed Growers Co.
P.O. Box 150
Rocky Ford, CO 81067
    herbs, flowers, and vegetables

DeGiorgi Seed Company
6011 N Street
Omaha, NE 68117
  herbs, grasses, wildflowers

Dixondale Farms
P.O. Box 127
Carrizo Springs, TX 78834
  onions

Henry Field's Seed & Nursery Co.
415 N. Burnett
Shenandoah, IA 51602
  vegetables, ornamentals

Garden City Seeds
1324 Red Crow Rd.
Victor, MT 59875
  seeds for northern gardens

Gardener's Choice
County Road 687
Hartford, MI 49057
  vegetables, fruit trees, and vines

Gleckler Seedmen
Metamora, OH 43540
  unusual vegetables

Golden River Farm
P.O. Box 73568
Fairbanks, AK 99707
  organic, certified, exotic potatoes

Gurney's Seed & Nursery Co.
110 Capital St.
Yankton, SD 57079
  general gardening, including herbs

Harris Seeds
P.O. Box 22960
Rochester, NY 14692
  vegetables, ornamentals

Hartmann's Plantation, Inc.
P.O. Box E
Grand Junction, MI 49056
  blueberries, fruits, miniature roses

Indiana Berry & Plant Co.
5218 W. 500 S.
Huntingburg, IN 47542
  berries and supplies

Johnny's Selected Seed
311 Foss Hill Road
Albion, ME 04910
  vegetables, flowers, herbs

Jung Seed Company
335 S. High Street
Randolph, WI 53957
  *vegetables, heirloom seeds, land-
  scape plants*

Kelly Nurseries
1706 Morrissey Drive
Bloomington, IL 61704
  landscaping plants

Kitazawa Seed Company
1111 Chapman Street
San Jose, CA 95126
  oriental vegetables

Orol Ledden & Sons
P.O. Box 7
Sewell, NY 08080
   new and heirloom varieties

Liberty Seed Company
P.O. Box 806
New Philadelphia, OH 44663
   unusual garden varieties

McFayden
30 Ninth Street
Brandon, Manitoba
Canada R7A-YA4
   Canada's largest mail-order seed company

Nourse Farms, Inc.
41 River Road
South Deerfield, MA 01373
   berries, asparagus, rhubarb

Park Seed
P.O. Box 31, Highway 254
Greenwood, SC 29648
   vegetables, flowers

The Pepper Gal
P.O. Box 23006
Fort Lauderdale, FL 33307
   peppers of all kinds

Pinetree Garden Seeds
Box 300
New Gloucester, ME 04260
   vegetables including ethnic varieties, herbs, heirloom seeds

Porter & Son
P.O. Box 104
Stephenville, TX 76401
   hard-to-find melons, tomatoes, peppers

Clyde Robin Seed Co., Inc.
P.O. Box 2366
Castro Valley, CA 94546
   hard-to-find wildflowers

Stark Bro's Nurseries & Orchards Co.
P.O. Box 10
Louisiana, MO 63353
   fruit trees, landscaping plants

Stokes Seeds
P.O. Box 548
Buffalo, NY 14240
   vegetables, flowers, herbs

Territorial Seed
P.O. Box 157
Cottage Grove, OR 97424
   year-round general gardening

Thompson & Morgan
P.O. Box 1308
Jackson, NJ 08527
   rare and unusual seed varieties

Tomato Growers Supply Company
P.O. Box 2237
Fort Myers, FL 33902
   exotic tomatoes, peppers, and more

Wildseed Farms
P.O. Box 308
Eagle Lake, TX 77434
wildflower seeds

Willhite Seed Company
P.O. Box 23
Poolville, TX 76487
melons and other vegetables

Wood Prairie Farm
RFD 1, Box 164
Bridgewater, ME 04735
*certified potatoes, including
heirloom varieties*

FREE GARDEN-SUPPLY CATALOGS

American Hydroponics
824 L Street
Arcata, CA 95521
hydroponic gardening

American Standard Co.
157 Water Street
Southington, CT 06489
pruning tools

Aqua Culture Inc.
700 West 1st Street
Tempe, AZ 95281
hydroponics, greenhouse gardening

ARBICO
P.O. Box 4247
Tucson, AZ 85738
ladybird beetles

Bozeman Bio-tech, Inc.
P.O. Box 3146
Bozeman, MT 59772
*biological control insects,
pheromone traps*

A. C. Burke & Company
2554 Lincoln Boulevard, Suite 1058
Marina Del Rey, CA 90291
gardening software, videos, books

Co-Op Gardening Group
P.O. Box 155
Red Lion, PA 17356
organic gardening products

Diamond
628 Lindaro Street
San Rafael, CA 94901
indoor gardening and hydroponics

Fox Hill Farm
20 Lawrence Street—D
Vermon, CT 06066
Hoop House greenhouse kits

Gardener's Supply Company
128 Intervale Road
Burlington, VT 05401
*extensive selection of gardening
products, including seed-
germination kits*

The Garden Pantry
Box 1145
Folsom, CA 95763
    fine tools and accessories

Gardens Alive!
5100 Schenley Place
Lawrenceburg, IN 47025
    organic gardening products

Garden-Ville of Austin
8648 Old Bee Caves Road
Austin, TX 78735
    organic gardening products

Great Lakes IPM
10220 Church Road NE
Vestaburg, MI 48891
    integrated pest management

Home Gardener
160 Koser Road
Lititz, PA 17543
    composters, irrigation supplies

Irrigro
P.O. Box 360
Niagara Falls, NY 14304
    garden irrigation supplies

Light Mfg. Co.
1634 S.E. Brooklyn
Portland, OR 97202
    hydroponic gardening

MacKenzie Nursery Supply, Inc.
P.O. Box 322
Perry, OH 44081
    tools

Mellinger's
W. South Range Rd.
North Lima, OH 44452
    general garden supplies

Naturally Scientific
726 Holcomb Bridge Road
Norcross, GA 30071
    *environmentally responsible
    pesticides*

Necessary Organics
One Nature's Way
New Castle, VA 24127
    composting, organic gardening

Ohio Earth Food, Inc.
5488 Swamp Street, N.E.
Hartville, OH 44632
    *organic fertilizers, soil
    amendments*

Peaceful Valley Farm Supply
P.O. Box 2209
Grass Valley, CA 95945
    organic gardening products

Plant Collectibles
103 Kenview Avenue
Buffalo, NY 14217
    *indoor gardening, greenhouse
    supplies*

Sea Born/Lane, Inc.
P.O. Box 204
Charles City, IA 50616
    *bone meal, rock phosphate, sea-
    weed*

Storey's Books for Country Living
Schoolhouse Road
Pownal, VT 05261
   books on gardening and herbs

Watermiser Drip Irrigation
P.O. Box 18157
Reno, NV 89511
   drip irrigation products

Turner Greenhouses
P.O. Box 1260
Goldsboro, NC 27533
   hobby greenhouses and supplies

Worm's Way, Inc.
3151 South Highway 446
Bloomington, IN 47401
   hydroponics, indoor gardening

Varmint Fence
70 Commerce Drive
Ivyland, PA 18974
   garden fences

Yeoman & Company
P.O. Box 30
Monticello, IA 52310
   general gardening

SELECTED GARDENING MAGAZINES

Flower & Garden. Home gardening and landscaping.
Horticulture. Gardening and botanical information.
Organic Gardening. Gardening without chemicals.

COMPLIMENTARY COPY OF *HORTICULTURAL DIGEST*

In a peaceful hollow in the hills of Kentucky, there's a gardening family with access to hundreds of international magazines, journals, and databases dealing with horticulture. Each month they issue a newsletter consisting of about twelve pages crammed with newspaper-size print, listing addresses and toll-free numbers; book references; and magazine article, product, and book reviews. It's hard to imagine a less expensive, more comprehensive, constantly updated peephole into the horticultural world. Annual U.S. subscription rate as of 1996 is $20. Write to *HortIdeas*, 460 Black Lick Road, Gravel Switch, KY 40328.

NOTES

NOTES

NOTES

NOTES

NOTES